C000125828

ALISTAIR FINDLAY worked as a frontline ... 973
until 2009, one of the first recruits to ... ork
profession which integrated all four prev[... ntal
health, childcare and welfare. Prior to sc ... onal
with Hibernian FC 1965–8. He worked as . ... neral
labourer until training for social work in 1970, when he began a three-year training
course at Moray House College, Edinburgh, then worked between 1973 and 1975 as
a social worker for Falkirk Burgh, becoming a Senior social worker there with Central
Region until 1977. He became an Emergency Duty Senior for Nottingham and then
Derbyshire 1977–80, after which he was intake Senior for Craigmillar in Edinburgh
from 1980 to 1984, and was Lothian Region's Coordinator for Child Protection from
1984 to 1991. He then joined West Lothian as a senior social worker in Broxburn
becoming a Children and Families Practice Team Manager in Livingston from 1992
to 2009. Active in NALGO, the local government trade union, he was Convener of the
Lothian Region Social Work Shop Stewards Committee and Branch Education Officer
between 1982 and 1986.

He qualified CQSW (Certificate of Qualification in Social Work) from Moray House
College in 1973, receiving the June Gordon Memorial Award for merit, then took
an MA in Applied Social Studies (Bradford University, 1979), an honours degree in
History and Literature (Open University, 1993), a certificate with distinction in Scottish
Cultural Studies (University of Edinburgh, 1995) and an MPhil with distinction in
Modern Poetry in English (University of Stirling, 1999). One of West Lothian's – and
Scotland's – finest poets, his first book was *Shale Voices*, an acclaimed social history of
West Lothian's shale mining communities, and he has since published three volumes
of poetry – one of which, *Dancing with Big Eunice: Missives from the Frontline of
a Fractured Society*, is a book of social work poems. His songs have featured on
Greentrax CDs produced by Ian McCalman, *No Pasaran! Scots in the Spanish Civil
War* (2012) and *Scotia Nova: Songs for the Early Days of a Better Nation* (2016). A
critical anthology *Lenin's Gramophone: Scotland's Left Poetry and Song 1860s–1990s*
is forthcoming from Luath.

Images
Left: Author, 1972. Photo Glynis Houston/McEwan. Centre: 'Big Eunice', drawing by Anne
Dickson. Right: Author and Big Tam, 1999. Photo Marion McWilliam.

Mollycoddling the Feckless
A Social Work Memoir

ALISTAIR FINDLAY

Luath Press Limited

EDINBURGH

www.luath.co.uk

First published 2019

ISBN: 978-1-913025-07-6

The author's right to be identified as author of this book
under the Copyright, Designs and Patents Act 1988 has been asserted.

The paper used in this book is recyclable. It is made
from low chlorine pulps produced in a low energy,
low emission manner from renewable forests.

Printed and bound by Bell & Bain Ltd, Glasgow

Typeset in 11 point Sabon by Main Point Books, Edinburgh

For Big Tam, Danny, Paul, all the Regent Roaders, Helen, Wee Marion, Raymond and all the Falkirk-burghers, Wee Jan and all the Craigmillar-ers, all the NALGO-ers, Gus and Les and all the Shrubhillers, all the Leith five-a-siders, Sheila, Big Grahame, Margaret Graham, Wee Jim and all the West Lothianers, Big Ronnie and Emma and also (in memory of) Iain Morrison, Douglas Carnegie, Walker Butler, Mary MacLeod, Ian Gilmour, Peter Harris, Bob Purvis, Ian Quigley, Bob Holman, Alex Ferrie, Sheila Maguire/Taylor and Joyce Gunn.

Contents

Glossary of Acronyms

ADSW   Association of Directors of Social Work, renamed Social Work Scotland

BAAF   British Association of Adoption and Fostering

BASW   British Association of Social Workers

CCETSW Central Council for Education and Training of Social Workers

CI   The Care Inspectorate (Scottish Government Inspection body)

CQSW   Certificate of Qualification in Social Work

IMF   International Monetary Fund

NAI   Non-Accidental Injury (Child Protection) Registers

NALGO   National Association of Local Government Officers, renamed UNISON

NHS   National Health Service

RSSPCC Royal Scottish Society for the Prevention of Cruelty to Children

SACRO   Scottish Association for the Care and Resettlement of Offenders

SSSC   Scottish Social Service Council (Scottish Government Regulatory Body)

SWSG   Social Work Services Group (old Scottish Office)

Note to the Reader

I HAVE ADOPTED what some readers may consider a rather free-wheeling tone not only to entertain but also to suggest something of the black humour that was commonly shared by social workers and their managers, no doubt to counteract the constantly unpredictable and emotionally draining situations we routinely faced. Frontline social workers can flit in the blink of an eye from the ordered calm of a courtroom to absurdist Beckett-like dialogues with psychotic individuals to struggles with distraught mothers – for example, one wielding a claw-hammer on a tenement landing, as happened to me. This is beyond the ken of most non-social workers, I suspect, and in trying to portray some of this I have sometimes taken the liberty of carnivalising some aspects of my own and colleagues' behaviour in certain situations. Some of the serio-comic passages given may invoke the slapstick of an 18th century novel by Henry Fielding in which the hero typically survives in a corrupt society by living on his or her wits. This is intended to illustrate the wider, more elusive truths and pressures often acting on individual workers and their managers. This depiction can range from the rueful to the comical but always with an eye on the intense pressures that the work can impose on everyone involved. Likewise, chapter introductions purporting to offer a brief synopsis of what each contains is highly unlikely to be found on any Scottish Government recruitment website. I have of course not named individual clients because of professional confidentiality.

Preface

My mother, ninety-three,
blames me and my kind
for mollycoddling the feckless.
'Mollycoddling', *Dancing with Big Eunice*

Comprising confident assertions as to the width and quality of the author's professional background; a depiction of social work's unique importance to the social care, child protection and criminal justice systems; a vigorous refutation of how it is portrayed by right-wing gobshites as a repository for simpering, liberal-minded idealists persistently duped by old cons, young thugs, paedophiles and general deadbeats which simply encourages more of them. The author points out how he managed many social workers, many of whom were female exponents of tough love and who he was pretty much afraid of himself for most of his four decades.

EVERYONE KNOWS WHAT a teacher or a doctor does because everyone has met one. Very few people meet social workers, unless they have committed quite a serious offence; appeared before a children's hearing; been taken into foster, residential or adoptive care; been admitted to a mental health facility; been abused or neglected by their parents; or have a significant level of disability or vulnerability through their youth, age or infirmity. Your chances of meeting a social worker increase the poorer you are; the more jobless; the more deprived the area you reside or are homeless in; the more addicted to substance or drug misuse; or the more liable to gang sub-cultures or low school attendance and performance levels. If you have been subject to some or all of these disadvantages, you could probably write a better book about social work than I have. But I did not set out to write about the people social workers deal with except to shed light on social workers and their mindsets, using my own practice and frontline management experience as a guide.

Social workers do not all think or react in exactly the same way when facing the same set of predicaments and decisions about the same kind of people as teachers, doctors and police officers. They call the people being discussed 'pupils', 'patients' or 'suspects' but we call them 'clients' and, although that is not brilliant, it is better than some later attempts to rebrand them as 'consumers', 'service users' or, heaven forbid, 'customers'. A client is not only a pupil, a patient, a tenant or a welfare recipient: a client is a person who may have all kinds of difficulties – and perhaps creates all kinds of difficulties for others – for which the state deploys social workers to support or supervise them, preferably on a voluntary basis but compulsorily if that is required. Clients are not always that easy to categorise or put in the same box. A recent survey (*Mental Health in Prisons*, National Audit Office, 2017, p9) shows that 80 per cent of people in prison have a history of mental health issues. Unfortunately clients do not come along with their destinations already stamped on their foreheads as buses and trams do.

Politically, the social work departments I joined in 1970 were part of a new social policy project, an integrated welfare profession strong enough to compete for resources with the established giants of health, social security, education and housing. Our remit was to build community-based services to replace the outmoded institutions and mindsets that had built huge prisons, mental hospitals, orphanages and approved schools. In that process, social work coordinated the new care system on an inter-agency basis which kept more people in the community than ever before. This 'holistic' approach slowly set up wider networks of community care, support and scrutiny than any single agency could have achieved alone, including 'one door' social work departments. My generation embedded inter-agency working practice where it mattered most – on the ground. What the 'one door' social work departments did was to take professional 'ownership' of the community-based care system at large. I know this because I was one of those who encountered that system before there was any effective coordination and cooperation operating between the main services – to which condition private market models threaten to return us.

This is not to imply that social workers act merely as hod-carriers for the social care and protection system. Social workers are in their own right central to the adult and juvenile justice and mental health systems charged with providing reports and assessments and recommendations to sheriffs and panels and tribunals which help determine whether individuals end up in prison or in residential or hospital care or are placed on supervision or probation orders in the community – which social workers are responsible for carrying out.

It is social workers who have the 'difficult conversations' with the people who are jailed or placed on probation or supervision; who visit them in their homes, institutions and communities; who explain stuff after panels have made their decisions and case conferences have placed their children's names on the Child Protection Register; or when children or old people are removed from home. That is social work's key skill set: to be supportive and authoritative, and often both, in the same difficult conversation. Too much of the one and not enough of the other is the tightrope that social workers have to walk routinely. That is what social workers do that no other professional group can or is trained for or better placed to carry out within the care and justice system as it has evolved over the last 50 years.

If this memoir has anything to offer today, it may be to remind people of how the modern social work system began and why, and what it faced over decades of experiment, conflict, bemusement and hostility, both within and outside the profession. What may surprise readers unfamiliar with social workers is the extent to which my depiction may not conform to the common right-wing caricatures of us as the naïve, idealistic, over-sympathetic and gullible 'do-gooders' of popular legend. That ignores the 'tough-love' reality which our role in respect of courts, hearings and tribunals often entails – including compulsory removal from home or the community, no matter how sympathetically that may be achieved.

Such selective vision I think has helped fuel some of the wrong-headed attempts by populist politicians and corporate executives to recast social work as some kind of local Government 'customer-friendly service provider', just like any other. This is not only untrue but has distorted the peculiar combination of 'care and control' that distinguishes statutory social work from private and third sector agency models which, though these can enhance certain aspects of public sector provision around the edges, can be used – as it has by mainly right-wing political forces – to dismantle the core 'public service' ethic and social funding infrastructure on which the welfare state was built and still essentially relies. That at least is what my generation of professionals understood and based our practice on from the very start and which many of us continued to believe up to the point I retired and published *Dancing with Big Eunice* in 2010, for which this memoir may be seen in many respects as its prose background. The respected social work academic and community worker Bob Holman made the following remarks in his *Champions for Children* (2013: 220).

> I have read thousands of pages about social work, brilliant research by academics, helpful analysis by practitioners, endless proposals by cabinet ministers for administrative reorganisations, yet none give the feel of social work like Alistair Findlay's poems. He conveys its sweat, its smell, its reality. He understands both its trivia and its enormity. He perceives why clients do what they do and what drives social workers to continue in their hard and thankless jobs.

I belonged to the generation that pioneered the new, large, 'one-door' (generic) social work departments of the 1970–90s. We took what were called at the time 'one-man-and-a-dog' town hall operations, typically comprising a childcare officer, a couple of welfare officer clerks (untrained), a mental health officer (hospital-based) and a few Probation Officers (Home Office trained) working through the local Sheriff Court and unified them into a single, modern welfare state apparatus. My generation was as cynical of this inheritance as a new generation of welfare staff are now no doubt as dismissive of our legacy to them. Indeed, it was one of the annoyances of my final years as a frontline manager to have to listen to a re-writing and junking of social work's actual history by a new breed of corporate management flunkies (mainly middle managers) who barely knew the period and who would not have lasted five minutes as managers through the tumultuous times leading up to Mrs Thatcher and then through and beyond her attack on the welfare state and local Government services. While I welcome informed criticism of my profession, this would have to exclude anyone whose perceptions of the 1970s are based largely on excerpts from *Life on Mars* and endless re-runs of the *Winter of Discontent* narrated by someone like Martin Amis.

As a student on placement in the brand new social work department of Hamilton Burgh in 1971, I recall being quizzed by a motley crew of ex-childcare, mental-health and welfare officers, all miraculously re-branded overnight as 'social workers', as to what this new 'generic' stuff was all about. Never before or since has a body of new recruits to a foundling profession exercised such influence in its development. There was no doubt plenty of scope for change and maybe even improvement in the old Burgh and county halls, in which this new breed of college and university trained social workers would set up our stalls to serve, in the parlance of the times, 'the mad, the bad, and the sad'. My generation were in effect 'upstarts' in a profession or, rather, a series of vocational specialisms established before the Second World War (apart from Children's Departments) still rooted in social policy assumptions and legislation reflecting widely held cultural ideas concerning the divide between the 'respectable' skilled working-class and the 'unrespectable' working-class poor, the work-shy, the criminal and the insane. These were now to be the collective concern of the one-door social work profession. My generation had grown up ourselves amongst such cultural beliefs which we would meet and take on, head-on, in the homes and lives of the people we encountered every day in the course of our working lives: clients.

The book's title comes from a poem in *Dancing with Big Eunice* called 'Mollycoddling' which conjures up the clash between the cultural mores of my parents' and grandparents' generations and my own, the 1960s generation. We were naïve but certainly not innocent as we hurled ourselves at the reforming task, fearless and bold in comparison to the professional cultures prevailing in education and health as much as in our own field of welfare.

In the event, whether by accident or design, and probably a lot of both, we would become the 'shock-troops' for a piece of late-1960s liberal social legislation, The Social Work (Scotland) Act, 1968 – much too progressive for those decrepit institutions waiting expectantly to absorb and contain us when we emerged, blinking in the sun. Many of these institutions would get broken and re-made in the course of the next decade, mostly because they needed to be. That decade and the following three are the subject of this memoir, a personal memoir about what is in fact a collective activity, welfare, whose trajectory from liberal caring vocation to political football should become clearer in the telling. I also discuss football.

For nearly four decades, I witnessed Scotland's small Burghs and Counties become large Regional Authorities in 1975. I was Convener of Lothian Region's Social Work Shop Stewards Committee during the strikes over Tory public-sector cuts in the 1980s and Lothian's first Child Protection Coordinator during the Cleveland (1988) and Orkney (1990) Sex Abuse Inquiries. I saw the return to Specialisms in 1992, the replacement of Regions by Districts in 1996 and the emergence of the new Scottish Parliament in 1999, which turned the public services into one huge political football. I worked for six different authorities, lived through nine external and internal reorganisations, occupied eight distinct roles and grades and worked through 22 changes of boss, roughly one every 18 months over 36 years. During this time, I never left the field of play, the frontline, in thought or deed except to dance, laugh, sing and even imbibe at the Christmas pairties.

I offer a personal account of what is a little understood and often deliberately maligned profession. Social work is in reality a diverse occupation, a collective activity relying as much on teamwork and difference within the profession and between professions – the police, health, education and voluntary organisations – as it does on the initiative and ability of individual workers. It has been a central part of the scapegoating of social workers from the outset for right-wing media to blame individual workers for 'failures' which are rooted in intractable social conditions – criminality, ill health, poverty, inequality, family breakdown – exacerbated by limited welfare funding. The continuing 'bad behaviour' of those whom social workers spend their time trying to help, stabilise, and turn their lives round is relentlessly blamed on them, and I explain why that is so above and beyond what my old granny would have called 'badness'.

I did not set out to defend the profession so much as write about myself and the people I worked and laughed with, who I now complain and tell awful or amusing tales about in the hope of showing us to be frail human beings taking on virtually impossible tasks which other professions and agencies have failed at before us, and will do so again – the police, judiciary, prison, lawyers, medics, teachers, charities, churches, chapels, RSSPCC, the Old Firm, Parliaments. I write about people who work every day with other people who can be threatening, hostile or the very opposite, suicidal or despairing or skint and at the end of their tethers, in need of genuine comfort or a metaphorical boot up the arse – whatever the worker thinks or feels is best at the time – in real time, that is, not after, at some lawyer-led special case review second-guessing already known outcomes. Anyone can do that, and, indeed, many have and in the process suggesting levels of certainty that social work – dealing with complicated and often messy individual lives – cannot offer, and which no social agency can offer.

Social work, I have tried to convey, is not a beige profession, dealing with beige people. The day it does you will know it has become what most of its critics insisted it was from the outset: a dead parrot. I never thought that and neither did most of the people I worked with or for.

Judges' Daughters

Yonder see the morning blink:
The sun is up and up must I,
To wash and dress and eat and drink
And look at things and talk and think
And work, and God knows why.
Oh often have I washed and dressed
And what's to show for all my pain?
Let me lie abed and rest:
Ten thousand times I've done my best
And all's to do again.
AE Housman, *Last Poems*

Showing the author being lifted from the streets of Bathgate in autumn 1970 by press-gang – through a local misunderstanding – and transported to Moray House College, Edinburgh, as an indentured student social worker for the next three years. He falls in with a rowdy crew of future senior managers becoming pally with a particular fellow apprentice cut-throat, Big Tam. They are taken on as cabin-boys by a right pair of old sea-dogs, tutors called Morrison and Carnegie, who give the impression of being respectable bank managers – which they patently are not.

I FIRST CAME across the term 'social work' in early 1970 speaking to Jack Ingles, who was in charge of community education in West Lothian. His granddaughter, Heather Reid, would become known to later generations of BBC Scotland viewers as 'Heather the Weather'. Heather's father was Peter Reid, a PE teacher at Broxburn Academy, West Lothian, who managed the County Schools football team which myself and John Gorman – another Winchburgh born lad, who became a professional player with Celtic, Carlyle United and Tottenham Hotspur, later chief coach for Glenn Hoddle's England squad – played for. I would last three years as a part-timer with Hibernian FC which, with Hearts of Midlothian, enjoyed the same kind of rivalry in Edinburgh as did Celtic and Rangers in Glasgow, and for much the same biblical reasons. I would still have been a writer though. (I write of my time with Hibernian FC in Andy MacVannan's *We Are Hibernian*, published by Luath Press in 2011.)

I was visiting Jack at my father's suggestion in his office at Wellpark, a stone-built mansion on the upper reaches of Bathgate which was also home to the District Library. I was hoping to arrange some voluntary youth work to put on my application for teacher training at Moray House College, Edinburgh. In the middle of our chat, Jack said, 'Why don't you apply for this new social work course they've started? They're looking for guys like you. It's full of judges' daughters.'

Twenty-one years old and just married, that did not sound too bad to me so I also applied for the Three Year Diploma Course in Social Work and Community Work Studies which would give me a Certificate of Qualification in Social Work (CQSW), a licence to practise whatever that was exactly.

I was duly called for interview at Regent Road, Edinburgh, the School of Community Studies, an annexe of Moray House, half a mile beyond the Canongate, just past what is now the Scottish Parliament building at Holyrood, and up towards Easter Road, my old stomping ground. The course organiser was Alan Smart, son of a former Moderator of the Church of Scotland. Alan was a bright, conscientious, self-deprecating academic in his early 30s. I think there were 50 or so places for several hundred applicants. The figure 700 sticks in my mind and of the group I was interviewed with, only Rosemary Taylor and I got through. We all received an individual interview before being placed in groups of about twelve to discuss topics introduced by Alan while being observed by a couple of other tutors sitting silently in an outer circle, making notes.

I think I impressed Alan no end when he asked the group to discuss whether we thought that individuals could 'change the system better from within or without'. I hung back to let the reckless, the verbally incontinent and the most desperate batter the subject to death before stepping down from the Olympian heights to offer an analogy taken from Ghandi and quoted by Aldous Huxley in *Ends and Means*: roughly that any individual who enters 'the machine' will almost certainly be misshapen by it but the machine will also be forced to alter its own shape, however slightly, in order to absorb them. Stunned silence. Alan's eyebrows shot up as he looked meaningfully across at the outer-seated observers. Killer blow, I thought, and so it proved. Letters from Moray House duly arrived offering me places on both the teaching and social work courses and I plumped for the latter, a decision I have never ever regretted.

I continued working the rest of the year as a labourer, building a huge reservoir near Slamannan, Falkirk, until a week before the course began in September. I and the 50 or so other successful applicants were gathered together for a residential week at Middleton Hall, an early 18th century historic pile standing in its own grounds a few miles south of Edinburgh. A semi-carnival atmosphere prevailed, half Jimmy Hendrix concert, half sixth-form debating society, well-lubricated in the evenings with drink, no doubt a little wacky-baccy and blethers, otherwise known as 'group discussions'. It was there I first set eyes upon my abiding pal, Big Tam, who had given up his job as a metallurgist in Ravenscraig Steelworks to tramp round the States in search of 'the blues'. Coming from Hamilton, I suggested, need he really have travelled that far? Big Tam looked like a young Karl Marx, with a mass of thick black curls, a dark green figure-hugging jersey and a reservoir of jokes and stories, the tang of which would later make Billy Connolly famous.

Tam Wallace was a couple of years older than me, not long married, and we discovered we were the oldest in the group whose gender balance was roughly 50:50. I was certainly startled by the youthfulness of some, many of them young women not long out of school. I need not have feared though, except perhaps for my own safety. Feminism was in the air along with revolution and beer. I met Big Billy Gorman, Big Rab Murray and Wee Mike Tait, not long after I met Big Tam. We were more sizeist than sexist, evidently. Indeed, some of the young men had longer hair and frillier shirts than some of the young women. Myself and Big Billy still had fairly short hair. He came to my notice one evening in a group sitting round discussing 'freedom'. Big Billy had thick black NHS glasses and was smoking a pipe. He made taciturn seem almost raucous. He said nothing even more often than I did. Eventually I decided to climb down once more from the mountain to announce that 'the only freedom worth having is economic'. Big Billy sprang into life, tapped out his pipe and said, 'Quite right, big man', which silenced everyone.

If my nemesis was Big Tam, then Big Billy's was to be Big Rab. Big Rab was as loud as Big Billy was not. Big Rab was one of the young men whose hair and shirts were longer and frillier than the lassies'. Later a Director of Social Work for Glasgow City, Big Rab is perhaps worth describing in some detail at this juncture: a pair of long thin Donald Dewar-type legs, Mick Jagger bouffant hair-do, Vietcong combat-jacket, John Lennon specs, a pair of distressed blue jeans before the term became confused with a fashion statement, white scuffed plimsoles ('gutties') complete with in-built ventilation ('holes'), and a voluble and constantly excited Easterhouse accent which got him (and Big Billy) lifted one night (completely maliciously) by Dunfermline's finest simply for being present at Harry Lister's stag night – but that's another story. The least said about Wee Mike the better. He would share a flat with Big Rab and Big Billy for the next three years in Edinburgh, about which he has sworn an oath of secrecy. Well, almost.

Needless to say, the induction week flashed past to a soundtrack provided largely by The Rolling Stones, Simon and Garfunkel, Joni Mitchell and Carole King. There were no judges' daughters at all but certainly the offspring of some doctors and ministers of religion. All the shires of Scotland seemed represented and a few from England and Ireland. Obvious hippies rubbed shoulders and other parts of the anatomy with obvious squares, boyscout leaders or anarcho-syndicalists from Banff or Buckie. There were people who were obvious misfits even for this course, like someone called Jim, a young working-class Tory from Castlemilk, a fluent talker who would abandon the course after a few terms to take up drama or possibly investment banking. Big Tam and Big Rab spent most evenings competing over who would run out of telling jokes on any chosen subject first. Unfortunately, neither did. Big Billy smoked his pipe and listened intently. Wee Mike donned a bushman's hat with corks dangling from strings and led some dancing maidens through moonlit groves playing his guitar, just to see 'who would follow'. Needless to say, Big Rab, Big Billy, Big Tam and myself never bothered.

Days were taken up with self-selected groups working on some kind of improvised play or spectacle to be performed on the closing night with the Principal of Moray House College present, a Dr McIntosh. If I remember right, my group's project seemed loosely related to the musical 'Hair' but without the nudity, punctuated by a scene which had Big Tam, hair streaked white, wearing a tartan shawl with his bare feet placed in a tin-bath pretending to be his coalminer grandfather from Hamilton. If this were not spooky enough, I was assigned the role of narrator which culminated with everyone on stage and a spotlight directed under my face while I recited the final words of the Sermon on the Mount. It was all judged to be a resounding success. Word went round that Dr McIntosh had been forced to abandon his pre-prepared speech in favour of some off-the-cuff remarks about being overwhelmed by youthful energy, excitement and social conscience. The tutors were obviously delighted too, though none of them had made much impression on me at this stage. All seemed reasonably calm and, well, rather normal individuals. This would change soon enough when the actual course began the following week.

Regent Road in fact trained over half the field and residential social work and youth and community work students in Scotland, a main feature being to mix us into weekly joint 'group-work' tutorial groups. Some were as young as 17 and some were in their 50s, including a couple of SWSG (Scottish Office) Prison Advisers, Harry Richmond and Jim McKiddie. In contrast, the universities offered about a dozen or so places only to social policy graduates – aged about 21 – and they undertook a one-year social work degree course focused mainly on 'casework' principles and practice but with only a passing academic critique of group-work and community work skills and methods. The Moray House course offered its recruits a core 'group-work' experience intended to make quiet people louder and loud people, well, quieter – though the failure rate for the latter must have been pretty high. After the first week of initial lectures at Regent Road and talks about timetables from the School's Principal, Brian Ashley, and his depute, Ross Flockhart, my tutorial group, comprising about 15 individuals between 18 to 21 years old, met on the Friday afternoon for something called 'Principles and Practice' or P and P – our initiation into group-work theories and dynamics, had we but known.

We sat gathered in a huge room, the September sunshine filtering through the high, elegant windows of Regent Road. The tutor was not there and, after five minutes, some were shifting about in their chairs, wondering whether to go. The door opened and a shortish, squarish middle-aged man in a grey suit came in and sat down. He had the large head, battered face and sturdy build of a boxer or perhaps ex-rugby player. He did not introduce himself. In fact, he said nothing, just smiled and looked round, looking everyone straight in the eye. If we were expecting a 'leader' or 'teacher', as most of those present had had until very recently, then we were about to be put right. Nobody spoke.

Eventually the wee guy said, 'Imagine there has been a nuclear war and everywhere outside this building has been obliterated but we still have good air to breathe and a clean water supply. What would we need to do to survive as a group?' I expected folk to laugh but not a bit of it.

For the next 45 minutes, ideas, suggestions and contraptions poured forth to which the wee guy raised practical or ethical questions which led to more and more convoluted modifications to our imaginary social schemes, utopian and dystopian, until I could stand it no longer. I spoke once more from the region of Mount Olympus.

'Just listen to yourselves,' I said. 'This wee guy comes in off the street, you don't know his name, if he's a janny or just let out for the day, and now, after voting to send out corpse-gathering parties to use the radiation in their bodies as a power-source, we have just agreed a proposal by a Church of Scotland minister's daughter (Francis) that part of our future food supply will include cannibalism, to be precise, eating every second male baby born to our little colony.'

The tutor, Iain Morrison, sat back, twinkling, and said, 'Perhaps that would be a useful note to end on?'

The P and P group broke up in a clamour of noise. Iain Morrison never moved from his seat. I slowly gathered up my haversack and slung it over my shoulder. Still he never moved, just sat there like a lighthouse beaming out. I shook my head and stared at him. He said nothing, just kept on beaming and staring back. Had the film *The Madness of King George* been made back then, this non-verbal exchange would have resembled the scene where the mad King says, 'I have you in my eye, sir' and the equally mad Doctor replies, 'No, I have you in my eye, sir'. As I chuckled and nodded my way out through the door, little did I suspect that the basic essentials and lessons of the last hour would repeat themselves and be reinforced between this wee guy and myself not only over the next three years but for the rest of my professional career and, indeed, my life, as, indeed, they still do. In that sense, Iain Morrison has never left me, or I him, in spirit.

* * *

When I started training as a social worker, I would describe myself as a sensible young working-class man who had grown up in West Lothian in a small pit village, then a large council housing scheme, a progression many made in 1950s and '60s Scotland. I attended local council schools, had working-class parents, three older and one younger brother, as well as grandparents who lived with us for all my life until they died by the time I was 16. We lived happily enough cheek-by-jowl with what sociologists then called 'a good social mix' of the 'respectable' and the 'unrespectable' working-class. The latter, to us, were simply 'the Stewarts' or 'the Parkers', who never gave us any bother, mostly because we were even more frightening than they were.

These were the kind of people I would later learn to call 'clients' but whom my mother knew as 'poor souls' and my second-oldest brother, Alan, uncharacteristically sympathetic for the times, called 'the pathetics'. I ran into many of them on the building sites and labouring jobs I worked in during the two years prior to my entering social work training, guys who had been in prison or on probation, who I had played football with, delivered papers to, heard stories about from friends or family. They were a relatively small part of the general scenery of ordinary working-class life in the housing schemes of Glasgow and Edinburgh such as Easterhouse and Craigmillar (where I worked in the 1980s) as much as they were in smoky Bathgate with the coalmine, the railyard, the steelworks and the factories which I also grew up amongst in the Central Belt of Scotland in the 1950s and '60s.

So far so typical. But what I should perhaps add about my own background is that my father had been a shale-miner for the first 25 years of his working life, then took up local journalism, becoming the editor of the weekly newspaper, *The West Lothian Courier*, in the mid-'60s. We were a decidedly political household, therefore, largely through my father's support for Harold Wilson type socialism, exemplified by our local MP, Tam Dalyell. My brother, Alan, on the other hand, was a Marxist shop steward involved in a strike for trade union recognition at Caterpillar, then an American-owned non-union tractor plant at Bellshill. The continuous soundtrack of reformist and revolutionary rhetoric I heard at home and in the pub emanating from my brother and my father and their like-minded friends and acquaintances no doubt influenced my future left-wing social and political attitudes, which later exposure to social work training and practice did nothing to reduce.

And so I landed in 1970 at the School of Community Studies which sat on a little island triangle precariously positioned between the east end of Regent Terrace, overlooking Edinburgh's Old Town, the vistas of Arthur's Seat and the top side of London Road just where it meets the traffic lights at the top of Easter Road. It seemed an unreal seat of learning waiting there just for me, a solid Victorian public school building on the outside, but with another world inside, where 'feelings' and 'beliefs' and 'intuitions' were spoken of as though they were as apparent as the lectures we received on society, sociology, psychology and law – the alleged real world. This sense of unreality was further added to by the fact that the building was in sight of the bus stop on London Road where I had alighted every Tuesday and Thursday evening for three years between the ages of 16 and 19 to then walk down Easter Road to train as a part-time professional footballer with 'the Hibs'. There, I had kicked a ball about with folk like Peter Marinello, Alex Cropley, John Brownlie, John Blackley and even such luminaries as Pat Stanton and Pat Quinn. One somewhat unlikely world thus collided with another equally uncanny one and their close proximity seemed initially quite odd to me. Once inside the Tardis that would become 'Regent Road', however, I knew that I had picked the right place or it had picked me.

I fell on the opportunity to read and study that social work training offered me like a flea on a mangy dog. University education had been denied me for the past three years, although I had left school with the requisite Highers to have allowed admittance. That is when I discovered that I was part of 'the bulge', the statistical name given to the huge birthrate upsurge in the wake of the war and which went through the country's existing provision for education, housing, employment and health like a size 10 foot trying to get into a bairn's bootee. Being knocked back from university despite having more than the required entry qualifications was more distressing and revelatory to me than being freed by professional football which, although largely commercially driven, was a skill-based 'meritocracy' nonetheless. Being deprived of further education for which I had felt both suited and eligible – indeed, entitled – was a real political awakening, deeply personal and, well, enraging. I would then end up taking a job as an apprentice quantity surveyor with an Edinburgh building firm until, square peg in round hole, I gave it all up, much to my mother's disappointment, for labouring on building sites until something better turned up, teaching most like, hence my interest in applying to Moray House.

Journalism was no doubt also in the frame then but I wanted to explore the world more widely before considering taking up my father's trade. Young middle-class people would later take sabbaticals prior to going to university and, in a sense, my enforced sabbatical would be three years long and spent in offices, mines, building-sites and factories. While labouring, I read all kinds of esoteric material from the existential novels of Camus and Sartre to the poetry of TS Eliot and WH Auden and the classic socialist-realist novels of Jack London, Patrick MacGill and John Steinbeck which, like Robert Tressell's *The Ragged-Trousered Philanthropists*, had once been standard fare for earlier generations of autodidacts (self-educated, working-class intellectuals) that swarmed round the socialist movement. I had no sense then of participating in that kind of tradition, which came later when I began writing myself. And so, at Moray House, I studied and read, discussed and debated and was exposed to a life of feeling and emotion that the intellectual life on offer at traditional universities, several of which I have since attended, rarely matches.

In sociology, we studied the Hawthorne Experiment in 1920s America, which subjected factory workers to psychological pressures and work-control methods designed to increase job satisfaction but only if it also increased productivity levels. Another behavioural study that impressed itself on me sought to test notions of decency and justice held by some university students having white-coated 'experts' telling them to apply electric shocks to fellow students who were suspected of being deviants or spies. This showed that the students were prepared to use voltage levels that would easily have killed the 'suspects'. George Orwell's 'Big Brother' thus met the McCarthyite witch-hunt trials of 1950s America, which chimed pretty much with what was also on the course reading lists: Marx's theories of 'alienation' and their role in reproducing capitalist social relations. Our group-work classes served to make the implications of such studies 'real' rather than remain intellectually interesting but dormant pieces of social information. In group-work, our personal relationships and values were exposed and examined not as theoretical constructs 'out there' – equality, fairness, justice – but personal factors rooted 'here', in this place, and continually going on 'inside' one's own unique 'self'. Needless to say, I found all of this intellectually stimulating and personally absorbing.

The first year of the three-year Diploma course seemed designed to broaden young people who had recently left school with little experience of life and people like myself who had some work experience but little or no exposure to social work in its various existing settings. Iain Morrison said we were a bit like tomatoes in a greenhouse, forced to grow a bit faster than nature had intended. But grow, I think, we did.

In our P and P group-work classes, there was great emphasis placed on keeping confidential any information shared or arising within the group to itself, rather like football teams now speak of training ground punch-ups 'staying in the dressing room'. Class soon emerged as a major driver of difference, or punch-ups, emotional and ideological, between group members. The intense nature of the feelings aroused in groups in which individuals were encouraged by other members to articulate their basic thoughts and feelings, and so 'own' them, was a very powerful mode of personal learning. The downside was the spectacle of young women, often the daughters of doctors or ministers, being regarded almost as 'class enemies' by young working-class men. I forcefully criticised this on several occasions, though I was struck by how composed many of these young women could be in defending themselves, hurling back a few good pelters of their own at the inverted working-class snobbery detected in their erstwhile assailants.

This pluck and verve was, of course, exactly why they had been selected for the course in the first place. There was a notable absence of sectarian religious conflict which may have been because the true religion of most of us was now the recently discovered hedonism of the age combined with the atheistic social liberation movements erupting all over the world, affecting even Zen-Calvinist Scotland. There were some evidently Catholic or 'churchy' young people amongst us, too, but they were all seen as rather similar, more soberly attired and restrained, more polite and mannerly, more conservative in their social attitudes compared to the larger student body with whom they nonetheless happily shared flats, classes, tutors and, of course, weekend parties.

Along with lectures and group-work classes, we performed role plays in drama classes run by Miss Milroy, an ageing thespian who seemed to me to be due for retirement but I was young myself then and the young really know very little about such things. Miss Milroy, who never said 'call me by my first name' (Alice), forced us by dint of her implacable will and personality to do two things. First, in her Communications classes, we had to write a speech of some sort and perform it for her and the rest of our group to comment on and constructively criticise. I chose Lenin, declaiming how the primary function of welfare in capitalist society is to keep the working-class from revolting. Miss Milroy said she was thrilled by my opening dramatic gesture of throwing my jerkin, the inside of which was a violent red, across the lectern before giving it laldy, what she called 'a vivid and energetic performance'. I was quite thrilled myself – my first public performance before an audience not linked either to playing football or singing at New Year.

Big Billy was also in our group. Miss Milroy had taken the precaution of stating that if people did not come up with their own ideas for role plays then she would provide them with some. I think this was how he ended up being 'a sergeant on parade'. Billy nodded his head, put his pipe in his pocket and stepped forward. He politely invited all the rest of us to also step forward onto the floor in front of him. When assembled, he suddenly screamed at the top of his voice, 'yeio 'orrible feckin' shower', so transforming himself into a bellowing psychopathic monster for the next five minutes that it still makes me shudder to think of it. The whole class was shell-shocked except Miss Milroy, who was splendidly agog and captivated, as we all were, really. She applauded Big Billy, who immediately subsided as quickly as he had erupted, retrieved his pipe from his jacket pocket and looked out resolutely once more into the middle distance.

The second thing that Miss Milroy forced and cajoled Big Tam and me into were 'observational visits' to a care establishment to record our impressions. This is how we ended up attending the local psychiatric hospital in West Lothian one night a week for the duration to play cards and dominoes with some of the old men in the long-stay wards. It had touches of the cult film *One Flew Over the Cuckoo's Nest* about it. As with Jack Nicholson's character McMurphy, Big Tam did not take too kindly to the inmates persistently cheating. It was not the Hamilton way. What really unnerved us, though, was the occasional flurry of activity to the side or behind us when nurses would suddenly rush towards some old guy standing in the middle of the floor and shake his waistband wildly until a perfectly formed wee jobby would appear magically down one leg and roll slowly and seemingly deliberately towards us. Another nurse would appear almost as magically with a shovel and a plastic bag and then wheech said object into it and the old guy responsible for it just as suddenly away. Big Tam and I looked on helplessly and just kept playing the cards until the visit's end.

This was all brought suddenly back to me a couple of decades later when I read a book called *Buster's Fired a Wobbler: A Week in a Psychiatric Hospital* by Geoff Burrell, a vivid factional account of a young man training to be a nurse in Victorian-built psychiatric hospitals in England in the early 1980s, which seemed even worse than the one Big Tam and myself visited in the early 1970s, albeit with our hands over our eyes. The wobbler that Buster fired was neither a jobby nor a strunt but a reasoned argument for closing institutional monoliths that had once housed the psychiatrically ill, the handicapped and children in care. Such places were what our generation of professionals met when we eventually entered the field and which we then began pushing to have replaced by community-based services. The closing paragraph of *Buster* shows the crux of the book's argument enacted between a young trainee and a veteran nurse, Sam, who has challenged the youngster to explain what can practically take the place of isolated 'looney bins' that the public might be prepared to accept and the politicians to pay for. It states the conundrum that also faced my generation and which we still face today – how to change cultures that are ingrained not only within professions, but also 'out there' in that fabled place, 'the community':

> To me though, the only way forward is in the community. A chance to break the power of the bin. It's not enough to tinker, to put out a new syllabus like they did in 1982, the one I trained under, if you're going to leave the institution intact. Learners will still come out the same as Sam because institutional life attracts people like Sam. What's needed is people like Jayne – risk-takers, thinkers, individuals, people with character, people who can develop the new skills needed to work out there, in the community, where people live. And that's why the kind of nurse needed can never be produced in a bin like this, where the skills they need to learn are virtually non-existent. Anyway, the best education in the world would always be destroyed by the attitudes fostered and perpetuated within these walls. Attitudes that Sam shows in the extreme and with which all of us are tainted to some degree. And if we can't produce the quality of nurse we require, in the quantities needed to be effective, then who is ever going to help the poor bloody patients?

This was a very good question for Buster to ask, the answer to which my generation of social workers, had we been asked it in 1971 and if 'patients' were changed to 'clients', would have given the resounding reply – 'us'! That's what we were being trained for, to dismantle and replace the existing institutions of health, care and incarceration, for society's benefit as much as for the client population we would have to deal with directly. As a codicil, a history of the hospital that Big Tam and me visited then (*The Bangour Story*, WF Hendrie and DAD MacLeod, Mercat Press, 1992: 166, 222) shows that the number of patients, drawn from Edinburgh and surrounding areas as well as West Lothian, peaked at 1,200 in the early 1970s. This then gradually fell back to around 500 beds. By spring of 1992, Bangour was closed and a new psychiatric ward set up in a wing of the new St John's General Hospital, Livingston, with 100 psychiatric assessment beds. That number is now reduced to 35 beds or so. Such an outcome was made possible only by improvements in drug treatments and the development of community-based support services over the intervening decades. But the demands this has made on community care services and the nursing staff who have to deal with the core of highly complex patients now filling these comparatively few beds are huge. Anyone doubting this can read Dennis O'Donnell's *The Locked Ward: Memoirs of a Psychiatric Orderly* (Jonathan Cape, 2012), an account of modern psychiatric in-patient treatment by a compassionate and untrained outsider to the nursing profession who, like myself, is a writer of West Lothian heritage.

The theme of large ancient institutions and their passing brings me to the 'duff-plate' that some of us encountered during an observational visit arranged by the college to a young offenders prison, probably Longriggend, since Glenochil had not been built then. Unfortunately, I missed it but Big Rab was pleased to describe it afterwards to me or anyone else that would listen. The students were taken round in a group by a prison warder of the type that would later become familiar to the nation through Fulton McKay playing Mr McKay in the prison comedy, *Porridge*. Big Rab and the group eventually reached the canteen, the door was opened, whereupon all the inmates sprang to attention. Mr McKay, played by Big Rab in his rendition of the story, his bouffant hair-do notwithstanding, interrogated some of them, asking if they enjoyed their food, was it good, did they get enough of it, all at the top of his voice. Finally, Mr McKay reaches out and picks up a huge plate from a pile which he flourishes and holds upwards on the palm of his hand as a top-class restaurant waiter would, then addressed the group in the following manner: 'This is a duff-plate. They get all the duff they want. If they want more, they just have to ask for more and they will get more.' At which point, Mr McKay narrowed his eyes and put his other hand side-on to the rim of the plate and balanced it there for a few seconds, to indicate depth, before barking out, 'Duff up to here!'

We all laughed at Big Rab's performance, of course, but we all knew by then that what was waiting for us out there was 'duff up to here' and as much as you could possibly want.

2

Mini Skirts and Scandals

a category-mistake
Dougie Carnegie, Moray House, 1970–3

The author is set adrift from the mothership with four other crew members to inhabit a large Glasgow housing scheme called Castlemilk to fraternise with the natives; a mega shtooshie erupts regarding the late arrival of living expenses which creates a minor mutiny and a great night out in the Blue Blanket pub; right-wing politicians are slated; tutors are observed closely and social work training revealed in mind numbing detail. No one dies, but a chance voyage to London results in an emotional incident for the author.

A GLIMPSE OF life beyond college slowly began to intrude upon us. Indeed, we were sent out in the final term of our first year on ten-week long 'community placements' the length and breadth of Britain in small groups of about five students. I was sent to Castlemilk in Glasgow in the company of four others to study it and write a report of our findings. We visited local schools, social work departments, day centres, employment offices and local projects of every description. Three of us – myself, Linda Joy/Race and Ian Neil – lodged with a young Church of Scotland minister for Castlemilk and his wife, John and Mary Miller, in a large manse in Rutherglen, which they eventually were allowed to leave after a struggle with the Glasgow Presbytery to take a council house in Castlemilk, where they lived for the next few decades bringing up their children at the local schools. Mary is the only judge's daughter I have ever met – her father, Lord Hope, was Scotland's Second Senior Law Lord – and though she was not a social worker in the professional sense, she was in most ways that mattered in that community. Both were.

Another dedicated character I met there was Bob Purvis, head of the Family Service Unit (FSU), a voluntary support service. I was so impressed with him and the work of the Unit that I would return there two years later to undertake a casework placement, which I will discuss later. The Unit was a converted council house – indeed, a couple of flats knocked together – which offered 'intensive support' to a few families rather than the 30–50 cases local authority social workers were commonly expected to deal with mostly on a statutory basis. The FSU therefore tried to reach out to struggling families on an early basis to avoid them being referred to the statutory services, which is what the families wanted too.

The report involved me interviewing the highly regarded local Tory MP, Teddy Taylor, a thorough and assiduous constituency MP, who gave the impression of being a One Nation Tory but he wanted to reintroduce capital punishment and birching. Teddy was charming and looked like a well-scrubbed RD Laing but he was really a wolf in sheep's clothing. He became a thoroughly Thatcherite MP for Southend East after the voters of Glasgow finally gave him the boot in the 1979 election, otherwise he might well have become Secretary of State for Scotland in Mrs Thatcher's Government instead of the affable and reputedly 'wet' George Younger. Indeed, as the Labour MP Brian Wilson once remarked, calling himself a nice cuddly name like 'Teddy' was like calling the Hound of the Baskervilles 'Rover'. Teddy was not the only hang-'em-and-flog-'em politician then trumpeting in Scotland. In Edinburgh, every ignorant utterance of the infamous populist local councillor, John Kidd, got headlined in the *Edinburgh Evening News*.

'Councillor Kidd' seems to have made his own way to Edinburgh from the depths of reactionary Northumberland in the mid-'60s to champion every cause so long as it was retrograde enough, from keeping public wash-houses open, to criticising the corporation for profligate spending and condemning sexual permissiveness, vandals, hippies, long-haired students and 'filth' wherever it appeared on screen or stage, particularly during the Edinburgh Festival. He was anathema to liberal, progressive opinion, though it is perhaps instructive to recall that the Tory Party in Scotland received over 50 per cent of the popular vote and over half the seats in Scotland in the 1955 election. Mrs Thatcher received 31 per cent of the Scottish vote and 22 seats in 1979 and, in the election of John Major in 1992, the Tories polled 26 per cent of the vote. It was under Major in 1997 that the Tories in fact lost all of their Westminster seats in Scotland. There continues to be a deeply reactionary seam inside Scottish civic society that is able to politically mobilise up to 25–30 per cent of the voting population, as the 2017 general election confirmed. That is the same political bloc my generation of welfare professionals faced half a century ago, and it remains intact.

In the early 1970s, Kidd's kind was rife in most councils in most parts of Scotland, rural or city, whether Labour, Tory or Liberal. It was his ilk that encouraged the right-wing press to coin the phrase 'mini skirts and sandals' to describe the dress and appearance of the new breed of dedicated young social workers being unleashed on the 'underclass'. Many were, of course, less bothered about the youth, gender or dress of those being trained to help 'wasters' than upset that any help was being offered at all. Media criticism was also fuelled by those with professional axes to grind, such as the courts, the parole board, directors of education, and the police. This is neatly summarised by Gill McMillan in *British Social Services: The Scottish Dimension* (John Murphy, Gill McMillan, Scottish Academic Press, 1992 179):

> One sheriff described the Social Work Act as 'a most bungled piece of legislation', another speaking of the disastrous decline in service, described the new social workers as mini-skirted 'Rosemarys and Gwendolines'. The chairman of the Parole Board, a very reverend gentleman, also troubled by mini skirted supervision of men sentenced for rape, complained that reports were now based on hearsay and 'worse than useless'. Reasonable claims as often, were devalued by unreasonable rhetoric, the shortage of dress unnecessarily diverted attention away from shortages of service. The directors of education viewed with suspicion the new 'semi-educated' upstarts, who seemed to question their primacy of knowledge with deviant children and difficult parents. The police were generally critical of social workers, not least for their poor performance with absconders, and tended to see the perceived soft line of children's hearings as largely social work inspired.

From such perspectives such folk had every right to be worried. We were being actively trained and encouraged to 'support' people, not just keep them 'in their place'. As part of that new breed, we were beginning to show that, as a body, we were prepared to stand up for ourselves, both as students and as future professional workers. Intimations of this surfaced at the end of our first year, when various financial cock-ups regarding board and lodgings payments not being received during our ten-week-long community placements, strung out across Britain, erupted as soon as we had all gathered for a fortnight's outward bound course at Glenmore Lodge, Aviemore. The first night passed in universal greetings and drink-related activities but a different mood set in the following morning. I was looking forward to the day's events (kayaking, I recall) when murmurs of discontent arose among the student fraternity. Big Rab and Wee Mike had been inflaming the troops about the iniquity of it all and calling for a mass show of hands to up-sticks and leave the Lodge immediately in protest.

Big Tam and myself, having actually worked for a living for three years since leaving school, were entitled to a 'mature' student's grant, unlike many of our younger colleagues who only received a token £50 per year, their parents being expected to effectively support their offspring for the duration of the course. Big Rab, Big Billy and Wee Mike stood resolutely with their hands held up. All eyes seemed to turn towards Big Tam and me, possibly because we had not yet put our hands up. We looked at each other. I saw the smokestacks of Ravenscraig flit briefly across Big Tam's eyes and he saw apprentice quantity surveying hover across mine as we slowly lifted our hands too. Every hand shot up, even those who had been looking forward to Gartmore the most – the track-suited ones who were even now preparing to show every kid how to play basketball in every community centre then spreading across the land like a rash on a baby's bottom. Now, no kayaking. We climbed into our buses and went home or to still-rented digs in the Edinburgh tenements round Moray House.

I remember a rather triumphant entry into the Blue Blanket pub next to the College, now The Canons' Gait, the local used by generations of Moray House students and lecturers. Gerry O'Regan and Harry Cohen, senior psychology and sociology lecturers respectively, were at the bar buying the drinks, both delighted at the reports of our walk-out. Gerry and Harry were everybody's idea of what late-1960s radical, progressive lecturers in their mid-30s were like – academically gifted and dressed much the same as their students. Sitting beside them was Douglas Carnegie, a recent recruit to the Regent Road tutorial staff, wearing a dark suit. Dougie was in his mid-40s and looked the very double of George Brown, deputy leader of the Labour Party under Harold Wilson, who had recently come to political and personal grief mainly through hubris and drink. Apart from coming from Leeds University, little was known of Dougie at that point, although this would change in the coming term when he would link up with Iain Morrison to form a kind of Regent Road double-act, almost joined at the hip, like Morecambe and Wise. I became tutored by Morrison and Big Tam by Carnegie to both our benefits as professionals and people, I think, since they each engaged with our different outlooks and temperaments.

I respected Dougie as a person but always felt that he was too obviously a games-player compared to Morrison and, well, a bit of a bully – without meaning to be – in his relentless pursuit of individuals whom he seemed to want to 'emote' just to show how much you cared. Needless to say, Dougie pursued me in this fashion for several years, both through and beyond college, to zilch effect. I think I felt that for someone employed to promote self-awareness in others, he could often display a surprising lack of awareness in himself. In Dougie's case, the promoting of self-awareness could turn readily into the provoking of it through some kind of emotional confrontation that Dougie seemed to get more out of than anyone else. Both Morrison and Carnegie would have been amused by the suggestion of them acting like Morecambe and Wise but I feel Dougie would have made the 'category-mistake' (one of his favoured expressions) of seeing himself as Morecambe rather than Wise. What both of them were not, clearly, were the conservative bank managers they appeared in dress and outward demeanour.

Both were, in fact, anti-authoritarian, self-directed, empathetic and deeply caring teachers, utterly committed to the task of taking raw youngsters like ourselves and preparing us emotionally and professionally for the demanding work that lay ahead. In effect, what I learned from them both is what actual revolutionaries looked like in the modern era in Scotland: not Che Guevara, more like what everybody else looks like given their age, gender and class. Morrison and Carnegie wore the same kind of suits as Jimmy Reid and Mick McGahey – my actual idea of revolutionary heroes. And what Morrison and Carnegie also did, rather like Reid and McGahey, was to emphasise that what one did rather than what one talked about doing was the real mark and measure of a person. In their own different styles, Morrison and Carnegie, in my book, embodied all of those precepts and, just as importantly, demanded all of them back from us in return.

So this is what lay ahead, but thankfully next term, as we made merry in the Blue Blanket pub. That first summer I would get a job labouring, loading lorries with huge red roof tiles down at Plean, Stirlingshire, courtesy of Stuart, my next-door neighbour in Armadale, an under-manager for Redlands. Roof tiles are heavy, insensitive and fairly uncomplaining objects which I turned to with some relief – indeed, almost gratitude – as my first year's training came to a fittingly unexpected close. Roof tiles were just roof tiles, endlessly replicated, unlike the human objects in the world I had now entered into, where everything was not necessarily what it seemed on the outside. This much I realised.

* * *

At some point that summer, I squeezed in a month's residential placement at a girls List D school in Haddington, East Lothian. I had long fair hair, a Frank Zappa moustache and an athletic build, which did not go unnoticed by some of the residents, and I was left a few anonymous but highly explicit notes and drawings. In turn, some of the staff began to chaperone me rather more closely than they did some of the girls. The emotional level in such places could rocket in the blink of an eye. The staff on duty would then run to the immediate source as though cordoning off an explosion, separate youngsters who were 'acting-out' – shouting, crying, spitting, attacking each other – and then take them off individually to quiet areas, perhaps their bedrooms, to 'talk it through'. There could also be repercussions arising from these outbursts, aftershocks amongst kids who had not been directly involved but had witnessed the incident, perhaps igniting violent feelings or grief memories of home lives that had brought them here in the first place.

At that time, the bulk of residential workers were unqualified, untrained and grossly under-paid. In 1989, says Murphy (4), there was a general level of qualification in residential care well below 20 per cent and the specific level for childcare was just above that figure. In 1971, it just seemed to me as a social work student on placement that these generally highly motivated and committed people were both brilliant and crackers. This remains my view some 40 years and more later.

In September 1971, the first term of the second year of our course commenced at Regent Road. The next term, after the New Year break, we would be sent out on our first ten-week block practice-placement, anywhere in Britain. This continuous in and out arrangement prevailed for the remaining two years, a pattern which provided a remarkably varied, almost disorientating, kind of learning experience for us as new professionals. Regent Road became something like a basecamp, a mothership, to which students would periodically return, meet and greet another year of students and then go back out again into the 'real world' of practice in myriad settings, anywhere in the country.

We were now joined in our second year of the Diploma course by the first year of the two-year Certificate course, comprising people even older than Big Tam. Many were 'seconded' (paid) by local authorities or the Government from posts in social work offices, residential units, hospitals, prisons and even the Scottish Office. They varied in age from late teens to early 50s. Our discussion groups were now enlivened by more factual practice information brought by folk from the frontline mixing with the pep, vim and utter idealism of our first year. Perhaps what was not quite so expected was the extent to which the older students were as inspired as we were by the intention of the Social Work (Scotland) Act 1968 to throw off all remnants of the old Poor Law mentality. An ethos of separating the 'deserving' from the 'undeserving' poor may still have lingered in some of the new social work departments now being reframed by that pioneering piece of social legislation, which placed a new duty on local authorities – 'to promote social welfare' (Section 12) – but it formed no part of the value-base being promulgated by the teaching staff at Regent Road.

Our lectures now included social policy principles, legislation analysis and practice issues of the type we would begin to meet in that 'field' waiting for us beyond the college gates. I recall one such early lecture taking place in the big hall in Regent Road, jam-packed with tutors and different years of student intakes. Its topic was the main sections of the new Social Work (Scotland) Act and what they meant in practice. We came to the bit about taking a 'place of safety order', which would allow officials to compulsorily remove a vulnerable person, a child or old person from some danger to 'a safe place'. The lecturer was asked to repeat the places to which such persons could be removed and so he began listing them – a hospital, a foster home, a police station – to which Big Tam suddenly gave out a resounding snort and the equally resounding comment, 'aye, it a' depends on whit ye think is 'a place o' safety!' Even the lecturer laughed, for who could not? In this way, the expectation that, as a professional group, we would have to insist on the spirit as well as the letter of social work legislation in the face of sceptical and powerful vested interests held by the already established professional groups was well understood and anticipated by most of us from the very start.

And so our training continued. If the mature students brought with them more specific knowledge of the existing social work world outside college, then we who already had some preliminary exposure to group-work were often better able or prepared to handle the emotional pressures released through it. Some of the older recruits were married with children and some marriages no doubt did result in strain and even breakdown through the personal change that only one of the parties in the marriage or relationship was going through. What the course was in fact putting everyone through was 'intrinsic' and 'extrinsic' learning combined. Extrinsic learning was what Dougie Carnegie would say was aimed at 'head-level': factual information of the kind offered at universities and colleges through social policy, sociology and psychology lectures. This was the type of didactic information we had all expected to receive when we arrived and we did receive it. But what we also got, more unexpectedly, was intrinsic learning, in which intellectual reasoning was integrated or combined with emotional understanding of one's 'self' as a professional person, promoted through small group-work and drawing further on our own personal beliefs and value-systems. Much of this involved matters of 'trust', not just talking about it but demonstrating its operation through our relationships with other members of the group.

Its pertinence for 'the field' was vividly drawn for Big Tam and me by Dougie in typically dramatised fashion. When Dougie had been a Probation Officer in Leeds before he came to Regent Road, he claimed he was sitting in his office one day when the door burst open and one of his charges, wild-eyed and raving, ran in declaring he was going to end it all by jumping out of Dougie's window, several floors up, and that Dougie need not try to stop him.

Quick as a flash, Dougie decided to go into role-reversal mode, so he shouted, 'You're right, man, we'll both end it all right here and now!' Then he brushed past the guy and started struggling to open the window, whereupon the guy suddenly calmed right down, now concerned about Dougie, and starts trying to persuade him not to jump.

On hearing this, I asked Dougie what he would have done if the guy had taken him up on his proposal and Dougie nonchalantly replied, 'Oh nothing, the window was absolutely nailed shut.'

Think what one may of this vignette, it does convey something of the heightened emotional states and scenes that professional social workers can get into in the course of an ordinary working day, and then go home to their children.

Thus the place where we often first encountered scenes involving heightened emotions between ourselves and others, real or imagined, were the group-work classes conducted by Morrison and Carnegie, not forgetting the other tutorial staff, like Hilda Courtney, a quick-silver Irish woman very popular with all but especially the young women. The other tutors, one might say, were possibly more 'orthodox' in their approach, a bit quieter and less ebullient or 'confrontational'. Together they catered for the different needs of a very wide-ranging group of students, the new recruits to a new profession. I was assigned to Iain Morrison's group. About the second week, Morrison confronted Big Davy Brown, a prominent Edinburgh councillor, an ex-miner and Convener of the Housing Committee, who was on the course on a 'community work' ticket. Davy was usually late arriving for the group and also usually had to leave early for some important council business.

He sat in the group mostly hugging his large briefcase while he was there. Readers can perhaps guess the rest, but the impeccable ray-gun accuracy with which Morrison sliced and diced Big Davy for his lack of commitment, empathy or contribution to the work and life of the group was eye-watering in its intensity. Big Davy admitted out of his own mouth that he was indeed only 'taking' from the group what he personally wanted or felt he needed for himself. He admitted he never really thought of what he may contribute or put in for the benefit of others in the group so that the 'message' he was giving out to the folk he was 'leaving behind' was that we were less important than the place he was off to next, or the place after that. This, of course, is exactly the kind of time-demand and emotional-demand that social workers in the field have to learn to juggle and cope with everyday in their work, going between clients and various other meetings. Big Davy finally let-go of his briefcase after that, well, at least for the rest of the term.

Around the middle of that term, Big Tam and myself ended up going to London for a weekend course that I had spotted – lectures on behavioural psychology and positive thinking by a large American – who else? – called Harvey. It so happened that the place we were staying was hosting some 'alternative' therapy workshops. Big Harvey was both huge and a big disappointment. He came out in a crew-cut and business-suit and spoke in an expansive drawl, opening with the quite promising analogy that a person's early learning imprints on them like a record and every time they get into emotional difficulties later in life, sure enough, they spin into that same little ol' groove they'd been spun in from the very start. The question Harvey then posed – how to break the cycle and change the record – Harvey failed to answer in any way meaningful or convincing either to Big Tam or myself.

'Never mind,' we said. 'Let's go to some of that alternative workshop stuff.'

We joined a small queue waiting to go through a wee curtain thing. Big Tam decided he wasn't for it but I went in anyway to be met by a small blonde woman, clad like some harem-girl out of the Arabian Nights. She asked me to close my eyes and 'trust' her – that word again – and not to open them until the experiences which lay ahead were over. She took both my hands in hers and I closed my eyes. She coaxed me forward, walking slowly, while these different experiences unfolded: flowers and grasses touching my face, my fingers gently placed in bowls filled with water or oils, scents wafting, perhaps also including waccy-baccy, and soft music playing as I was passed from one pair of leading hands to another and then another, all with my eyes kept firmly shut and trusting myself and my helpers until, finally, I stopped, only to be kissed full on the mouth by a gorgeous pair of lips which, when I opened my eyes, realised belonged to a large hairy guy dressed like Ziggy Stardust.

Later, in the bar, Big Tam and I were ruminating on what the day had brought us. I began telling him all about the different experiences that the 'trust tour' had involved and, just as I got to the punch-line about the kiss, he said, 'I'll tell ye somethin', Al, yon big guy sure looked a good kisser!'

I said, 'Whit dae ye mean?'

Big Tam said, 'I was standin' there watchin' ye's. It was just a big gym hall behind thon wee curtain. There was a crowd o' us standin' watchin'. I don't suppose ye could see, but, ye'd have had yir eyes closed.'

We returned from London pretty much the same individuals as before we'd left. Trust, or its lack, continued to be encountered in the old classrooms of Regent Road, Morrison making astute observations usually beginning with the same phrase, 'as my old granny used to say'. He seemed to have a photographic memory for every word that anyone and everyone in the group had ever said or thought of saying, even if they had not got round to saying it yet. If Morrison's chosen weapon was the stiletto, then Dougie's was very definitely the cleaver. His group sessions tended to end in high crescendo with Big Tam comforting distressed women in the corridor or canteen afterwards. Some things just cannot be taught. Big Tam had four sisters and seemed attuned to the female psyche in a way that I, having four brothers, could only gawp at, for Tam intuits female emotion the way a Steinway piano-tuner calibrates scales. And all the while Dougie, like Vincent Price in yon film about

a demented Witch-Finder General in Cromwell's Model Army, continued on
his one-man crusade to root out what he termed 'emotional vampires' and
'charismatic leadership', these evidently being amongst the most dangerous
tendencies to which humankind is prone in general, and social work and
community work students in particular. Well, not on Dougie's watch – not
by a long chalk.

It would be too facile to suggest that, throughout our training years, I
was 'thinking' my way round social work while Big Tam was 'feeling' his,
but there is a modicum of truth in this at least. Professional development
involves integrating both thought and feeling and people tend to start out
from one end of the spectrum and hopefully work towards the other end.
The same was true of everyone on the course. Tam's own view of himself as
a person as well as a social worker was created not simply by being reared in
a largely female household headed by a strong matriarchal mother but of her
being widowed in her mid-30s when his coalminer father died early of heart
disease and having to struggle with the material poverty this brought in its
train. Tam would say they were 'poor' in a way that my thoroughly working-
class family never was and I believe him.

It showed in the way Tam could communicate immediately with what
the textbooks called 'the client group', sometimes using what the textbooks
would have called 'bad language'. But what the client group got was what it
saw, someone who cared enough to swear back if he was sworn at but then
sticking by them too, when it came to the 'bit' – which it always would, nine
times out of ten. The textbooks might call this 'a strong sense of compassion
and social justice' but, to us on the course, it was just Big Tam.

What I am trying to recall is how, back in 1971, we were mostly trying to
come to terms with our own thoughts and feelings – our own truths – across
a whole range of matters. Questions of trust were being writ large not only
in the classrooms of Regent Road but echoing down its corridors, often in
the form of Rod Stewart's 'Maggie May' which topped the charts in October
1971 and drifted constantly out of the canteen. Its pulsating beat and lyrics
provided an unlikely backing track and almost sardonic commentary on the
explosion of Scottish working-class resentment that had broken out that
summer against the Heath Government's attack on public sector industries,
notably ship-building on the Clyde. The UCS work-in galvanised popular
opinion in Scotland, even Tory opinion, for the Scottish Conservative Party
contributed to the work-in's fighting fund, along with John Lennon and
Yoko Ono and all of Scotland's churches, from June 1971 to October 1972.

And so, as Morrison and Carnegie were questioning us, and we were
questioning ourselves and each other, and students on university campuses
all over the world were questioning America's War in Vietnam, the organised

British working-class was questioning the capitalist system on Clydeside in the shape of the Tory Government. As Wordsworth had written when he was still a young radical at the outbreak of the French Revolution:

> Bliss it was in that dawn to be alive,
> But to be young was very heaven!

And, indeed, so it was.

3

Hammer-Throwers

My first placement, 1971, Hamilton Burgh,
Joe Gillen asked me to do a process recording,
a detailed report on a visit I had made
…Godot, alive, and waiting, in Hamilton.
'Process Recording', *Dancing with Big Eunice*

*The author paddles out alone in a coracle to the island of Hamilton Burgh
for a practice-placement and finds himself trapped in an ordinary client's
house whom he cannot help. He is lured to Falkirk Burgh with the promise
of easy money by two experienced mariners who will prove important in his
career, Danny Deans and Paul Morron. He visits the seaport of Liverpool
with another band of rascally buccaneer community workers and learns
lots about Beethoven and where he has a verbal punch-up with a Militant
Trot over the UCS work-in. He gets caught up in a College campus sit-in
demanding more training places for more social workers otherwise they'll
be totally run-off their feet as soon as they reach the end of their training
(which they are in any case).*

I WAS SENT out of Regent Road to my first ten-week block practice-placement
in Hamilton Burgh social work department at the beginning of January
1972 under the supervision of Joe Gillen, a former Probation Officer, and
the training officer for the Area Team. I still have Joe's report written at the
end of my placement, in which he mentions my absence for the first few days
of the placement through 'injury', no doubt football-related. Joe helpfully
lists the half-a-dozen cases, what we may call low-level cases, which I mainly
picked up on duty and followed up by visits thereafter. It is safe to say that
I can remember absolutely nothing about any of them save the one which I
relate in detail below in the 'process-recording' cited.

At this stage I had absolutely no experience of directly interviewing
people in need, far less being familiar with the legislation which qualified
them for help or support and so I was completely reliant on getting as much
relevant information as I could from them and then checking this out either
with my supervisor or the other more experienced workers in the office at
the time. This is still largely the case in social work today, which has always
been a team activity in this sense. Experienced workers assist inexperienced

workers but they also help each other no matter how experienced they are themselves. The complexity of cases experienced workers have to deal with often requires deliberation and consultation with a Senior or experienced peer since these decisions can be as much a matter of balance and judgement as of statute, regulation or precedent.

On the placement, I spent my days reading files, sitting in on 'duty' cases and talking about the stuff which arose on a daily basis. Early on, I spotted a rather veteran social worker lacing himself into a long blue gabardine raincoat that nearly reached the floor. He had his trousers tucked into his socks and a leather helmet with flaps that resembled those shown in old films of bomber pilots during the war, which he looked like he could have been in. On my enquiry, he said he was going out to visit one of his mental health cases, for he was indeed what was once called a Mental Welfare Officer. They had been based in hospitals before becoming drafted into the new social work service that was now up and running. He offered me the following basic advice about the visiting of 'dirty' homes, the likes of which he was about to visit himself: never accept a cup of tea and never sit down. I thought he was slightly mad himself, about which I am not quite certain to this day.

Come the day, however, and Joe suggested that I arrange a home-visit to a case that had cropped up through the duty system: a single-mother about to give birth but still living at home, who had been turned down by the DHSS for a grant to buy some baby clothes. My first ever unaccompanied home-visit to a client, Joe asked me to write it up in full in the form of a 'process-recording', a device possibly defunct but then extensively used by trainers to alert them as to what students are actually doing, thinking, feeling and saying while interacting with a particular client. My write-up has survived and is offered here for posterity. I note the date of my visit was 1 February 1972, my 23rd birthday:

Miss G answered the door, I assumed it was Miss G because she did not deny it when I introduced myself and asked her, but the young lady was pregnant and appeared to be in the age-category I knew Miss G to be in – 20 to 21. She opened the door wider and said, not to me particularly, 'my faither's in the kitchen', and as I proceeded along the hall, she bellowed out behind me 'there's a man here daddy'! By this time I had arrived at the kitchen door which led off left from the hall. A closed door terminated the hall, immediately adjacent to the kitchen door.

As I stood framed in the kitchen doorway, I saw a man of about 50–55 years, short, rotund, gray-whitish hair stooping over a huge pot of soup. He raised a ladle to his mouth and started drinking the soup but apart from a glance out of the corner of his left eye he gave no indication that he was aware of my presence. The young lady whom I assumed was Miss G brushed past me into the kitchen and there was what must have been a couple of minutes of confused activity, at least on my part. They moved to-and-fro not speaking or looking at each other or at me in particular. I stood there, brief-case in hand, motionless, apart from my mind which said 'scrub it and we'll start again from the door – take two, action'! I felt myself screaming with laughter somewhere in the region of my mid-riff, or perhaps it was nerves, but anyway I stood there, uncomprehending and, seemingly, uncomprehended.

The closed door opened and a big guy about 20 years old came out, looked at me as though I wasn't there. I nodded my head. He spoke to no one, diddled about, entered back through the door he had just come out of, paused momentarily, looked at me, still without any expression on his face or interest in who I was and what there doing. I, of course, was standing. He closed the door.

My gaze moved back to the occupants of the kitchen. By this time, the man was rubbing his hands on a cloth and his body and head were slanting forward in my direction, although his eyes were lowered, in a manner which suggested that my presence was in danger of being acknowledged. I squeezed past a large wooden dresser and found myself almost in the centre of the living room. Seated round either side of a gas-fire were two youths, one the large fellow I had encountered earlier was sitting with his back towards me and turned his head half-round to look at me. The other guy looked slightly younger with a mop of thick, black curly hair, was sitting directly facing me in an armchair on the far side of the fire. I watched Miss G skirt round the back of the couch to occupy a wooden chair with its back to a window looking inwards. Still nobody had spoken to me and I stood. Still nothing, so I decided to sit down on the couch.

I started talking to Miss G about what action I had taken concerning her case and the conclusions which had been reached. I paused. Nothing. I looked round. The two guys were looking at me. The older man was standing leaning on the back of the big guy's armchair looking half at me and half at the floor. The living room walls were filthy, furniture, what there was, dilapidated. Without much experience of such places, it is the dirtiest place I have been in. The young dark, curly haired guy turned round in his chair and shouted to his sister, for so she was – 'did you no hear the man talking to you?' Miss G was moved to say something to him which I did not quite catch, but it was only a few words. Her father started to talk, something about the putative father running away and so on and what he'd get when he came out (of jail), then spoke about the possibility of getting a pram from somewhere from a neighbour. I turned back to Miss G and asked her about the money she was getting from the social security, perhaps she could put some aside for a layette or part of one. She looked away again. I heard her father say behind me – 'she doesn't know what a layette is'. I re-interpreted my question but still nothing. Her father started talking again about how he was on social security and what was going to happen to this guy when he came out. I again addressed Miss G, explaining the limits of our powers to assist financially but to call back if she was having difficulty with clothes or any other problem. She said nothing. Her father showed me out, repeated at the door most of what he had said before and I left. Miss G has yet to speak to me.

The only thing unusual about this case is that it involved a home-visit. It was a typical duty-case that would have ordinarily been dealt with by inviting Miss G into the office but, a student needing 'experience', I was dispatched accordingly. I had in fact been in touch with DHSS and discovered that a baby was entitled to a clothing grant only if it survived the first six weeks of life. What the Government thought a parent without means should do to clothe a child meantime remained unanswered for several years to come. In such cases, Salvation Army clothing was often available but why this was not offered in this situation or in this area now escapes me. Charity provision did vary from place to place as did the interpretation of Section 12 payments or money grants that local authorities felt able to pay out in the absence of national social security entitlements. This kind of cat-and-mouse payment conflict between local councils and central Government departments responsible for social security still continues today. The gap between what is entitled and what is given as 'discretionary' is nowadays often filled by food banks or food parcels which social workers may supply but only in what are deemed absolutely emergency situations.

As Joe Gillen put it in his placement report:

There were no particular areas of difficulty encountered during the placement, although it must be said that Mr Findlay's placement here was essentially one which considerably resolved many of the general questions which existed in the student's mind regarding the basic concepts of the profession.

Safe to say that for the next four decades, Mr Findlay would continue to mull over in his mind the basic concepts of the profession and, in many ways, unaccountably, he is still doing so.

After the Hamilton placement, I returned to Regent Road for my final term of the second year. On 9 February, the National Union of Mineworkers, led in Scotland by the communist Mick McGahey, had struck for the first time since 1926, resulting in a three-day working week imposed throughout the country. The strike lasted for all of 18 days with a complete victory for the miners and for anybody else who had the brains to see through the Tory Government and its anti-working-class intentions, such as restricting the power of the trade union movement through the 1971 Industrial Relations Act. There was a rally against this held outside New St Andrew's House Square, Edinburgh, a tight little space that got completely filled by protesting trade unionists, students and the police. The usual suspects from Regent Road were there, as we would be too at the rally in Glasgow in support of the UCS work-in. Wee Mike busied himself going round with a flash camera taking photographs of the Special Branch officers who were busy taking photographs of the demonstrators. I wrote a poem about the Edinburgh rally, later published in *A Rose Loupt Oot: Poetry and Song Celebrating the UCS Work-in* (Smokestack Books, 2011), edited by David Betteridge, four decades after the event – the Industrial Relations Act, 1971 (repealed 1974) which begins:

> We were part of a big demonstration,
> New St Andrew's House Square jam-pack'd,
> the Tories Industrial Relations –
> the dole and a knife in the back.

College life continued against this backing track. The Heath Government and the way it was trying to impose unwelcome authority and 'austerity' on ordinary working people was an inescapable theme of the day. This invigorated our own demonstration regarding Regent Road needing to expand the number of training places to meet the new social work responsibilities but, before that, I spotted another event that Big Tam and myself decided to go along to, this time in Glasgow. It was a conference on 'Truancy and School Phobia', the main speaker being Fred Stone, an eminent child psychiatrist who provided assessments and consultation for List D schools in the West of Scotland. So we got the train through from Waverley and when it stopped at Falkirk High station, a wee guy boarded and sat beside us. He looked like an office clerk, had a Liverpool accent and a bright manner about him. When we got off, so did he, and we discovered that he was to speak at the conference – Geoff Evans, Director of Social Work for Falkirk Burgh. Fred Stone gave a brilliant talk about the differences between 'school phobia', affecting middle-class children who were over-sheltered, almost to suffocation, by over-protective parents, and 'truants', usually working class kids acting 'normally' by mimicking highly anti-authority attitudes held by their parents, and receiving little parental interest at all.

The best joke was told by Geoff Evans, who had formerly been a Probation Officer in Liverpool. He said his old boss used to compare social workers to 'dung' because – 'when spread out thinly on the ground they might do some good but when gathered altogether they just stink'.

Near the end of my second year on the course, it suddenly dawned on me that I was over halfway towards becoming a qualified professional social worker. The field was presently stuffed with unqualified folk waiting on folk like me to finish our training. I was aware, too, that Joe Gillen had suggested that I seek an intensive casework experience in my next placement, and where better to get it than in nearby Falkirk social work office? I therefore phoned Geoff, who was delighted to offer me a couple of months' well-paid summer employment.

And so, in July 1972, I found myself in Newmarket Street in the old Burgh hall building in the centre of Falkirk, the town's social work department. I met my Senior, Danny Deans, who was seven years older than me and had been a Probation Officer for all of six months before the new generic, one-door social work departments opened their doors on 17 November 1969. He had only been a Senior social worker for a few months and I would work with and for him, off and on, over the next 30 years. Danny was smartly dressed in bluish blazer and flannels and he looked you straight in the eye. He was friendliness itself but with a bounce you knew wasn't going to make him back down easily, if ever.

Danny introduced me to Paul Morron, whose tiny office I would share, looking out onto the main street, which had benches and rose-beds in the centre where the local 'jaikies' (alcoholic homeless men) sat beneath the Great War memorial. Paul was a lawyer, brought up in Glasgow as part of the strong Jewish community there, and worked for Danny as an unqualified social worker. He was a very able, thoroughly organised, stringently honest, fair and deliberative kind of character, certainly in formal and official settings, for which he dressed the part in a suit and tie. He also had a huge propensity to crack up laughing at the slightest provocation, almost without warning. This meant that later he would laugh a lot with – or at – Big Tam, for Tam too would do a placement in Falkirk and also join the department at the end of the course. Paul was perhaps a couple of years older than me and we got on like a house on fire. He would later decide not to train for a professional social work qualification, which did not prevent him from becoming the lead Criminal Justice manager for Strathclyde Regional Council when

Community Service Orders, which Paul helped pioneer through his role with the Scottish Association for the Care and Resettlement of Offenders (SACRO) in 1978–9. I think Paul appreciated discussing casework theories and practice with me and my attempts to incorporate these into my own practice. At this point, he helped ground my practice by discussing some of his own cases and those I encountered on duty.

Between Danny and Paul, I was suddenly being treated like a fellow colleague, not as a student or a trainee, and I was expected to get on with it, although they offered me advice whenever I asked for it. They perhaps felt I was 'sound' compared to some of the other unqualified workers they had had dealings with before I arrived. I think they saw in me something they possessed in large measure themselves: a lack of basic 'fear', either of the people we had to work with or the emotional demands the job involved. They might even have seen in me, in football parlance, someone who could put the boot in, run all day and make the occasional telling pass. Danny had indeed played football with his home village team, Bonnybridge Juniors, famous in those circles as 'hammer-throwers' – in a league which greatly relied on 'hammer-throwers' (that is, people who believe in taking the man as well as the ball, but certainly the man if not the ball). Paul was, of course, a referee. Both of them, in their own ways, made the job real to me, as well as enjoyable.

And so the summer passed, after which I would complete my third and final year of the course, first a placement in Liverpool in a voluntary casework agency until Christmas, then a final term at Regent Road for more lectures and final exams and then a final placement, the Family Service Unit in Castlemilk, another voluntary casework agency. Both Danny and Geoff were persistent in asking me to return to Falkirk Burgh when I qualified for what it had to offer me as a new worker starting out. I was pleased to be asked, of course, but the roller-coaster that I felt I was on had not yet come to a halt and I was still pretty curious as to what might yet lie ahead around the next bend.

What lay around it was Liverpool, where I found myself in September 1972 working on placement for a voluntary agency on cases drawn from the 'tough' Speke housing estate. The agency had a duty-desk in a local surgery in a small shopping-centre for a couple of days a week, though the main office remained in the city centre, about which I remember very little. The duty-room was tiny and cramped, just large enough for my chair and table and a couple of other chairs. A charity box stood menacingly on the end of the table, silently expecting donations that were never forthcoming.

It was a shoe-string affair compared to Falkirk Burgh, tiny compared to the volume and range of work and staff employed by the local authorities.

My lack of recollection of the cases I dealt with in voluntary agencies in Liverpool and then Glasgow in the following spring may partly stem from the lack of focus such work tends to have compared to most statutory social work intervention. Helpful and interesting as it no doubt was for my professional development, voluntary agency work did not compare to the experience I felt I had been offered in Falkirk Burgh. I soon realised that local authority work attracted me far more, both for what I got out of it and for the scope and variation it offered my career. Small-scale voluntary agency work did not suit or attract me, just as I knew that, at some point, I would end up working in a city environment to complete my experience.

What Liverpool gave me more than intensive casework was the opportunity to live with four other Regent Road students, all of us sent there on different placements, a couple of them in the much vaunted 'Vauxhall Project', a so-called community project. Pooling our expenses, five of us jointly rented a huge detached house in the Aintree area of the city – Big Rab Murray, Ed Finlayson, Alec Davidson, Glynis Houston/McEwan and me. We had separate bedrooms and a communal lounge and kitchen. There was a massive 1950s gramophone with a deep sonorous bass sound which, with the volume up full, rocked the place, the foundations, the street and the horses running around the racetrack.

Big Rab was initially a bit unnerving to live with. Sitting in the lounge on the settee, he never just got up and left the room, made himself a cup of tea or offered to make you a cup of tea. No, Big Rab stood up and then announced to the whole room what he was about to do, I suspect even when there was nobody else in it. And so we lived, talking of different placement experiences, socialism, politics, films and pop music, punctuated by Big Rab standing up and announcing, 'I'm away for a paper' or 'I'm away for a dump' or 'I'm going to fart'. If there was no resulting blast, he would add a rather apologetic codicil, again in the form of an announcement – 'sorry, that came oot wi' its slippers on'.

Surprising as it may seem from that description, Big Rab was also something of a 'culture-vulture' when it came to classical music, especially that of his 'socialist' hero, Ludwig van Beethoven. If Big Rab told us once, he told us many times how Beethoven had left his music 'to my brothers' – 'That's us', says Big Rab, 'we're his brothers, the working class! He left his music to us!' Beethoven did in fact have two brothers, one of whom survived him, so strictly speaking, according to Big Rab, he would have said 'my brother', singular, if he had only meant him. But he said 'brothers', plural, so, he meant us!

As luck would have it, the Liverpool Philharmonic Orchestra put on a performance of Handel's *Messiah* as our placements ended, and so we were dragged along mid-week in the middle of winter to a huge hall with wooden floors, wooden chairs and absolutely no heating. When the conductor walked on stage, a large portly character, Big Rab leapt to his feet and began clapping wildly, saying more to himself than to us, 'A big gallus conductor. I like nothing better than a big effing gallus conductor!' The place may have been half-empty and freezing but Big Rab glowed through the whole of the recital.

The lead male and female singers sang their hearts out dressed to the nines, and the big effing gallus conductor conducted gallusly until, near the end, came the one transforming moment of the evening for me. In the middle of Part III of the *Messiah* there is a section called 'The Trumpet Shall Sound' and when the orchestra came to that bit, the male singer sang poignantly, 'And did those trumpets sound?' In response, he was expecting to hear a solo trumpet toot crisply back the melody of the phrase he had just sung, but what came out was more like one of Rab's strangled farts. The orchestra could not stop, of course, so when the female lead singer sang immediately after the very same poignant question 'And did those trumpets sound?', the solo trumpet tooted back the very same strangled fart noise. Unhappily, this charade had to be repeated several more times in quick succession, a superbly sung, 'And did those trumpets sound?' with the same awful strangulated solo trumpet response. I thought I might die, but Big Rab shrugged it off matter-of-factly, explaining that it was all to do with the cold air in the concert hall because a trumpet needs to be warmed up enough to be able to trumpet effectively. On our way home, eating our sausage and chip suppers, Big Rab talked about his favourite musical hero, Ludwig van, who, Big Rab told us, had become so engrossed in composing the *Eroica* symphony that he had lost all track of personal hygiene. Indeed, as Big Rab explained, 'Beethoven never wiped his arse for a year!' before adding, 'Imagine that!'

We also went to a film, I recall, a rather rude Italian semi-pornographic film version of Boccaccio's *The Decameron* (1971), a book which inspired Chaucer and Shakespeare in their bawdier moments. The film had abundant nudity, graphic sex, slapstick, scatological humour and English sub-titles, which were not really necessary, for there was about as much 'plot' as the *Kama Sutra*. I also remember some of us going in Edinburgh to see Stanley Kubrick's *A Clockwork Orange* (1971), based on Anthony Burgess' 1962 novel about a group of hedonistic skinheads led by an exceptionally charismatic and violent character, played by Malcolm McDowell. The sex and violence reached almost cartoon proportions, and there was much laughter as well as moments of panic and revulsion in the audience. Each scene of mindless violence seemed to call forth an even more terrible response, culminating in McDowell finally being strapped in a chair and made to watch horrific human atrocities while listening to his beloved Beethoven, the only human and potentially civilising trait he seemed to possess – music – being deliberately used against him by the state. To me it clearly showed how the state should not respond in kind to individual violence and murder, if it wanted seriously to break with the cycles of violence and alienation which lay at the root of human violence. I remember being staggered by the impact, how all the acts of violence perpetrated by persons on each other, were as nothing compared to the violence which the state was capable of inflicting on individuals, whether through capital punishment or brain-washing. I remember thinking how Kubrick was extraordinarily effective in raising the kind of issues that Carnegie kept on about – revenge, retribution and rehabilitation. The only film I remember Dougie telling me he loved was in fact Ken Russell's *Tommy* (1975), because of the soundtrack. Big Tam did not believe him, but I thought that was Dougie all over – a middle-aged punk in a suit.

In Liverpool we collectively pooled our resources to hire a car every couple of weekends to return home, Ed driving us back via Dumfries, Lanark, Glasgow, Armadale and Edinburgh respectively. Just before Christmas 1972, the end-of-placement party became a massive group event since we invited workers and students from all five placements to our pad in Aintree. During the stramash, the 1950s gramophone blaring away, a group of Goldsmith College (London) community work students arrived and I was soon locked in argument with a young scouser with huge dreadlocks and wild-staring eyes about how he thought the UCS work-in, Communist-led, had 'sold-out' the working class. I forget his exact logic for this, other than that the workers' leaders had not somehow held out for 'real socialism', despite a Tory Government being in power. The next time I saw him was on television in the early 1980s, Derek Hatton, leader of the Militant-led Labour Council in Liverpool, whom Neil Kinnock would effectively kebab from the platform at the Labour Party Conference in a manner he never achieved against his real opponent, Mrs Thatcher. Derek may have lost his dreadlocks in the intervening years but sadly nothing regarding his smirking, self-righteous conception of 'real socialism' – what it was, or how to go about achieving it, certainly in modern democratic Britain. He was, in short, an ultra-Left poseur and hence part of the problem, not the solution. Such folk still annoy me, mostly because the Tory media just love them because they help confirm the 'Red' caricature.

I received an A-pass for my Liverpool placement and returned to Regent Road in January 1973 for final exams and to help organise a sit-in protest at Moray House College over the lack of training places for social and community work students. In conjunction with Moray House Student's Union and its President, Keith Simpson, who later became a local Labour councillor, the sit-in lasted a couple of weeks and involved boycotting official lectures and groups at Regent Road and Moray House. Our 'cause for concern' turned on the need to increase the number of social work and community work students required to cope adequately with the new welfare provisions introduced by the Social Work (Scotland) Act. A few of us appeared on a BBC television discussion on the subject chaired by the respected TV journalist, Donald MacCormack. *The Daily Express* reported the event in the following manner on 1 February 1973, in fact my 24th birthday:

About 180 student social workers and 15 lecturers walked out of the School of Community Studies in Edinburgh yesterday in protest against 'overcrowding and antiquated working conditions'. They continued their classes in the Student Union of Edinburgh University where they arranged temporary accommodation. The community studies school is a department of Moray House College of Education. It is responsible for training above 60 per cent of the social workers who qualify in Scotland and is housed in what was formerly a Victorian primary school in Regent Road. Students and staff complained yesterday that the premises were totally inadequate. Because of staff shortages and lack of space, more than half of the suitable candidates who applied for training had been refused.

The demonstrators said: 'We still have to make a straight choice between breathing and hearing in lectures and tutorials. While a staff of 15 tries to cope with the training needs of 315 students, the 315 try to eat and study simultaneously on 42 chairs.' They also expressed concern about the low priority given nationally to social work training. Recent student research they said had shown that the already inadequate staff in the social work departments throughout the country would deteriorate further because of insufficient training facilities in Scotland. Dr Douglas McIntosh, the principal of Moray House, said he has offered to meet the staff and students to discuss the problems of accommodation. The college, he said, was negotiating for a site for a new building and had promises of financial support from the Government when one was available. Mr Brian Ashley, the director of the school, said that staff and students could no longer be expected to bear the brunt of unfavourable comparison with similar courses elsewhere. If the protesters returned to the school he would set up a staff-student committee.

I like the bit about 42 chairs – very precise – and I wonder if they really counted them. It is worth noting how so much of our youthful energy was being directed at crucial matters such as the number of professionals employed in an expanding welfare state. We obviously understood very clearly just how central the creation of the welfare state was – public health, education, housing, social security and welfare – not only to our parents' generation but to our own. Our sit-in emulated other demonstrations then occurring in university campuses across the country prompted by the recently concluded UCS work-in on Clydebank forcing the Heath Government to U-turn on closing the shipyards. We arranged through the Student's Union to have speakers from UCS come to Moray House to speak and collect money for the workers' occupation of the yards. It was therefore in 1972–3 that young white-collar professionals like ourselves were becoming aware that we were not only part of the welfare state but also part of the 'public-sector' workforce responsible for its delivery and, when necessary, defending it, from right-wing political forces from Ted Heath through to Mrs Thatcher and so on right down to the present Tory Government.

In May 1973, we were sent out of Regent Road to our final practice placements. I returned to the Family Service Unit in Castlemilk, headed by the quietly charismatic Bob Purvis, the legendary manager of the Unit. Neither of them was that much to look at on the surface but both had a huge beating heart underneath. An important role the FSU played was to work with hard to reach clients – those who avoided or refused to cooperate with the statutory services in the area.

Gus Campbell, who will figure at various points in this narrative, worked for the FSU for a couple of years after qualifying in the early 1970s before entering the local authority arena in Greenock. He learned much from Bob and his ways, especially in his attitude to the marginalised client group this local neighbourhood style of working was geared to try and get alongside. One was an elderly man, unusually a beer-drinking alcoholic, who periodically called in for a chat with Bob and he sometimes tapped him for a 'loan', which Bob always gave him. Bob told Gus that he often asked the guy for a 'loan', too, if he knew he had money and the guy always obliged. Bob would say that he was not due his wages for a few days and he was short of cash, and would ask if the man could lend him a couple of quid to see him through. Bob's rationale was that this fitted with the working-class culture and assumptions of the area, allowing the relationship between the workers and people to be more even and hopefully less hierarchical and patronising. It would probably get him sacked today.

On completing our final placements in June, we returned for a few days to Regent Road for the graduation ceremony. There was some talk being whipped up by Big Rab and others against the convention that the Principal of Moray House, the haunted Dr Douglas McIntosh, would only offer his hand to those graduates who were to receive honours or distinctions of some sort. There was also some aggravation about the cost and flummery of graduates having to wear the traditional black scholar's cap and gown for the ceremony. While chewing this over, I was called to see the Director of the School, Brian Ashley, to be informed that the tutors had voted to award me something called the June Gordon Memorial Award, dedicated by the parents of a former student who had since died. According to Brian, this award was not given annually but only to a student whom staff felt merited it. I thanked Brian but refused the award since it was a distinction I did not feel I merited. He asked me to think about it for an hour or so. When I left his office, Morrison and Carnegie were waiting for me and, for the next half-hour, I was given the full treatment: this might help get me a job I wanted or was particularly suited for and so on. In the end, I finally succumbed and told Brian I would accept the award.

Wee Mike has since told me that he was offered the award first but stuck to his principles and so refused it. I told him he should write his own memoir. Besides, it was something to tell the parents, who had come along for my graduation. Afterwards I introduced them to Iain Morrison, having prompted my father about how important he had been to me. As for the June Gordon Memorial Award, it never helped me get any job in the future, though it did perhaps reflect how much of myself I had put into the course. I cannot now remember if Dr McIntosh shook my hand but I do recall Big Rab, *sans* scholar's cap and gown, making his own personal protest during the ceremony, offering his hand to Dr McIntosh from a distance of 20 feet and walking slowly across the stage towards him, which the good Doctor studiously ignored. I was, of course, hoping that Dr McIntosh might have been foolish enough to have reached for the outstretched limb, only for it to have been whipped away at the last moment, for a thumb to have been stuck on the end of Big Rab's nose and for the rest of his fingers to have been wiggled profanely. This would have been a fitting symbol, perhaps, for what many of this new generation would soon make of the traditional institutions we were about to be released into, some of which were half-expecting change but not quite sure what it would look like. I smile now because it looked like Big Rab, but also many who did not look like him at all, but who still wanted much the same kind of changes he did and, indeed, most of us did.

In those final days at college, representatives from every local authority and voluntary agency in Scotland and beyond came to make their pitch to recruit those graduates still looking for jobs. Indeed, it was a bit like a cattle auction in reverse, the people with the money and jobs in the centre of the ring that had been the lecture hall in Regent Road, now being weighed up by the very people they were hoping to employ. The best speaker was definitely the Depute Director for Coatbridge social work department, an area with very high levels of poverty and unemployment. He had the burly look of an ex-miner squeezed into a tightly rumpled suit, and he was as broad in his speech as he was in his build. He began brightly: 'Ah'm fae Coatbrigg. Some say it's the "Ersehole O' Lanarkshire", but I can tell ye's this, if ye's come tae us ye's'll no be wantin' for work!' He was a great hit with the whole student body, though I noticed nobody actually signed up for 'Coatbrigg'.

I had already signed up for Falkirk Burgh and so had Big Tam, who had gone there for a final practice placement. He came back quoting a phrase used in the workplace to denote his supervisor – 'keep me posted' – who, needless to say, was rarely to be found whenever needed most.

In fact, six Regent Roaders would end up working in Falkirk that summer: me, Big Tam, Les Barnaby, who had been seconded by Falkirk Burgh to the course, Helen Petrie, Davis Mitchell and Alex Thain. Together with a trainee, Janet Campbell, and a Senior, this in effect comprised a whole Area Team. As our Moray House 'sit-in' had helped expose, the staffing levels for the new social work service mirrored exactly the existing staffing levels for the old specialist services combined, about 1,000 posts. When these were divided amongst the Scottish population of 5 million it gave a ratio of about ten social workers to a 50,000 population area. Magically, this Scottish Office back-of-an-envelope calculation roughly matched the English Seebohm recommendations (Murphy: 169), in which there was no change planned to the juvenile court system, unlike the major increase in caseloads that the new Hearing system would create.

On the night of our graduation, a bunch of us ended up drinking in Carnegie's local hotel, The Abbey, just up from Regent Road. I was button-holed by, let's call him Big D, who Dougie had spent the best part of two years trying to make a less 'dangerous' worker because Big D had all the charismatic qualities of a born leader but not a scoobie as to where he wanted to lead anyone or, indeed, why. Big D, in his cups, thus hailed me across and told me that he had managed to swing the Scottish Office and a large local authority into funding a new day-facility for youngsters that would have group-work at the core of its approach. The only trouble, Big D said, was that he knew 'eff-all' about group-work. But me, he said, I knew everything about group-work, for I had gone to the classes. Would I work for him?

There is a moral here somewhere, I suppose, but I am no longer sure what it is. Big D did set up the resource and it was pretty successful for a number of years as it changed its shape and function over the coming decades. And it was a new resource, something different from what existed, if anything, before then. Perhaps that is the moral: simply that my generation were being sent out into existing institutions and expected to change them, part of that being to invent what had hitherto not existed or not in adequate form or sufficiency. And this we did.

What became of Big D? Still leading but to where, God alone knows. As for Big Tam and myself, we did not spend time mourning the loss of Morrison and Carnegie, who we would see soon enough in our future careers. What came now was Falkirk Burgh and Orchard Street, our local office, which covered the Bog Road, our local 'patch' – a place where much patching up was indeed needed, and which it got, usually without the aid of anaesthetics, either for us or the clients.

4

Are You Laughin' At Me?

Panels, the Children's Hearings, set up
as instruments of God by Lord Wheatley
to lead Scotland out of darkness in 1971
whereupon the number of children sent
away rocketed up, peaked in 1974, after which
Miss Gee retired, thank Christ, satiated, Chair
of Falkirk Burgh's Panel, an ex-headmistress,
everybody's granny, tho' the smell of burning
sulphur followed her about

'Panels', *Dancing with Big Eunice*

Many stirring adventures unfold with the author observing clients in their natural habitats, progressive managers and team meetings, what an area office looks like on the inside, the frightening power of Admin, Children's Panels and the Reporter Charlie, the author's frightful ignorance as a new professional, the numbers of very young mainly poor and working-class children trapped in residential establishments some with histories of retribution rather than reform, rehabilitation and therapeutic support – leavened by a couple of very good ones too.

I LEARNED TO be a basic grader in Falkirk Burgh in the remaining months of its existence as a local authority between 4 August 1973 and its replacement by Central Regional Council on 1 April 1975. I started at the top of the salary-scale as did everyone else. To attract and keep professional staff, smaller provincial authorities like Falkirk Burgh and its successor, Central Region, often used higher pay levels to attract and retain workers and managers who might otherwise have gravitated towards the cities and larger authorities. Better pay formed no part of my own calculations, although neither was it a disincentive. What Falkirk Burgh offered me professionally was a sorted Senior in Danny, a more experienced and trusted colleague in Paul, a progressive Director in Geoff Evans (who went on to become Director of Social Work for the Borders Region) and Ian Gilmour, later an Acting Director of Social Work for Glasgow City in the 1990s. And all of it was conveniently located 13 miles away from my home in Armadale, West Lothian, where my wife was a newly qualified teacher at the new local comprehensive.

Falkirk Burgh uncommonly also acted as an adoption agency, whereas cities and larger authorities often leased out this function to specialist voluntary bodies like Barnardo's or the Catholic Adoption Society, as many still do. I was now in a workplace that offered the full range of professional childcare provision from taking children into care, to placing them in foster care or adoption through the local Sheriff Court. Falkirk had a population of 40,000, the size of the city of Perth. It was thus large enough to have local 'gangs' based on traditional territorial rivalries between the young denizens of Camelon in the west and Bog Road in the east towards Grangemouth. Grangemouth and its docks also added a smattering of drugs and prostitution to the traditional mix of large families, unemployment, ill health, criminality and misfortune which had provided most of the clientele of the old welfare agencies and child rescue societies like the Royal Scottish Society for the Prevention of Cruelty to Children (RSSPCC) for at least the last half-century. I was therefore aware from the very start that here was a place in which I could learn my trade and keep my professional interests alive for longer than a fortnight.

Falkirk's Directorate took the new duty bestowed on local authorities 'to promote social welfare' surprisingly seriously. There was a community development section based in Newmarket Street which set up and ran everything from day centres and lunch clubs, to crèches and meals-on-wheels and similar communal provision. There was a 'detached community worker', Craig Robertson, who lived in the local community he served, a 40-year-old humanitarian idealist who was to alienated youth in Falkirk what tree-hugging would become later to Swampy and the Green movement. In the air, there was a general feel of feverish activity and a sense that something was moving forward and going to happen, which doubtless related to the two general elections that would occur in 1974, resulting in Harold Wilson's Labour Party winning an overall majority of three seats. The Scottish National Party (SNP) would poll 30 per cent of the Scottish popular vote and gain 11 Westminster seats, then its highest ever total. Like most industrial central-belt towns, Falkirk Burgh was solid Labour, its local MP the well-liked and respected Harry Ewing, a junior Scottish Office minister responsible for Devolution in the 1970s. But he was no firebrand and quite willing to accept a peerage to the Lords in due course.

Our weekly team meetings, chaired by Geoff Evans in his large office in Newmarket Street, seemed to pack everyone in: the development section, both Area Teams plus the whole of Admin if they wanted to come. It was an eye-opener. Everything got debated, from paper clips to the legality of certain practices (usually raised by Paul and usually at great length) to making everyone Director-for-the-day (usually raised by Big Craig and also at great length), even including Big Eunice, admin assistant under the ever watchful eye of Miss M. Every social work workplace has a formal and informal communication system, an official and unofficial level of information exchange, which management must tap into if it is to keep functioning effectively. The weekly Falkirk Burgh team meeting chaired by the Director on an open basis brought these information flows together, which achieved a certain degree of clarity and congruence between higher policy aims and daily service delivery and practice. It helped resolve glitches arising between these levels. In those early days, Falkirk Burgh got it about right by harnessing the energy, enthusiasm and confusion of just about everyone under the professional leadership of a liberal and progress minded boss like Geoff Evans and, later, Ian Gilmour. If it looked like chaos to outsiders, the workplace itself thrummed and hummed and got on with the basic business of delivering welfare in all its tedious, frightening, occasionally heartbreaking aspects. What would result when this empowered workplace came up against an out-of-its-depth and defensively minded regional management will be detailed later. For now, we had something much more important to deal with – Admin.

If, as Napoleon famously said, 'an army marches on its stomach', until the recent advent of new technology, social work departments were also largely in debt to the quality of its Admin almost as much as to its professional staff. The person nominally in charge of it was Wee Bill, whose beatific face and gentle manner seemed to me magnified by the thick bottle-glass wire spectacles he wore. Wee Bill reminded me of Master Po, the blind old Buddha-like philosopher who used to say 'ahh, grasshopper' in the long-running American TV series, *Kung Fu*, in which Cane (played by David Carradine) is a half-white/Chinese boy raised by Shaolin monks. Master Po mentored Cane and brought him to worldly wisdom by uttering gnomic, unworldly paradoxes like 'Fear is the only darkness, grasshopper' and 'What is more forceful than quiet water, grasshopper?' Maybe these were the kind of conversations I would have liked to have had with Wee Bill, who was discretion and graciousness itself but, in the four years I was in Falkirk, we never got much beyond 'Yes, Alistair' or 'We'll see what we can do about that, Alistair'.

That 'we' obviously included Miss M, not so much the power behind Wee Bill, more a lioness prowling round the entrance to the cashroom where sat Miss M's junior assistant, Big Eunice. A bit like Miss Milroy at Regent Road, Miss M was always called by her surname, except by Big Eunice, who called her plenty of other names. Big Eunice could do half an hour of wicked stand-up impersonating Miss M, behind her back and beyond ear-shot, a difficult feat to achieve given the vigilance she attached to keeping

Eunice close by her desk and close by herself as well. Miss M tended to wear the stiff, crinolene dresses once popular in the '50s and was always immaculately coiffed, a bit like Mrs Thatcher, and she had evidently been a fine-looking woman in her day. At Christmas, with a fair amount of sherry under the bridge, Miss M seemed to shed her chaperoning of Big Eunice and go to the other extreme, confiding *risqué* stories of her time in the Women's Auxilliary Air Force (WAAFs), telling Big Eunice, who then told everyone else, 'I won't die wondering, you know'. Miss M was thus in charge of the cash and ran a very tight ship but kept herself mostly out of sight round the back, unlike her periodically office-wandering charge Eunice, who never kept herself in the dark if it could at all be avoided.

The benign rulers of Admin in Newmarket Street were Rita the Receptionist and Jean the Director's Secretary. Thankfully, they were great friends and they combined the official and unofficial communication systems mentioned earlier, since Jean knew everything that was happening upstairs and Rita knew everything that was going on at street level. Given the size of their personalities, it was fortunate they did get on but they ruled jointly through their competence, good humour and 'upfrontness'. Everything was taken in their stride. Rita held the key vantage point, the gatekeeper of the phones and all the people coming in off the street. Rita could juggle three phone calls at a time; advise the duty-worker where the proper forms were and how to fill them in; entertain two allocated cases waiting on their social workers; redirect several passers-by to their correct destinations; and send Old Willie, the local flasher, off with a flea in his ear, all the while talking to Jean about arranging a visit by some new Panel members the following week, without missing a beat. Old Willie, in regulation dirty old raincoat, had made himself famous by shuffling up to Rita one day, busy in her reception booth, and saying, 'What do you think, Rita?', flitting his eyes mysteriously downwards, so that Rita, always curious, stretched over the counter only to see Willie's bared member looking back at her with a pink ribbon tied round its middle. Rita did not scream, as Willie was hoping, but said firmly, 'Put that away, Willie, and behave yourself,' and turned back to her other tasks. Old Willie slouched off, deflated, never to bare his all again, at least not to Rita.

After a short period based in Newmarket Street, the Bog Road team to which both Big Tam and myself had been assigned under Danny's leadership, moved about 200 yards along the road to a new office, a detached Victorian villa in Orchard Street, as fragrant and sunlit as its name suggests. It was a bit like entering another Tardis for me, another Regent Road, with its own ambience and internal rules of governance belying its stolid, bourgeois appearance. It had a long hallway with wooden stairs halfway along, which led up to a half-landing doorway, the entrance to my huge office overlooking the back garden. At the top of the next flight of stairs were two large rooms either side, one to the right for Danny and one to the left for Paul and Helen, a Regent Roader like Big Tam and me. At the foot of the stairs, on either side of the hall, were other huge rooms, one of which housed Alex, another Regent Roader, and Agnes, an unqualified social worker who was, like Alex, a late entrant to the profession, she being in her mid-30s and Alex in his early 40s. Agnes would soon be replaced by Kate Peart, an English rose, her haircut like Rod Stewart's and with an understated way of conducting herself that combined firm resolve with an elegant demeanour, a good contrast, therefore, to Alex, her voluble and sometimes slightly tense roommate. When Alex was on form, he was great, but when he was not, he could be downcast verging on suicidal but we liked him. The reason we liked him most and also the reason he was most often downcast verging on suicidal, was that he had a case that we did not, called, let us say, Dora.

My first encounter with Dora was, like everybody else's encounter with Dora, always memorable and always the same. Dora was a spinster in her 50s and suffered from paranoia. She was also thick-built, strident, confrontational in both speech and manner and had unruly, curly, rather garish red hair which kept escaping from beneath a kind of 'pork-pie' hat plonked onto her head, complete with the same constant hard-wearing raincoat and bag. I had walked downstairs from my office to enter reception and there stood Dora, blocking the way. I tried to walk round her. She blocked my way again, then stuck her rather round and puffy face menacingly close to my own, then stared straight into my eyes and said, in a very loud voice, 'You laughin' at me?'

I was taken aback, and stepped back, whereupon Dora immediately stepped forward and adopted the very same stance, that is, one inch from the end of my nose and enquired again, in the same loud voice, 'You laughin' at me?' By this time, my face was probably creased into something that maybe looked like a smile, as fear can sometimes be confused with laughter. Dora continued her harangue, her face thrust menacingly close to mine – 'See! Ye're laughin' at me?' – which she followed up by appealing to the crowded queue of clients sitting in reception enjoying the spectacle of a social worker being kebabed in front of them. 'See! He's laughin' at me! Urn't ye?'

I dared not retreat back up the stairs to my office and I dared not retreat out of the front door but I managed to wade my way past Dora's accusations and hanging face which now resembled the gigantic proportions of Charles Laughton playing Quasimodo in *The Hunchback of Notre Dame*, only I had suddenly become the hunchback and Dora the howling mob in vengeful pursuit.

Thankfully, Alex emerged from his room and whisked Dora away to the privacy of his office, while Denise and Wee Marion smirked and laughed at me in much the same way that Dora had been accusing me of a few moments earlier. When Alex eventually left the team for pastures new some 18 months later, we were all sorry but petrified, too, as to who was going to take over Dora. We had seen the effect she had had on Alex, reduced from the supportive Titan he had been in the beginning, to climbing out of his office window whenever he heard Dora's voice in the hall demanding to see him – 'Ah ken ye're in there! Ah kin hear ye breathe!' – her ear pressed tight against the solid door to which Alex had wisely had a lock fitted to prevent her from barging straight into his office when he was with other clients. Dora's emotional state, of course, went up and down according to her preparedness to take her medication. Oh Dora! Oh Alex!

Across the hall from Alex's room lay reception, which had an internal wooden and glass partition dividing the room, two-thirds of which had two desks for the typists, Denise, the senior one, and Wee Marion, the junior one – our Admin section – which left just enough room on the other side of the partition for a row of about six chairs for clients to sit on while waiting to see their allocated social workers or the duty-worker, just as they would at a dentist or GP surgery. A small sliding-door hatch just above waist level prevented Denise and Wee Marion being gawped at directly by the clients but conversations could still be heard over the top of the partition either side. Conversations between me and Denise and Wee Marion usually occurred when the waiting area was empty, me hovering over their shoulders finalising a late report, often dictating it straight onto the typewriter. Denise was an exceptional typist, demandingly exact, with curly blonde hair and big blue eyes and a compulsive desire to correct my grammar, spelling and any unfamiliar words and expressions.

Like some downmarket 'Rumpole of the Bailey', I would spice some of my banter with favoured quotes, such as Oliver Goldsmith's *The Man in Black* – 'a prodigy of parsimony and prudence' – or Dr Johnson's advice to James Boswell – 'as for poverty, sir, avoid it' etc. Thus, what Denise might have conceded as regards obscure words she soon regained in spats over spelling. Wee Marion was 18, tall and slim, and had dark shoulder-length hair and a knack for spirited repartee that belied her years. She also had a flare for finishing arguments if one were foolish enough to start any. If Denise was ever losing ground against 'Rumpole' impersonations, Wee Marion would wade into the fray with some well-chosen remark that began somewhere below the knees and travelled unerringly towards its target, the solar-plexus. Which reminds me, she was also an excellent typist and great administrator.

Next door to Reception, at the foot of the stairs, was Big Tam's lair which he shared with Janet Campbell, the trainee, a cavern that could easily have taken another four desks and which had a large window looking onto the back garden. Past Tam's door and past the stairs, the hallway led through to the back of the building to the kitchen, a back lounge, bathroom and shower room, and out into the back garden itself, in which we could sit in the sun eating sandwiches and catching half an hour's repose. Danny would talk later about the many mornings he came into Orchard Street after dropping his kids off at school to the smell of frying bacon wafting through the hall, me shaving at the sink and Alex singing in the shower, which we were obliged to keep in full working order under some old Poor Law legislation for the purposes of de-lousing vagrants or other infirm persons coming into care. Alex merely kept it in full working order.

I took over the caseload of Liz, Craig's girlfriend as it turned out, who had been working for a year or so as an unqualified social worker. We managed a couple of weeks' overlap, during which she was able to introduce me to some of the families I would be taking on. The received wisdom was that this was a good thing, a kind of 'laying on of hands' from one worker to the next but, since we were of the laity and not the priesthood, I always doubted the value of this in practice. Besides, no modern council would now pay two workers two salaries to do the same job for two hours, let alone two weeks, especially since there is now an in-built gap of about three months, a neat salary-saving device, between a worker leaving and being replaced by another. In this gap, the burden of the caseload is carried by the rest of the team, including the frontline manager, with salary savings to the employer, the council.

The reality of practice shows in any case that different social workers respond to clients differently and vice-versa, depending on such basic factors as age, gender, appearance, class and personality. There is also the fact that new social workers often have different ideas of priority from the outgoing caseworker, one worker deciding a certain case needs more visiting than before and another case less visiting and so on. In some ways, a new social worker will be rather like a new football manager arriving at a struggling club, relegating some of the old first-team regulars to the reserves, while plucking others from the obscurity in which they have been languishing. Indeed, some cases might suddenly become more active because of some change in family dynamics, irrespective of the comings and goings of the social workers, whose arrival and departure rates would in any case soon go through the roof compared to the days when children's officers spent most or all of their careers with the same authority. In my later experience, the departure of a social worker entailed the immediate closing of lower priority cases, especially those held open by the worker who feared that some undoubted 'progress' might not be sustained, and so had kept it open, just in case. Anyway, like most new social workers, I started by trying to visit all the 35–40 cases Liz had left me until, six months later, having gained a dozen or so new cases, I sent letters to any non-statutory cases that had not been in touch since she had left asking them to make an appointment with the duty-worker should the need arise again. Big Tam recalls that there was some insistence at the time that this was too narrow an interpretation of 'statutory cases' because under the general duty of Section 12 to 'promote social welfare' all cases were capable of being considered 'statutory'.

In a similar way, because of the variety of social workers and their practices, I became quite sceptical about the store that other workers and managers put on reading the case file before meeting clients, as though this would make the slightest difference as to how one perceived or acted towards them or they towards you, simply because you had read something of their past. Their past is only what has been recorded of it, often by a succession of professionals, including non-social workers of uncertain training, ability, experience, judgement, observational skills and something my old granny called 'nous'. Regent Road had prepared me effectively to come to my own professional judgements, albeit tentative and constantly open to review, about the people I worked with because that is what I was expected by statute and regulation to do and, by professional training and professional experience, equipped to offer – honest and informed perceptions of them and their personal, family and social situations. Social work is focused on the present and the future primarily, informed by the historical personal past, but it cannot allow itself and the people it works with to be over-determined by that past. Otherwise it will risk losing its main function, which is its helpfulness to people trying to live their lives now, in the present. This was the way I myself attempted to work with clients and those social workers whom I would later supervise as a Senior and frontline manager. Indeed, much of my initial contact with new cases or social workers involved ironing out this stuff by making explicit that whatever their previous experience had been of social workers or supervisors, good or bad, would not count with me and I expected the same attitude back from them. I would treat as I found and I would defend only my own involvement with them, nobody else's – not the agency's, not the Panel's or the Sheriff's, just me and them, as client or worker or manager.

In supervision with Danny, I went through the 30-odd cases on Liz's case list. It is important to comprehend that the question of caseloads and their 'weight' or 'complexity' would require the genius of whoever invented calculus combined with the creative accountancy of Del Boy to define that highly mythical beast, the 'average caseload'. I speak from four decades of low-level guerrilla warfare wandering round such terrain, both as a frontline manager and as a National Association of Local Government Officers (NALGO) shop steward. Reports from this period often cited caseloads reaching over 70 cases and this being 'double the recommended level' (Murphy, 1992: 180). This should be taken as allegorical mainly, for I personally never worked for any authority that ever stated a caseload level until 1992, when Lothian Region reverted to the specialisms reinstated by the Community Care Act 1990, implemented in 1993. It was judged at that point that the maximum number of cases for the complex work involving children should be 25 while community care social workers could take about ten cases more than that. Frontline managers were limited to supervising up to nine staff.

In the summer of 1973 in Orchard Street, Danny supervised six social workers and a trainee. He dutifully went through Liz's old case list with me, chuckling and replying to questions regarding legislative or statutory matters. I cannot remember him offering professional insights into any of the clients, even those known to him. This was clearly to be my job. The new Hearing system was still a matter of some conjecture to all, including Danny and Charlie, the new Reporter, who looked to me like the Scottish comic actor Alistair Sim, only much less amusing. I recall Danny fuming about having to allocate a Hearing report requested on a nine-year-old who had removed soft putty from a new window frame just installed in a house across the road. Danny then had a frank exchange of views with Charlie, the report requester, which was always useless.

We were all on some kind of learning curve, especially Charlie and especially the Children's Panels. The Hearing system had only recently replaced the juvenile court system which was not the case in England, where the Probation service and Juvenile Court continued as a central Government responsibility quite separate from local Government social services. Although welcomed and admired internationally as a radical innovation in social justice, the new Hearing system unleashed a barrage of report requests and lay-Panel evangelism such that 'child-rescue' admissions to care and supervision orders immediately shot up, threatening to sink the new ship before it got halfway out of harbour. A new ship but sailing across the same old tides.

And thus I sat in 1973, going over my case list with Danny. The probation service had stamped Danny's professional assumptions which marked his supervision style which, in turn, marked mine. A Probation Officer was officially an 'officer of the court', primarily the Sheriff Court, for which he was obliged to supply background reports with courteous 'recommendations' to Sheriffs regarding 'sentencing' options. If there were subsequent 'breaches' of Probation Orders or Care or Supervision Orders, the Probation Officer could take it back to the Sheriff for further sentencing or amendment of Orders. Otherwise, the officer was free to supervise in any way s/he thought fit. This gave Probation Officers extensive professional discretion and control, answerable only to the legal authority of a court, not to local councillors, ratepayers, corporate executives, budget-holders, the press or even to parliament once it had passed the relevant legislation and handed it over to the judiciary for implementation. In reality, professional power was circumscribed only by the resources that local councils and the Government were prepared to make available to those carrying out their statutory duties and responsibilities. This was the actual power that local councils had – the allocation of resources – and these could vary widely across Britain. Barbara Kahan was Children's Officer for Oxfordshire in 1951, a large county which had 400 children in care, and her experience is cited by Bob Holman in *Champions for Children* (2013: 54–5), as illustrative of the petty punitive attitudes local Children's committees could display on either side of the Border, whether Labour, Tory or Liberal led:

> Barbara explained: The chair of the county council was an earl who nominated all the chairs of committees. In a deeply Tory county, the Labour party appeared to be allowed anything that was not considered important and that included the children's committee. Its chairman was a railway signalman and I was told to go to the signal box if I wanted to talk with him. (Kahan, 1999, interview with Bob Holman). Barbara soon felt that not all the committee members were sympathetic.
>
> Some of the Labour members held the view, 'These kids have had a rough time but so did I and I managed'. The Conservative attitude was reflected in the councillor who objected to children in children's homes having treats such as ice-cream.

Such attitudes were as much cultural as political. Faced with these ingrained prejudices, progressive Directors of social work in the 1970s to the 1980s sought to cultivate 'alliances' with Social Work Committee chairs so that they dominated the committees rather than the other way about. This allowed Depute Directors and other senior managers to concentrate on providing professional leadership to frontline staff trying to deliver practical support: day centres, home-helps, residential and foster care and so on. Those local councillors from the Children's Committee in Falkirk Burgh who had once annually visited foster homes in the company of the Children's Officer, Miss Hendry, no longer did so when the new social work departments arrived. Some loss of local political understanding may have occurred but, in general, my generation looked askance whenever we encountered the older breed of local councillor, usually as Justices of the Peace, whenever we were looking for a warrant to be signed. Many called us 'the Social Works Department', I often thought confusing us with the 'Sewage Works Department', only less useful. For our part, we had little use for the paternalistic and residual notions of the 'deserving' and 'undeserving' poor which shaped their views. The parochialism that was integral to the operation of local Government during this period is described by John Murphy, Director of Stirling County and then Central Region, who was at the interface between the new Social Work (Scotland) Act and the local political machinery (Murphy:10,168-9):

> Until the reorganisation of 1975 local Government salaries, like wages in the country, were kept comparatively low, as were staff ratios and the level of supporting services… Content with the old order and old loyalties to welfare and children, not all authorities welcomed the change, and some were sceptical if not hostile. Their natural resistances were not mollified by the dawning awareness that the White Paper's bland assurance of little extra expenditure were misleading, and that implementation of the new service must perforce be costly.

But as social workers we rarely engaged with local councillors directly and we were much too busy dealing with individual 'clients', whom we spoke about amongst ourselves constantly, for ideas, support, confirmation. The 'court officer' model of social work was thus applied to the new Hearing system as another legal 'authority' that we were absolutely accountable to but which required 'nurturing' in a way foreign to the Sheriff Court. Hearings were meant to be places of discussion to involve children and families and the social workers who were doing the detailed work with them. As regards children who were in care outwith the Hearing system legislation, these were run past your own Senior and then the adoption and fostering Panel to see if it entailed long-term care (fostering or residential) and whether on a voluntary or compulsorily basis. The deliberations and recommendations were passed to the Depute Director, Ian Gilmour, a former Children's Officer, to approve and take to the Committee/Sheriff when it involved adoption or the assumption of parental rights.

The whole area of approving adoptive and foster parents and of 'matching' babies to adoptive parents was delegated to the 'adoption and fostering panel' setup within the social work department, chaired by Danny, with myself as his deputy once I had learned the ropes. Danny in his turn was indebted to Ian Gilmour, acknowledged by all as highly competent and experienced in childcare matters, legal and professional.

My first case concerning adoption in Falkirk Burgh was to undertake a supervision visit to a couple a few weeks after the infant had been placed with them. They reported me to Ian Gilmour for being 'over-intrusive' in my questioning. Ian laughed as he explained that the purpose of the legislation was merely to enquire if any further supports were needed, not a full review of the whole placement. All local authorities needed to have people with this kind of specific professional childcare background and expertise in order to advise both frontline managers and basic-graders on the fine details of work which was so crucial to the lives of children and families. Dick Poor, Director of Lanark, who contributed to the framing of the Social Work Scotland Act, was a well-respected figure often referred to by Ian Gilmour himself, while a new generation would produce folk like Gus Campbell and Anne Black, both of whom I worked with when I joined Lothian Region in the 1980s. Anne served as a member of the Orkney Inquiry and later chaired an Inquiry Report on the death of a child much praised for its comprehensive and well-balanced judgements.

In Falkirk Burgh and then Central Region between 1973 and 1977, our adoption and fostering panel was regularly approving foster parents who wanted children under five years old and adoptive parents who wanted newborn infants. In my early days in Falkirk Burgh, we could approve an adoptive couple one week and offer them an infant a few weeks later. The adoption manuals of the day were suggesting that the 'optimum wait' for a baby should be nine months after the couple had been 'approved' since this would allow them to 'psychologically' prepare for parenthood in the same way that the 'normal gestation period' prepares natural parents for birth. Grangemouth Docks provided a steady supply of babies, aided by the religious, social and parental stigma that still attached to single and unmarried mothers who conceived children 'out of wedlock'. Whatever one's own doubts about the regressive nature of the social circumstances which resulted in such a plentiful supply of young babies being offered up for adoption, it made many childless couples very happy nevertheless. I also began to notice the regularity with which many adoptive couples, after trying for years to have a child of their own, often conceived immediately after adopting a child. The psychological really can have physical consequences. As for those mothers who gave up their children for adoption at this time, I wrote a poem called 'My First Adoption', every word of it true:

> My first adoption came three months
> into the job
> a woman had walked into the Infirmary
> with a concealed pregnancy

gave birth, discharged herself
and went back to work, same day.
She lived with her parents
already had a child
was afraid her father would put her out
if he knew, especially
as she'd been drunk and could not
remember who the father was.
I wrote a letter to be opened
by the child when she was sixteen
assuming her new parents would tell her
she had been adopted, which began:
your mother wanted to keep you
but of your father little is known
except he was tall, had black hair
and blue eyes and perhaps came from Glasgow.

Adoption law was not introduced into Scotland until 1930, before which birth parents could take back their children when they were of an age to work. The Adoption Act was thus mainly designed to 'provide security for the adoptive parents and children' (*Adoption and Fostering in Scotland*, Gary Clapton and Pauline Hoggan, Dunedin, 2012:xv). The annual number of adoptions in Scotland peaked in 1946 at 2,298 and remained around that level until the next peak in 1969 at 2,268, just as I was about to embark on my social work career. When I retired in 2009, the figure had dropped to 455, roughly 1 per cent of all 'looked after' children. In 1969, 69 per cent of adopted children were under two years of age compared to 14 per cent by 2009. The fall is probably explained by the wider availability of the contraceptive pill which women could control and a change in the moral climate which allowed young women to keep their babies. Indeed, the term 'illegitimacy' was made illegal in 1987 when the law was changed to allow no distinction between a child born to married or unmarried parents. As the supply of newborns increasingly dried up older children in care and those with various forms of disability began to be considered for adoption by an ever wider group of possible parents, including unmarried couples, single people and same-sex couples as set out in the 2007 Adoption and Children (Scotland) Act, implemented in 2009, the year I retired. Figures for England between 2004 and 2007 suggest 74 per cent of children adopted had been abused or neglected prior to entering care (Clapton: 10–11, 21, 44–54).

All this lay before me as I continued my own rite-of-passage through the courts, hearings, children's homes, List D schools, council schemes and

occasional howffs and drinking-dens of downtown Falkirk. I plied my trade
as best I could, trying to do whatever I could with what training I had been
given, now undergoing a massive learning curve and working overtime most
nights except weekends, without getting paid for it either. I may have spent
only 19 months or so as a basic-grader before being promoted to Senior
at Regionalisation but you could probably add another year (and another
lifetime's worth of experience) onto that tally. I gave up playing semi-pro
football, not having the time to train twice a week – but sometimes turned
out for the social work football team, run in a totally unpredictable fashion
by Walker Butler, Danny's old Probation boss, who sometimes arranged
games on Sunday afternoons down at Victoria Park. Paul, a qualified referee,
booked Big Tam in the first friendly with DHSS for 'ungentlemanly conduct'
– which also included 'swearing at the referee'.

'Risk' was something I soon learned social workers had to evaluate
every day, mostly in circumstances of moral greyness. We had studied
'rule-governed behaviour' through sociology and psychology lectures
we had received at Regent Road. Classic texts such as Erving Goffman's
The Presentation of Self in Society (1959), Howard Becker's *Outsiders:
Studies in the Sociology of Deviance* (1963) and Eric Berne's transactional
analysis *What Do You Say After You Say Hello* (1973) provided the basis
for 'labelling theory'. These were the staple diet of most university sociology
booklists of the time and they served to contextualise risk-related behaviour
in ways that questioned the authority and power of those who made the rules
and enforced them as well as those who subverted them. In our professional
training, such texts were supplemented by social-psychology perspectives
drawn from Erik Erikson's *Childhood and Society* (1950), Eric Fromm's
The Fear of Freedom (1941), Abraham Maslow's *Towards a Psychology of
Being* (1962) and RD Laing's writings, especially *The Divided Self* (1960).
All of these texts questioned the prevailing clinical, medical, legal and
cultural orthodoxies.

Such studies revealed the extent to which 'reified objects', like the Law,
were not only made or manufactured by politics but were themselves
the subject of institutional and localised practices, interpretations and
enforcements. The law itself was an institution and as such required to
be questioned, as did our own social work values and practices, however
benign its moral intentions. We learned, in effect, that all behaviour is
rule-governed and that all rules and modes of behaviour are themselves
open to question depending on the social context and circumstances of
their implementation. And this applied whether or not one was a judge, a
juvenile delinquent or a judge's daughter. We learned that the state, of which
we were part, needed to patrol its own boundaries and question its own

procedures and morality every bit as vigilantly as it employed people like us to interrogate the assumptions, lifestyles and value-bases of some of the wee neds living down the Bog Road.

As a social worker in the 1970s, one did not need to go as far as reading all these texts for we encountered the reality of which they spoke every day. The professional journals and job adverts in magazines like *Social Work Today* and *Community Care* were full of their consequences and implications, often in the form of criticising the existing institutions – DHSS, Housing, Policing, Courts. These publications pushed continually for more extensive community-based provision, for refuges for 'battered women' and the like. The extent to which we were dealing with a kind of 'underclass' was clearly evident though it was nowhere near the proportions it would reach under Thatcher or is visible today with food banks in every town and city. The central-belt working-class backgrounds of Danny, Big Tam and myself informed our dealings with clients and enabled us to make measured readings of them and their sub-cultures intuitively as well as theoretically and professionally. We dealt with individuals, certainly, but in the context of their social lives and circumstances, their social being, which we understood ourselves from the 'inside'. As Big Tam said, 'we came with the wing-mirrors attached'.

So, in Falkirk Burgh in 1973, I felt pretty well-placed professionally. We had two fully established teams of six qualified social workers, each with a trainee, Janet and Susan Hamilton, and each with solid Seniors, Danny and Sheila. By contrast, our colleagues in Edinburgh had 70 out of 150 social work posts filled. In Glasgow, the lack of staff and resources resulted in Section 12 cash being paid out in 'crisis' situations rather than using casework to avoid evictions and the loss of heating and lighting and so on. In 1969, the sum that had been paid out nationally for Section 12 amounted to £60,000. From 1970 to 1975, Section 12 funding was over £200,000 year on year and especially high in the urban areas of Scotland (John Murphy: 178, 180, 182). There were clearly a lot worse places to be in 1973 to 1975 than Falkirk Burgh's Orchard Street office and the Bog Road, and we knew it.

We weren't exactly under worked either. The Panels and Courts made sure of that.

But over the coming decades, we began reducing the total number of 'looked after' children aged 0–17 from 14,788 (0.93 per cent) in 1971 to 11,675 (1.09 per cent) in 2004, overall a significant 35 per cent reduction in the number of children in care between 1976 and 2010. The percentage in residential care would also be reduced by 77 per cent over the period while the percentage in family care went up 33 per cent (Gary Clapton and Pauline Hoggan, *Adoption and Fostering in Scotland*, 2012: 3). In stark terms, in 1976 there were 10,005 children in care, 62 per cent of whom were in residential care while in 2010, the year *Dancing with Big Eunice* was published, there were 6,476, of whom 77 per cent were in families. As Mrs Thatcher said of a rather different kind of war: 'Rejoice!'

I had also inherited from Liz a couple of children in long-term care up at Redding House, the local children's home, a 15-bed all-purpose unit, which took babies to early teenagers. The place was run by Miss MacLeod, a soft-spoken, lilting-voiced Gaelic spinster from Skye, a gem of a woman, who had been there for decades and had a brilliant rapport with the children. It was something of a truism, but true nonetheless, that Highlanders and Islanders had long come South to the Lowlands for employment, men often joining the Glasgow police and women entering the nursing and care field, which had the added incentive of offering accommodation and meals on the premises. Miss MacLeod had a family home in Skye which she drove up to as often as she could on weekends off. Her deputy, Miss MacCrae, was made of stricter stuff, possibly forming a 'good cop-bad cop' partnership. If there had to be places for that purpose, then Redding House offered basic security, structure and old fashioned female warmth and affection, as well as it could be in such places in such times, to its too-wide range of children.

When the Redding House youngsters reached their teens and began to 'act out', that was usually the signal for them to be 'moved on' to other establishments, List D schools or hostels, since the vast bulk of the children were under 12 and their protection and control was the main priority. On Thursday evenings, when the traditional weekly 'reporting night' for Probation and Panel cases was over, I would drive up to Redding House for tea and buns with Miss MacLeod to hear reports of the children and speak to them, alone and with her. They all usually lined up outside her door to be called in after their tea. When it became known that I was making valiant efforts to get families for the kids I had, some of the other kids whose social workers did not visit so regularly let it be known that they would not mind joining the growing band lining up to talk to Miss MacLeod and myself, a Thursday night routine that would last for the next four years solid.

Social workers cannot work with the same intensity or make the same connections or relationships with every client they encounter. Reciprocity may not be possible for a hundred different reasons whatever one's hopes. However, every social worker meets cases that will always remain part of their professional and personal lives, wedged in their memory banks and in their future practice until they hang up their boots and often beyond. The early years of practice is the period of maximum impact for these kinds of cases and situations to take root, when one is both more open to casework experiences and also professionally less 'well-defended'. For a social worker, the development of a 'professional self' helps stop them merging or over-identifying with certain clients, while still enabling them to focus their attention more on the client's feelings and life situation than their own, though one's own feelings and intuitions will always remain vital in guiding the worker in handling these cases. In the early years of practice, the openness to feelings which your training so assiduously devoted itself needs a period of 'running-in'. The new social worker becomes like a recently qualified driver, competent to drive on the open roads but still developing skill. Like driving, the more one does certain things in social work, the more automatic these become and a 'routinisation of feeling' rather than a continuous openness to feelings in each new case may set in, especially in the kind of cases one may have dealt with a hundred times before. This was the business – the messy emotional business – I had now entered and was cutting my professional teeth on. And professional social workers do need teeth, every bit as much now as we did then.

In my first caseloads, women tended to feature more frequently as 'put upon' wives and mothers, struggling to cope with out-of-control children or drunken violent partners or husbands. This was the start of the modern era of 'battered women's refuges', a nation-wide network created through the initiative of a burgeoning women's movement which increasingly pressurised central and local Governments and their housing departments to re-house women and their children fleeing from domestic violence. This led to reciprocal arrangements developing between authorities in Glasgow, Edinburgh, Dundee, Falkirk and so on, re-housing women and children in this predicament in new areas – kept secret – and therefore safer – from abusive men, meaning husbands and fathers. I remember reading some of the literature around this period produced by the women's movement which explained that the common term 'rule of thumb' was derived from 19th century social and legal norms permitting husbands to chastise wives or children with a stick – without fear of prosecution – so long as the stick was no thicker than 'a man's thumb'.

Big Tam recalls he sometimes favoured what might be termed 'direct action' when he came across 'wife-beaters' in the Bog Road in the early 1970s, one of them being the wife of a labourer who got 'bevvied' every Friday after work. Tam was waiting for him one evening when he arrived home 'sloshed' carrying a bottle of vodka. The wife and six weans assembled behind Big Tam who stood up from the kitchen table. The conversation went something like this:

Wife Beater: 'Who the fuck are you?'
Big Tam: 'I'm here to take these weans into care and get the polis

	to charge you with child neglect and beating up your wife regular.'
Wife Beater:	'Fuck off!'
Big Tam:	'I'll fuck off and bring the polis back unless you pour that doon the sink – the noo.'
Wife Beater:	'Whit?'
Big Tam:	'The vodka, doon the sink, the noo!'
Wife Beater:	'Are you fucking mad?'
Big Tam:	'Naw, but I'm getting that way! Pour that drink doon the sink and if I hear that you've laid one finger on your wife or any of the weans, I'll be straight doon here wi' the polis. I'm coming doon here next Friday night to see whit state yer in, so, gie's the bottle!'

Tam did indeed visit again and would discover the guy could not read or write, which he deduced from seeing him in a pub one night pretending to read the paper, holding it upside-down. People know themselves if they are struggling with life, the appearance of a social worker on the doorstep mostly just confirms the fact. As Big Vince used to say, 'Ali, you don't need to tell anybody they're having a bad game'. Aye, well Big Tam did anyway.

Regressive social-cultural pockets were particularly evident in the deprived and poor communities in which we worked, although, as the women's movement strongly asserted at the time, repressive relations between the sexes crossed class boundaries. Middle-class men were often better able to conceal their violence from public agencies like the police, social work and schools because physical control of children and young people was still a central part of 1970s culture. An indication of this can be seen in the furious public debate that erupted around 1980 over the banning of corporal punishment in schools, the infamous tawse, a metre-long cured leather strap cut into thongs at one end, that teachers were paid to wield in the classroom *in loco parentis*, allegedly necessary to keep control. Legally permitted physical chastisement still bedevils the prosecution of abusing parents today, for the law still permits the 'reasonable chastisement' of children. The birching of young offenders was banned in 1948 and the use of corporal punishment in approved schools phased out in the late 1960s, decades before it disappeared in mainstream schools in 1982. But that cultural legacy which endorses the rights of parents to resort to physical chastisement – no doubt from the old biblical mantra, 'spare the rod, spoil the child' – still lives on in Scottish civil society.

Legally sanctioned parental 'violence' is still a serious social issue. In the early days of the Scottish Parliament around 2000, the Scottish Government issued consultation drafts proposing to phase out the beating of children with an implement – cane, belt and shoe being the most common – only for this to be watered down and removed altogether when Parliament voted on it. As I recall, even a partial amendment was voted down which would have banned the use of implements against children who were under 3 years of age. One of the arguments put forward by one MSP I remember was his concern that parents who were 'handicapped', meaning actually having something wrong with their hands, might not then be able to batter their offspring to the same extent as their more able-bodied neighbours. An implement, so the logic of this tribune of the people ran, helps restore any such imbalance amongst the electorate. Suddenly, the Scottish chamber was convincing itself that inflicting corporal punishment on children, however small, including the use of implements, ought to be upheld like it was some kind of universal human parental right. But what about the human rights of the child, you may ask? What about the fact that police, teachers, social workers, doctors, nurses and hospital casualty wards are daily inundated with queries about children being hit, which all of these agencies must investigate fully at great public expense as to whether such punishment was excessive or not because they would get hung out to dry by the media when, lo and behold, some parent does 'over chastise' their offspring to their permanent injury or even death. At such moments, all one hears is, 'Isn't that dreadful? Somebody should be doing something about it.' Yes, the politicians and those who vote for them!

Health and social work professionals despair at the false nature of this debate. Enlightened opinion does not advocate a lack of control over and discipline of children, but suggests that there are many other non-physical, non-violent means that every parent resorts to every day, such as diversion, play, treats, encouragement, routine, affection and love. The time and money that currently goes into investigating referrals about levels of physical chastisement could be diverted into educating people more widely in using other forms of discipline, which in effect is what social workers currently do with parents whose children have been identified as at risk and placed on Child Protection Registers. We know, therefore, that showing parents that other methods work can in fact change the parenting skills and outlooks of even very abusive parents. When schools banned the use of the tawse in Scotland in the early 1980s, for example, the classroom mayhem that was promised and predicted, especially by teaching unions, did not ensue. Now, a return to corporal punishment in schools seems unthinkable, unless of course another Tory education minister emerges – populist, authoritarian, small-minded, Scottish.

My generation had to discover for ourselves the full extent of the physical and sexual abuse of women and children as would the other professions. It may seem inexplicable today but, in the course of three years' professional training at Moray House, no one ever mentioned child abuse to us. I qualified in 1973, two years before the Maria Colwell Report appeared and the first Child Protection Registers were set up in Central Region. Even then, abuse was seen as applicable only to seriously physically injured infants, conveyed by the term, 'battered baby syndrome', which entered our professional orbit based on American medical research. The identification of 'non-accidental injury' (NAI) thus relied on medical diagnosis and the medical profession became the lead agency in identifying and confirming NAI cases over the next decade, until the spectacular emergence of child sexual abuse was revealed by the Cleveland Inquiry Report in 1988. Cleveland was in fact a massive mis-identification of child sexual abuse cases but it did a good job alerting everyone – press, politicians, public, professionals – to its reality and extent. It also alerted courts and professionals to the challenges of establishing child sexual abuse on medical grounds alone, which ushered in a highly investigative approach involving far more scrutiny but also a lot less humility about the complexities of abuse and the difficulties of its detection and proof.

Scotland's equivalent to the Maria Colwell Inquiry would be the Richard Clarke Inquiry, a Perth child. The social worker was in our year at Regent Road. We were all stunned and I knew within myself this could have happened to any or all of us. It also stunned the tutors and word reached us in 1974, when the child died, that one of them was wondering aloud if the problem of not spotting bruising on the child may have been because the unfortunate worker had very poor eyesight. As I recall, the problem had not been as specific or individual as that; it was more a question of several agencies being involved, there being poor or no communication and assumptions made that others were 'doing something' when they were actually not. It soon led social workers, certainly in Falkirk, to refer all questions of bruising to medical staff, doctors or health visitors, instead of 'having a look' ourselves without having any medical training as to what we were supposed to be looking for. Neither did many of the medics, it appears.

Back in 1973, in Orchard Street, we sometimes came across police reports of young women prostituting themselves at the Grangemouth Docks but sexual abuse cases rarely surfaced and, if it did, it was more likely to be 'stranger abuse', which the police dealt with, rather than incest within the family, which psychiatrists dealt with. I can really only recall one case that Helen dealt with: the aftermath of a father who was prosecuted for incest with his several daughters, most of whom still maintained contact with him despite having children of their own, which was the focus of our concern. One of these daughters suddenly appeared on a Friday afternoon up at Redding House just as the office was closing, asking for her four-year-old daughter to be taken into care and threatening to leave the building without taking the child with her. I drove up to deal with the mother, a leggy, startlingly good-looking woman in her early 20s, confident to the point of brazen in her leather skirt (what there was of it) and knee-length boots, with an absolutely beautiful daughter in tow. The story was that she was on her way back to Amsterdam and had recently been reunited with the girl's father, a seaman, whose ship happened to be docked in Grangemouth, and she needed to meet with him to secure their passage back to Amsterdam. The story had more holes than a string vest but the lateness and the image of her young daughter, whose father was clearly from furth of Scotland, perhaps being dragged round Grangemouth Docks over the weekend was too much for me, and certainly Miss MacLeod, who said there was room at the inn for the wee girl at least for the weekend. So we agreed to take the child until Monday morning when the mother had to meet me at the office in Orchard Street.

Of course, Monday came and went and the mother never showed. Another worrying feature was that Miss MacLeod reported that the child seemed perfectly happy and content and was not crying for her mother. The thought struck me: was that person her mother? By Wednesday, I had got permission from Ian Gilmour to contact International Social Services (ISS), a charity organisation based in London that helps with family breakdown and divorce across 140 countries. It offered a translation service between countries and I wanted to get the Dutch authorities to check out the background and address details I had been given on admitting the child to care. By the end of the week, the mother blew into the office, taxi outside waiting to whisk her up to Redding House to collect the child and whisk her back to Amsterdam that very night. Her story was that she had managed to contact the father and was now booked to travel.

Despite misgivings, it was an uncertain legal situation if I tried to prevent the mother discharging the child from voluntary care. I could easily have asked a Justice of the Peace, a local councillor, to sign a warrant to hold the child in Redding House but, when the Reporter to the Children's Hearings, Charlie, received it on Monday morning, the legal grounds that he would require to frame for the making of a supervision order was, at best, scant. The child was perfectly healthy and well-cared-for, certainly physically, and emotionally she had got on well with the staff and children at Redding House. Even if the textbooks might suggest that this might have been 'too well', possibly a sign of poor attachment to the mother, I was not a child therapist and therefore not qualified to put that kind of assessment to a court.

The child had been placed voluntarily in care, which any defence lawyer would have argued was what a responsible parent would have done in the circumstances, and we had no proof of legal convictions for soliciting and the like. Plus – and it was a very big plus – what if the mother got into the waiting taxi and, instead of going to Redding House, simply disappeared and left us with the little girl with no other known family history? The purists and child-rescuers might carp or groan but I would do the same again, faced with the resources, the law and the accepted standard of care at the time – 'good enough parenting'. I was already witnessing the reality of what became of children routinely stuck in long-term residential care for whom I was now desperately trying to find substitute homes, attempting to trace long-gone parents and other relatives. When I got information back from the ISS, it revealed the addresses given by the mother were real but her current residence was not, so we would probably have had to contact Interpol to track her down had she gone off without taking the child with her.

And so, I agreed to return the child just as the mother had confidently expected I would. She uncrossed her leggy legs and flashed her knickers at me, reminiscent of that scene made famous by Sharon Stone in *Basic Instinct*. She purred how grateful she was for my assistance and if there was anything she could do to repay me – anything – well, I just had to say. I looked steadily at her and said that she should not drag her daughter round places like Grangemouth Docks or dump her in places like Redding House and then abandon her for a week. She suddenly became very placatory, which confirmed my suspicion that the justice and Hearing system would have been a complete cakewalk for her had it come to our trying to impose a care order. This smart young woman, with the transnational transient lifestyle now more commonly seen today, was not what the framers of the Social Work (Scotland) Act had ever imagined Section 15 being used for. Nor indeed had I. In retrospect, and with 45 years of sexual abuse research and practice to consider, might this mother have thought that placing the child in Redding House was the safest option during this visit back to her sexually abusive father and family?

The kind of transient cases that Section 15 legislation was actually intended for usually cropped up on office duty or out-of-hours over evenings and weekends, when our office was closed, like all the other offices relevant to the daily needs of clients – DHSS, health visitors, schools, day centres, housing. Only a skeletal emergency call-out service from us and the DHSS was available via the police for emergencies, roughly 'life and limb' situations. Every basic-grader did a week's turn on the out-of-hours rota, from Monday evening to the following Monday morning, for which we received a (very) nominal sum, enhanced by a call-out rate if we were actually forced to take some action on some case. On average, this meant one week's duty cover every three months, since there were about a dozen social workers in the Burgh. I was rarely called, never mind called out, no doubt because the police just looked at my Armadale phone number, 13 miles away, and found some other solution – or none – to whatever the problem was. This was before Child Protection took off in a serious way after 1975. Indeed, the only case I can remember being called out to was a transient, a mother with a 12-year-old daughter, who had been put off the Glasgow train at Falkirk High station for being drunk and incapable – the mother, not the daughter. Without funds, they now needed emergency accommodation. The dividing line then between housing responsibilities and welfare cases was hotly contested but the social work department still had keys for an old poor-house building, Windsor House, available for just such predicaments for the last hundred years or so.

And so, there we were, 10.00pm on a Sunday night, this rickle of bones, a wee woman who looked more like the girl's granny than her mother, myself letting them into their lodgings for the night, like some character from Dickens – Mr Bumble perhaps – opening a place I had never been before and would never see again. The young girl was what we would later call a caretaker child, destined to look after parents and younger children from a too-early age because of their parent's ill-health, psychiatric illness, disability or, as in this case, total inebriation. The mother, for so the girl claimed she was, looked rather like Old Mother Riley, a character from children's Saturday film matinees in the 1930s but still popular during the 1950s and '60s, played by a man in drag. She wore an Aunty Beanie hat and had delicate, bird-like features made even more vulnerable by a pair of brown and amber spectacle frames with one lens missing, coggling over her face and hanging first by one arm over one ear and then over the other, which her quiet and dutiful daughter kept straightening silently and without fuss. The woman was barely conscious but I had no qualms about leaving her in the capable hands of that young lassie. They both met me at the office the next morning, none the worse for wear, and I gave them money for the train to continue back to Glasgow. I probably did not even notify the relevant social work team in Glasgow, as we would now, if only to claim the money back because everyone knew Glasgow was stretched further than anywhere else in Scotland – and by far more serious cases than this.

These were what were called duty-cases, stuff dealt with on the same or following day. If that girl and mother had lived in the Falkirk area, a phone call to the local school and GP would perhaps have been made and, if further concern was felt, maybe a home-visit and a referral to the Reporter. The Reporter was supposed to be interested in cases where a supervision order might be necessary, voluntary or compulsory, by a social worker. This was a relatively high tariff but in those early years, Charlie was cautious as a Swiss banker and would exercise little discretion. Thus everything seemed to require a full report and cases put to Hearings even when social workers had not recommended any form of supervision at all. Early Panels seemed equally gung-ho and punitive. Supervision orders were given out like jelly beans, a cure-all for everything from truancy to whooping cough.

The Scottish figures show that the total number of looked after children, which included those placed in residential and foster care as well as home supervision through Hearings, was 14,788 in 1971, which increased incrementally to 20,553 in 1974, then down to 18,936 in 1975. There had, in fact, been a falling trend in the percentage of the 0–14 population of children in all forms of care in Scotland between 1952 and 1969, falling from 13,340 (1.06 per cent) in 1952 to 11,221 (0.83 per cent) in 1969. 1976 was the first year that separate figures were given for those placed on home supervision orders under the Hearings (5,883). (Statistics for looked after children were compiled by Denise MacLeod at SWSG at my request in 2005, some of which involved best estimates.) It is difficult to make comparisons between pre- and post-Hearing system figures, which extended the age of a child from under-16 to under-18 years but it is probable that Sheriffs who controlled the Juvenile Courts had a higher 'tariff' for putting kids on probation or supervision than did the new Panel system with its lay-membership and higher sense of 'child rescue' mission.

In 1973, the Chair of the Children's Panel in Falkirk was the formidable former head of a school for kids with learning difficulties, Miss G, who seemed predisposed to treat everyone as though they were a bit 'dim' themselves, especially social workers, who, like their clients, needed constant guidance and correction. She chaired a Panel which sent one of my truants off to List D school while I was on holiday so I could not attend, despite a request for it to be delayed a week so that I might suggest a contrary disposal. I then encouraged the family to get Paddy Imrie, a sympathetic defence lawyer, to appeal the decision to Sheriff Reid Kerr, who rolled up grandly in his Rolls-Royce every day from Stirling. He ruled that the legislation stated that the local authority had to provide only a report, nothing about the writer of the report presenting it to the Panel in person. Such pedantry disregarded the whole spirit of the Wheatley reforms, of course. Sheriffs as a body had been strongly opposed to doing away with Juvenile Courts and integrating the Probation service with social work which they envisaged, correctly, would result in a much-diluted service to them. Miss G was symptomatic of a far broader malaise not confined to Falkirk, a national upsurge in Panel members who were prepared to send mostly poor working-class children away from home in droves. The figures prove it.

Beds in residential units were now set at a premium. Waiting lists became central to the system. Social workers had to check for places in Assessment Centres and List D schools just before a Panel, even when we made no recommendation for removal from home. We checked not if there was a bed available in a certain Secure Unit or in a particular List D school which dealt with a specific kind of problem but how long the waiting lists for all of the schools were, approximately. Panels could make the supervision orders naming specific places but the Scottish Education Department had to provide the beds and the local authorities had to agree to fund them. A classic market dilemma: demand exceeded supply. Kids were condemned to removal by the Panel then sent home with the Sword of Damocles hanging over them – that is, with the threat of being 'taken away' whenever a place became available. Sometimes kids had to wait so long that some even earned a reprieve by changing their behaviour, perhaps by not stealing for a few months or going back to school. Panels began factoring some of this delay into their unhinged calculations, using the pending-removal-waiting-for-a-bed syndrome rather like a suspended sentence in the criminal courts. This sucking of marginal, low-end cases into residential care thus led many institutions – many of them private – to start picking and choosing, accepting or keeping the cases that suited them, and rejecting or ejecting those that did not, usually the most difficult. List D schools would often hold onto less troublesome cases for longer which thus delayed the admission of more serious cases, which in turn led to more kids requiring Secure Units. Secure Units were, of course, the most expensive resource imaginable, often costing more than Eton and Harrow, a statistic which social workers often noted ironically and angrily amongst ourselves.

Details of the subsequent turnaround from residential to foster care are in *Another Kind of Home: A Review of Residential Childcare* (SWSG, 1992, 26, 103) by Angus Skinner, future head of the Care Inspectorate. It showed that, between 1980 and 1990, the number of residential homes in Scotland (mostly in the private and voluntary sector) fell from 294 to 154 (52 per cent of the 1980 level). It also shows that, in 1977, one third of children in care under the age of five were in residential establishments but, by 1989, less than one in 20 were. By 1989, the vast majority of children in residential care (86 per cent) were between 12 and 17 years of age. Behind these figures are changes in social work and Panel-Reporter practice in certain local authorities, such as Lothian Region, which decided that children under 11 should only ever be admitted to foster care. This policy soon began to show regional variations: Strathclyde in 1990 had 13 per cent of children under 11 in residential care compared to 2 per cent in Lothian, with none in the

Borders and Fife. The duration of residential placements also became shorter: for example, the proportion of children in residential care for three years or more fell from 31 per cent in 1986 to 24 per cent in 1990 (Skinner: 25).

It all seems a kind of madness now. Back in 1973–75, I hoped that Panels might stop sending children away from home so easily or place them so often on supervision 'for their own good'. The Calvinism that ran so deeply and punitively in Scottish culture threatened to sink the whole ethos of reform before it could take off. Despite the abolition of the birching of young offenders in 1948, corporal punishment survived in Approved Schools until the late 1960s. The belt or tawse would continue to be used in mainstream schools until 1982 and in private ones until 1988. Commenting on the release of Scottish Office records from 30 years earlier in the teaching paper, TES, on 8 January 1999, David Henderson gives a vivid account of the debates that surrounded the banning of corporal punishment in Approved Schools in the late 1960s. The same attitudes were largely shared by mainstream teachers and Panel members – who were heavily recruited from the teaching profession, whether retired or still in the classroom:

> But whipping boys in approved schools was strongly supported by heads and school managers in the late sixties. Bruce Millan, the Education Minister, sought to bring approved schools into line with the code of practice and encountered strong resistance. Corporal punishment was used in Scotland 10 times as often as in English approved schools. Heads had mostly stalled following a Scottish Office circular in 1967. 'Over-hasty withdrawal may lead to a general breakdown of discipline and force the acceptance of standards that would not be accepted at home or day school' the Approved Schools Association (Scotland) advised in January 1968. Private letters between psychologists who worked in approved schools and HMI tell a different tale. Max Paterson wrote to John McPherson, HMI responsible for approved schools, about the true picture of beatings. 'On one visit to another school, I was told by the headmaster as a 'joke' that a child, an 11-year-old, bent over the desk to receive his punishment, had soiled himself after two strokes. The child panicked, jumped and run around the room. The head said, 'you should have seen the job I had before I caught him to give him the rest'. The school was Dr Guthrie's Boys' in Edinburgh.
>
> Punishment books in approved schools did not reflect the actual number of beatings or that some pupils were held down, Mr Paterson wrote. He urged ministers to bring in an immediate ban on belting on the buttocks which he described as 'vicious in the realm of punishment or of attitude'. It also had sexual undertones. Heads and managers largely

defended continued beatings. The head of St Andrew's School, Rhu, said corporal punishment 'should be to the eventual benefit of the boy'. In 1967, 28 boys [there] were belted for violence towards each other and 38 for insolence. Thirteen absconders enjoyed the benefits of the tawse. 'In each of these, the application of corporal punishment was meant as a therapeutic aid', the head said... J. Hill, head of Balgowan School, Dundee, wrote: 'We have been trying since 1959 to phase out the belt. It is inevitable, with modern thinking, modern methods of treatment – the accent constantly on understanding the individual child – that the future will see approved schools managed well without corporal punishment. I look forward to that day. But not in 1968.

You can almost smell it, the burning sulphur, the kind of forces we were up against in the old institutions throughout the 1970s with the same old staff with the same old mindsets, apart from pockets of progressive thought and determination provided by the likes of Max Paterson and a few others, some dotting about in this memoir.

5

Tasty-Toaster Tins

we came with the wing-mirrors attached
Big Tam, Falkirk, circa 1973

*The author's professional voyage of discovery sails on with the curious
internal lives of children and examples given of progressive and therapeutic
residential schools and of Big Tam's and his own attempts to find foster
families for kids in local children's homes – with some unexpected
outcomes some years later.*

FACTS AND FIGURES may tell us a certain amount about childcare but nothing
much about children. Their inner lives remain a mystery, even to themselves,
especially when they grow up, as do the inner workings of their parents' lives.
Big Tam had his first child, Kate, in Falkirk in 1976. I have often asked him
since how he first surmised that the tail-pipe of his Moskvitch, which started
to blow through a small hole that appeared in it, could be fixed, for a few
miles at least, by placing a small empty tin of his daughter's baby food over
the tailpiece, the diameter of which fitted over the pipe exactly. Seen initially
as a temporary fix, the Moskvitch's boot was soon filled to overflowing with
empty Tasty-Toaster tins until Kate finally moved on to solids, a day that
her father had almost come to dread. For this ritual had become a way of
life, a kind of denial that the blooming thing needed to go to a garage for
a new tailpiece. Big Tam had become so used to stopping every few miles
when the exhaust started to roar so loudly that even he could not ignore it
because the tin of the can had melted with the heat of the exhaust. Then the
boot was opened once more, another tin was extracted and made to fit with
all the honed dexterity of a Rolls-Royce engineer. To this day, Big Tam has
never provided a satisfactory answer to questions about how all this began,
a mystery, even to himself.

If an intelligent citizen and more than competent parent like Big Tam
finds it difficult to answer seemingly straightforward questions about fairly
trivial events in his past life, whether as a parent or a motorist, imagine the
incomprehension that social workers are often met with when they ask
parents or children to recount seemly ordinary events from pasts which were
dislocated, disordered and anything but straightforward. The question of
engaging with or relating to clients in my first social work post now came

up big time. I soon discovered that, apart from being on office duty when people came in with specific problems or doing reports and assessments, unless you spoke, you could have sat in silence for an hour, especially with teenagers on Panel home supervision, often for truancy or minor theft. Iain Morrison was wont to refer to a whole book that had been written about what took place in the first few minutes of meeting someone – probably Eric Berne's *What Do You Say After You Say Hello?* It now dawned fully on me that, unless I spoke, and continued to speak, little happened at all – just a wall of silence.

Myself being basically a 'listener' unlike Big Tam who was basically a 'talker', I began to develop my own style of interviewing and supervising silent clients. I began to enunciate propositions about a client's possible fears and worries based on what was known of their family history and situation, their peer group, their school and locality. Asking a teenager who truanted or shoplifted or got into gang fights at the weekend 'why questions' produced only blank stares and revealed what the casework textbooks termed 'a lack of personal insight'. I discovered that asking for descriptive statements – 'what happens when you and your mother fall out?' – or 'how questions' were far less threatening than, say, 'why are you shouting at your mother?' The 'why question' is often impossible to answer, even for adults. Of course, most of the textbooks were based on American experience, written by Helen Pearlman and the like, drawn from private practice with people able to pay for a chance to 'talk'. The truanting, thieving and territorially minded youth of Falkirk's underclass generally did not want to open up to a supervising officer who would report their conversations to the next Children's Panel, which might very well either extend their existing supervision orders or send them away from home altogether. The youths in the Bog Road certainly had enough personal insight to figure that one out.

You basically had to develop your own means of communication, client-wise. Unlike Big Tam, who lived in the same neighbourhood and had a great rapport with local youths and their families very similar to a detached community worker, I lived 13 miles and another world away in Armadale. Big Tam's nickname among the youths, 'Jungle', maybe reflects his personal standing, for they certainly found him approachable but someone you might not want to tangle with either. I, on the other hand, had shoulder-length hair, a Frank Zappa moustache, flared-trousers, pink and lime Paisley-patterned shirts with matching ties that my wife bought me, platform shoes that made me over six-feet tall, an athletic build and a studied way of speaking. Would you have spoken to me if you didn't have to? Fortunately, some did, mainly kids in long-term care.

I soon became aware that my encounters with the client population were structured in many cases by the business in hand, rather than being expansive, open-ended discourses about early lives or the forces that may have shaped their character or personality. As for choosing between different methods of intervention or therapy for different clients as I had read about in college – gestalt, person-centred, behavioural, group – I found what subsequent reading and practice would later confirm: the most effective approach across a wide range of clients came down to offering 'unconditional positive regard'. In other words, approaches which enable people to feel listened to and validated to some degree as a person. I found it reassuring in fact as a practitioner, supervisor and frontline manager that no matter how much fancy footwork skilled therapists, psychologists and psychiatrists could bring to the task of helping – especially children in residential or foster care – what people valued above all was a basic sense of reliability, consistency and integrity from everyone, whether social workers, care workers, foster parents or psychiatrists. Basically, troubled kids, like troubled adults, can spot a phony at 40 paces in a gale.

A key word used in social work assessment of risk today is 'resilience' – the strengths and weaknesses of a person perceived by the agencies involved and some of the youngsters on my caseload showed me what that statement meant in their actual lives. It was often the child who was an exception within their own family, either too 'thick' or too 'bright' to put it bluntly, who ended up on supervision or removed from home. The teenagers I had on supervision often fell into these extremes, the intelligent child of limited parents or parents who were once sensible enough but became so reduced by drink and drudgery that the textbook proposal of a worker forming an alliance to help them adjust to the needs or personality of a particular child was a non-starter. I discovered that a child who was physically over-chastised by a parent often had a better prognosis than one who was chronically neglected – because the former might denote a distorted parental concern which could be worked on by a social worker. But I also learned that some parents were so apathetic that their children had to rely on themselves, which could create either resilience or apathy in the child depending on a conglomeration of other factors.

Resilience. What does that mean in one's own life? I found myself thinking about this some 15 years later reading a book by Sula Wolff, the prominent child psychiatrist based at Edinburgh Sick Children's Hospital, *Children Under Stress* (1969). She had made a passing comment about the often serious emotional implications that sometimes arose for children of my generation who had been routinely hospitalised for a few weeks back in the 1950s and '60s to have their tonsils out. Suddenly, it all came back, myself three years old and bent over the GP's knee, feeling miserable, getting a jab in the bum then being whisked off to hospital, wrapped up extremely tightly before the operation, waking up in the men's ward with a burning throat and being given ice cream and jam to swallow painfully, my mother visiting then leaving, myself hysterical about not leaving with her. Sula mentioned that trauma like this might surface in some form in the future given other separations from parents, even mild ones like going to school, triggering minor panic or anxiety attacks.

In my case, when I was four years old, a kind of panic reaction did occur which was probably related to my family leaving the small mining village where we had lived, within sight of the small primary school at the end of the street that me and my pals knew we were going to go to at the end of the summer. Instead, I ended up in a half-built housing scheme on the edge of a fairly large town, Bathgate, which required a bus to take me to a rather forbidding primary school with a rather forbidding headteacher, Miss Orr. Luckily, my class teacher was Mrs Muir, a kind, matronly woman, who let me sit at her desk for the first few weeks. At home, I locked myself in the bathroom every morning for a fortnight refusing to leave the house unless my grandfather, who lived with us, took me to school in person. This was going fine until Mrs Muir was absent for a day and so our class was combined with Miss Orr's, thus making it a group of about 70 five-year-olds squeezed into a huge classroom. I remember sitting contentedly counting out beads on a small contraption, then hearing a scuffle somewhere and then all of us being lined up, our hands held out for Miss Orr to strike them with the tawse. I stood there, petrified, bewildered, mystified, my hand aflame and a wee voice inside saying, in my grandfather's Borders accent, 'whit the hell jist happened there, man?' And that was me, resilient, from a patently secure and stable home!

I was not at all sure what to do with a lot of the kids I had in various kinds of care and supervision. There was virtually nothing between home and residential List D schools except removal to foster or residential care or child therapy clinics attached to major hospitals. Another of the least commented on virtues of generic social work was the insight it gave children's social workers of the kind of future that awaited those who did not find a stable and secure placement in care – an endless progression through borstal or prison or mental hospital and sometimes all three. It was probably around this time that I vowed to myself that if I was not sure I could make the lives of a child or teenager better, then I would do my utmost not to make them any worse. It was a kind of pact between my personal and professional selves, a mini Hippocratic Oath – 'First do no harm'.

And so I began learning my trade working with troubled youngsters and families. In this regard, the most impressive place I encountered along the way was Ballikinrain List D School, Balfron, Stirlingshire, a Church of Scotland establishment for about 30 boys over 12 years of age. I immediately recognised the quality of the headmaster, Doug Davies, and his deputy, John Weatherhead. John later become head of Loaningdale List D school in Biggar, also noted as a 'progressive' school in the 1970s, partly through its association with the innovative and radical child psychologist mentioned earlier, Max Paterson. Max would soon become the controversial headmaster of Wellington List D school, near Edinburgh, after local Government Reorganisation in 1975. He created a veritable outcry with his innovative child-centred ideas, such as asking youngsters what punishment they felt they merited themselves. Max's contract was not renewed after a brief spell in charge, or not in charge, the latter being held by many of the old staff who had survived from the old regime.

I met Max a few years after this on the occasion of taking a young teenager to a List D school for assessment when I was a Senior social worker in Broxburn, West Lothian, in the early 1990s. I sat in while Max interviewed the boy and his father after I had briefed him about my views on the case. The son said his piece and left the room and Max started on the father, an aggressive, belligerent character. Max, smoking a fag, went straight at him, staring him in the face and speaking quietly while the man fumed and blustered. Max told him simply what he had seen in the brief session when his son had been present. The father dissolved into tears, completely disarmed, when Max said he was a parent who was totally behind his son and wanted to protect and defend him but he was going about it the wrong way. The boy saw him as constantly criticising and blaming him which, of course, he was, and so Max turned to the father's own upbringing, a veritable catalogue of violence which, he said, he did not want to inflict on his son. It was a masterclass of a kind I had sometimes read about in casework texts but never witnessed before, even after two decades or so in the field. Max could not only talk a good game, he could do it where it mattered, 'on the field'. I noticed, too, that during the hour-long assessment session, three quarters of it had been focused intently on the parent rather than on the son, the alleged subject of everyone's concern, including the father's. This was another gobbet of insight I would tap into through the course of my career: the power of direct, empathetic, authoritative truth-telling. It was a piece of theatre, a performance almost, and I would borrow from it for my own role as a supervisor and later frontline manager.

Doug Davies, the headmaster of Ballikinrain, was another exemplary professional in the List D school world, a mellow-voiced Welshman who looked like the Tory politician, Ken Clarke. He had a similar bluff persona and exhibited complete candour in speaking directly and warmly to and with, rather than at, youngsters and their parents and carers. Doug forged true alliances with the parents and foster parents of the youngsters who attended the school, some as day pupils. What was not on offer was a kind of stand-alone, 'boot-camp' experience, one that almost wilfully separated children from their home life. Ballikinrain staff attempted to help both the child and the parents understand each other better so they could relate and live together in a more satisfying way. Sounds simple to ordinary ears but, given the fractured lives of many of the children and their parents, it was often the equivalent of asking them to climb the north face of the Eiger. Doug was full of sharp professional childcare insights which inspired confidence, both in myself and in the children placed there and their families. John Weatherhead was likewise astute and direct in his dealings with youngsters, with the rugged look of a mountaineer and the warmth and humour to go with it. Teamwork, including parents, social workers and children, was really what underlaid their approach and brought home to me the skilled nature of this kind of work with these kinds of troubled children and their on-the-edge families.

The first child I placed in Ballikinrain was a wee timid boy from the Bog Road, a 'school refuser', from an overprotected and sheltered home. Timid had made friends when he was at primary school, so some elements of 'school phobia' seemed to me fairly obviously related to his mother's anxiety about him now starting at secondary school. She was a young, highly intense woman, whom I observed standing by the window curtains constantly looking out whenever the boy went into the garden or along to the shops and so on. I wrote a very comprehensive Hearing Report and took them to Ballikinrain to meet Doug and John which resulted in a relatively brief and successful placement, as a day pupil. I found out a couple of years later that John, who lectured at Regent Road for the residential social work course, was handing out my report with the identifying details blanked out, as a specimen of the kind of background report he wanted. Needless to say, I was not a little heartened that some of my early efforts at helping youngsters were not too wide of the mark.

I was, of course, hungry for practical professional childcare experience and working with people like them and these youngsters is how I acquired it, including my involvement with some in long-term residential care at Redding House. I will discuss three children in particular, one dealt with by Big Tam. I begin with Blondy, who I inherited from Liz's caseload when she left Falkirk. He was about six years old when we met, spiky blonde hair and a cheeky face. He had been at Redding House for about a year and had a still very young older sister who visited him monthly. His parents had separated and taken up with different partners. His father was a manual worker and had moved in with a younger woman who had young children but she could not cope with the lad too. His mother had left to live with an older man who was adamantly not prepared to look after another man's child. And thus it had been for over a year: Blondy in voluntary care and languishing up at Redding House with neither parent visiting.

I arranged to meet the parents in their current abodes. I was struck immediately by the sense of powerlessness that the father evoked in his attempt to explain the situation that he was in, as opposed to his son. It was as though fate was responsible for these circumstances, not him. There was no question of him bringing his son up on his own, even with support, or of him getting a job that would enable him to do so. The 'blame' was with the mother for having left and not taken the boy. He had at least tried with the lad, he felt, but it had proved too much for his partner, whereas the mother and her partner were not prepared to lift a finger. He had visited the boy at Redding House at first but the boy was so upset when he left that he thought it best just to stop visiting to let his son 'settle down'. But no, he would not give it another go and, anyway, what about his mother?

I visited the mother, a slim, nervous woman, who blubbered through the whole interview. We sat in the living room, her new partner sitting in the kitchen refusing to discuss it with me. The same fatalistic mindset inhabited both parents, no question of her attempting to set up on her own to care for her son. Both seemed trapped in relationships they could neither change nor leave, so their son was 'abandoned to care'. I was shaken to the bone by this kind of brazen obstinacy which wished to excuse itself simply by suggesting that the other parent should 'do something' about the child. These were both respectable working-class homes. One part of my brain was raging at this complete disregard of parental responsibility – without legal or financial penalty – while the other part of my brain, the professional side, was thinking that even if I managed to force the boy back into the care of either of these parents and their respective partners, what kind of care would that be exactly? Probably a lot worse than that on offer at Redding House, the dependable and affectionate regime under Miss MacLeod and Miss McCrae. But no foster carer was interested in a child of that age and, in any case, Blondy exhibited much the same kind of obstinacy as his birth parents in his conviction that one of them would come and take him back home, and soon. I wished I shared his belief, of course, but it never came to pass. I told him what his parents had said but I could see that, inside, he did not really believe it. Neither parent had been prepared to meet with him to convey directly that they could not have him back, which might have freed him to accept another family should the opportunity arise.

This situation is one that the Hearing system in theory might have handled well but, in those early years, it seemed impossible for a child received into voluntary care through Section 15 of the Social Work (Scotland) Act to be dealt with through the Hearing system under Section 44. This was despite Panels being strongly mooted as places where children's needs could be discussed in depth with parents and child present, the situation to be reviewed after three months then every six months thereafter. Voluntary care under Section 15 was thus left entirely to the local authority to administer and review annually, parents rarely attending. A parent could also take the child back any time within the first 12 months and, after that, by giving one month's notice. If the local authority was unhappy with this, they could apply to the Sheriff Court to assume full parental rights under Section 16, a legal process that also bypassed the Hearing system completely. It would be years before this parallel track was rectified. Blondy and other children like him often got lost within local authority voluntary care especially when Children's Officers departed the scene in the early 1970s when they were replaced by temporary, unqualified workers and managers unfamiliar with childcare legislation and practice.

After months of trying to arrange long-term foster parents for Blondy, I finally managed to contact a distantly related young couple with young children who lived in a nearby village. The attempt to place him with them broke down fairly quickly after a few weeks, the child's soiling being the biggest bugbear for them to overcome. Back to Redding House.

Blondy seemed neither up nor down with these developments. Then word came that his maternal grandmother had heard about his plight and wanted to take him. This had not been explored much before since she had reputedly had a heart condition. I met her, a cheery old grandmother wanting to do right by her grandson and to hell with what the GP might say. The GP was not obstructive but was doubtful as to how long she would be able to provide care for the boy. Enough said, so we allowed him to spend weekends with his gran for a few weeks, until she took him back full time. School reports had been good and all seemed fair, until she had a massive haemorrhage and died. Blondy returned to Redding House.

We discovered that he had been soiling repeatedly while with his grandmother but she had not reported this in case we took him away again. I insisted that he be allowed to attend the funeral. His experience so far had been of his mother and father disappearing from his life for reasons that he neither understood nor acknowledged. I therefore wanted to ensure that he 'knew' that his grandmother was dead and that it was not simply another fiction invented by grown ups. Indeed, I wanted him to see the coffin actually going into the ground – which he did, accompanied by Miss MacLeod. On his return to Redding House, he stopped soiling immediately. Indeed, he had never ever soiled while there, both before and after his grandmother's death.

While all of this was going on, I also took on another young boy, Shorty, who had been in Redding House for about seven years, basically from birth. Shorty had been removed from home as a baby under a Place of Safety Order taken out by the local RSSPCC Officer, badly scalded. It seemed that the parents were not allowed, and certainly not encouraged, by the RSPCC Officer to maintain contact with the baby once received into care. Indeed, cold fury over the parents' negligence and the severity of the child's injuries was expressed by the same officer when I asked about the circumstances of Shorty's admission to care. From this it was clear that no thought had ever been given to allowing the child to go back home. Why the child had not then been placed for adoption escapes me now but the local authority assumed parental rights and so could have placed him with long-term foster parents, had any been available. This was all several years before the development of Child Abuse Registers (1975) and the Hearing system, both of which introduced greater external scrutiny of childcare and child protection decision-making. Shorty had thus been dealt with by the pre-1968 charmed circle of Children's Officer, Children's Committee and Sheriff Court.

I remember Ian Gilmour commenting at this time that he hoped that all children removed from parental care might become subject to Hearing supervision and review, certainly until they were placed in long-term alternative families. He would have said this in regard to 'drift', the term then being coined to describe children who had been taken into care but then kept in institutions rather than returning them to their parents or placing them with relatives or foster or adoptive parents. Redding House was full of such children and sibling groups. Such children had almost uniformally been taken into care in 'reactive' or 'rescue' situations but kept there for years in the absence of fostering/adoptive placements. The route which I had taken with regard to Blondy – trying to renew contact with his parents and relatives – was thus ruled out in respect of Shorty given his severe injuries and estrangement from his birth family for so many years. In his case, my objective was simply stated: find him a long-term foster or adoptive family.

Miss MacLeod was pleased at this proposal and so was Shorty, a delightful wee boy, with huge spectacles, fragile appearance and an old-fashioned manner of talking and engaging that owed everything to Miss MacLeod, who had nursed him back to health, and the female regime at Redding House. There is little doubt in my mind that Shorty was Miss MacLeod's favourite and that this affection was mutually felt and returned by the boy. Given the success that eventually did transpire in finding an older couple who would foster and possibly adopt Shorty, the basis for the bonding which took place between the boy and his carers was undoubtedly due in large part to the quality of attachment he had acquired during his seven or eight years' stay at Redding House. In many ways, the family who came forward were an older couple who were as 'old-fashioned' as the boy they were taking into their home and I was overjoyed, as was Miss MacLeod, that such an outcome was possible given the circumstances of his birth and upbringing in public care which I shall return to in due course.

I will comment here on Bob Holman's remarks on the 1973 study, *Children Who Wait* (BAAF) by Jane Rowe and Lydia Lambert, which estimated that 6,000 children had been allowed to 'drift' in residential care without decisions being made for their permanent futures, in turn stimulating a pro-adoption lobby as part of the response. Social workers generally thought more foster care was necessary and there was no let up in their being urged to remove more children from their parents, just as they were beginning to be urged to 'protect' children from parental abuse, also by removal. The 1975 Children's Act in fact expanded the powers to remove children and dispense with parental consent for their adoption. Together with Jane Streather of the Child Poverty Action Group (CPAG) and Jo Tunnard, the director of the Family Rights Group, Bob Holman, a former children's officer turned academic turned Easterhouse community work activist, urged that the Act contain more preventative provisions directed at poor parents who might keep their children given higher incomes and more intensive social work support, possibly along the lines of Family Service Units (*Champions For Children*, 2013:174–6).

Holman urged that the differences between the pro-adoption and preventative lobbies should not be overstated and that improvements in both are necessary but the former frequently hold right-wing political positions that oppose or minimise state welfare provision on the grounds that it weakens families' 'sense of responsibility'. He also cites the fact that New Labour under Tony Blair in 2001 proposed the speed-up of adoptions while the Tory leader, William Hague, stated in 1999 that, 'Ideally, we would like every child to at least be considered for adoption'. Social workers focus, of course, on 'poor parenting' and its improvement but it is essential to consider what Holman and the preventative lobby were/are pointing out – the extent to which parenting is linked to the poverty of parents who may be 'poor' materially, educationally, socially and culturally. Of course, paying better incomes is not cheap in comparison to adoption but adoption and fostering can fail too and so what price a child's – many children's – lifelong security and stability? These are still crucially relevant questions and issues to ask and resolve today.

Back in 1975, Wee Dee, a child dealt with by Big Tam, helps illustrate the extent to which a child's family background is crucial to his fate when coming into care, particularly regarding the question of ongoing family contact. Wee Dee was about six years old and cared for by his father, who had mental health problems that sometimes required admission to a local hospital. When it became apparent after a few months that the father would possibly never be able to resume care of his six-year-old son, the social worker, Big Tam, set to work. What this meant was, yes, he spoke to me. By this time, our fostering and adoption Panel was running pretty smoothly and we had devised set procedures for most things: for approving carers and adoptive couples; for approving children who required long-term placements; for matching them to specific carers; and we also offered consultation sessions to workers to discuss complex childcare situations that were possibly coming the Panel's way further down the road.

Planning, planning and ever more planning, was the watchword, as I told Big Tam, who listened to me attentively on the Friday afternoon. On the Monday, he somehow got hold of the name and address of a couple newly approved for the short-term fostering of a female baby. He went to visit them the next night and was impressed, the couple already having two boys, the guy a long-distance lorry driver and the wife a salt-of-the-earth matriarch. This would be on the Tuesday. On the Wednesday, he took the boy down to them for his tea and then again on the Saturday, when he said he wanted to stay and they decided to keep him. He is still there today. That at least is how I remember it, although Big Tam insists the placement planning was far more intricate in that he left Wee Dee there after a third visit, never to return to Redding House except to collect his suitcase and say goodbye to Miss MacLeod, the staff and all the other kids, a third still mine.

Trying to fathom how Big Tam knew this placement would work is like wondering how he knew that Tasty-Toaster tins would work on his Moskvitch, only this time the fix for Wee Dee would turn out to be permanent rather than a pit-stop every few miles. Some of the work I attempted with the kids in Redding House had this stop-start quality but the family relationships involved all had crucial differences. Wee Dee had a good attachment to his father and contact had been kept up despite his hospitalisation. The carers had their own children and, after some initial sibling rivalry between Wee Dee and their eldest, which Tam quickly sorted out, the family never looked back. The couple felt no need to take over exclusive care or cut the child off from contact with his father. Likewise, the boy had not been abused or rejected by his father, whose inability to continue caring for his son was the perfectly understandable, commonly accepted one of ill health – not criminality, drugs or abuse. This is often reassuring to carers, especially those with young children of their own. So the prognosis for Wee Dee was very good from the start and all it needed was the right foster family and the right social worker and the right child to make it work.

I have described all of these children's cases in part to emphasise the lottery that faces children who come into care, not just then but still today. There is simply a lack of adequate resources available across the land, despite the best efforts of social workers who are now held responsible for this by the press, egged-on by snake-oil politicians like Tony Blair, carping about over-cautious adoption procedures. Foster and adoptive families have to be recruited, adequately supported, valued and paid more generously. That is all there is to it. In view of the experience I have just related, it was very interesting for me to read Bob Holman's commentary on John Stroud (1923–89) who, as a Children's Officer in Hertfordshire in the 1950s and '60s, pioneered the re-establishing of links between children who had been taken into care and had then lost touch with their birth families in circumstances similar to those I have cited. I had never heard of him before but he became a popular writer of fictionalised but realistic accounts of the poverty and complexity that care professionals and Probation Officers encountered in the post-war period. I had never heard either of his efforts to trace the families of children 'abandoned' to care, the same kind of children that I met in Redding House a decade or so after his own pioneering efforts (Bob Holman, *Champions For Children*, 2013: 90–2).

As I would discover for myself a decade or so later, tracing can also work in reverse, not just between child and former family but between child and former social worker. In the late 1980s, by which time I was living in Edinburgh and working as Child Protection Coordinator for Lothian Region based in Shrubhill House, the Social Work Department HQ in Leith Walk, there came a knock upon my front door. I opened it to find a tall, broad-shouldered, blonde-haired young man, propping up a racing bike and removing a crash helmet. I recognised him instantly as Blondy. He exhaled sharply and said, 'At last!'

We chatted for a while and from this I gleaned that his older sister had eventually been able to take him out of care to live with her until he was old enough to fend for himself. I did not ask any searching questions as to the intervening years or the present situation but understood that he had at least one child though he was separated from the mother. He seemed perfectly happy that we had met again but there was no expectation that he wanted us to resume contact and we simply parted with good wishes on both sides.

Whatever our meeting meant for this young man, it reminded me that my original wish for him had been that, should he not be able to obtain a secure family life, then at least he would not end up either in prison or hospital. If my expectations for his future seem now rather low, verging on pessimistic, I too exhaled an inward sigh of relief when I saw him, just as he had on seeing me. Here at least was one of my young charges who did not seem to have been damaged by exposure to my early inexperience and limited professional craft as a social worker. In that respect, I found myself not just pleased but grateful. It reminded me of just how much I had committed myself to these children and how much I had wanted all of them to have had a better start in life, the kind that we, the general public, mostly have and which we simply and quite rightly take for granted because it is surely every child's entitlement.

As a codicil, I received a letter shortly after this from Miss MacLeod, Skye, post-marked 14 February 1990 in response to a card I must have sent her, probably at Christmas, with no doubt a note inside mentioning the visit from Blondy. Her reply mentioned him in return:

> I saw him a year last April at a 'Wee Do' in Polmont which 'Crae' [her old Deputy] gave a few of her colleagues plus some of the older children we had with us in Redding House, shortly after she retired. He looked well though quiet and somewhat serious. We hope all will go well with him in his marriage.

She also enclosed a longer note concerning Shorty:

> It is over *ten years* since I last saw him, and he is now 25 years old, slim and *short*. I don't know whether you heard that he was a time served tradesman and got his City and Guilds with credit. He started working in the village before he left school, doing a full day Saturday. After leaving school he was taken on permanently and the then boss took quite an interest in him and gave him Day Release to Glasgow every week till he served his time. In all he worked seven years there, and I wish he had had enough sense to have carried on working there...The 'new boss' on occasions asked him to work late some evenings and although he got the 'odd £10', as he put it, he was not all that keen to comply with the request. So he gave in his notice. Following on this he got two temporary periods of employment but in each job he was classed as too slow in his work... Personally, I don't think he has the physical stamina to work at an acceptable speed for a full day. Around the time these changes overtook him... he got to know that [a local hotel] was looking for a porter and he was successful in getting a start there. He does on occasion do a *little* [of his trade] for them. He works morning and afternoon shifts and gets all his meals free while at work, including his breakfast if he is

on a morning shift. He referred to the meals as 'super, the same as goes into the dining room'. This is very important in his case. Now, lastly, without any prompting from me he disclosed how he came to get such horrific burns on his buttocks. He even gave me a demonstration of how his *father* held him by a *wrist* and an *ankle* against the fire. There was an inclination or leaning towards self pity some days while he was with me, which I did my best to counteract, could this be the explanation to him making such a disclosure after such a very, very long time, what do you think? I found it quite difficult to make a comment, and just said 'why should your Dad do that to you', and his reply was 'I suppose it was because I was crying'. It really all adds up – a fractured femur, bruises etc, as well as the awful burns. For however feebly he would struggle – a struggle there would be.

It is humbling to get a letter like that, appreciated more from this distance than perhaps was grasped at the time. Reading it now, one can remark on the 'continuity of care' which that small residential home provided for at least some of the generations of children who passed through it (most of whom remained there during their early and primary years) with much the same staff in attendance. It reads a bit like an extended family reunion in some ways – 'Crae's Wee Do' – old fashioned, maiden-auntish, personal, intuitive, commonsensical, untheoretical. Some of it contains the attention to detail Miss MacLeod gave me and other social workers or wrote in review reports or gave in the witness box at the Sheriff Court or to the Children's Committee. Certain key words are italicised, notably in respect of the lad's health, lack of stature, stamina and physical capacity, linking these directly to the horrific injuries he obtained at the hands of his father and which degraded and compromised his physical ability to earn a living equal to his skilled trade. One also sees signs of his institutional upbringing in later life, the recreating of the conditions of that upbringing in the sanctuary he found in a local hotel, another residential institution: a place also of 'routines', of people coming and going constantly, of cooked meals served on the premises, where one could blether and interact with the 'staff' – for which read 'visitors'/'guests'. This kind of gregarious sociability became an enduring aspect of the boy's personality, got him a new family and helped him survive. It shows the kind of resilience children can develop with support but also its absolute limitations.

When it comes to the admission of the abuse itself, it is sobering to realise the extent to which children may remain loyal to their parents even when they have been terribly treated. No one could have been more trusted by a child in her care than that boy in relation to Miss MacLeod, yet he was 25 years old, living independently and staying with her over a few days in her own home and only in a reflective, despondent mood did he feel able to open up.

What makes society or, indeed, the care profession assume that simply asking children if they have been injured by their parent or carer will make them 'disclose' (another professional term that is not also part of a child or teenager's routine vocabulary)? If children later speak up, why is the default position that they were either not listened to or not 'heard' by my or earlier generations? Someone as long in the tooth as Miss MacLeod found it difficult to know what to say to him for the best, partly because she could not imagine the full horror of the attack on a defenceless child. The whole of the social work profession in 1990 was going through much the same process – though the watershed of the events in Orkney were still another year away. It is a reminder too that Shorty is still a real person, not a character in a novel written by someone like John Stroud or, indeed, a poem written by me.

6

New Dawn

destroying old case files, sifting through,
fragments, crumbling manila folders,
records of visits, tissue-thin carbon-copies,
letters, black Remington-type, scribbles,
notes, Dear Sir, I am, most grateful for
'Case Histories', *Dancing with Big Eunice*

Being a brief account of the origins of SACRO *and some tales verging on the sentimental concerning the old style administration of justice at both ends of the scale – meaning Falkirk Burgh and Sheriff Courts, the author attends a client wedding and participates in the last football match and final office party of old Falkirk Burgh which made local news.*

IN OCTOBER 1973, Dougie Carnegie appeared, trailing Iain Morrison and something called the Scottish Association for the Care and Resettlement of Offenders (SACRO) in his wake. Dougie had kept up contact with Big Tam as he would for many years after. Political change hung in the air as Edward Heath called a snap general election during a miners' strike to answer the basic question, 'who governs Britain?' He received the basic reply: Harold Wilson and Mick McGahey, that's who. Dougie, it seemed, was now bent on revolutionising the Scottish Criminal Justice system via the voluntary sector. Word was received that Big Tam and I were to muster as many of our Falkirk Burgh buddies as possible to a Thursday night AGM of SACRO in Edinburgh, just down from the Castle. Nobody knew why, least of all Big Tam and me.

I remember arriving, Dougie patrolling the pavement outside the meeting place, excited and puffing a fag. As Danny walked towards the door, Dougie, who had never met him, stepped forward and said, 'Who the fuck are you?'

Danny looked at him and replied, 'Who the fuck are you?'

Dougie roared with laughter and patted Danny on the shoulder, ushering him inside. Danny entered, with the look of a man who had just won a free ticket to the opening night of Dante's *Inferno*. Iain Morrison was already inside, looking rather sheepish I thought. I recognised some other old and new Regent Road faces who indeed formed the bulk of the audience. In effect, Dougie had packed the meeting to vote out the old SACRO Committee and replace it with one more in tune with Dougie's thinking, whatever that might be exactly. I may have ended up as Secretary of Falkirk's new SACRO branch, which consisted of me, Big Tam, Danny, Paul, Walker, Helen, possibly Kate and Wee Marion, who unofficially typed its letters in the coming months while the hitherto rather spectral organisation kicked into life and sprouted actual branches across the land.

It was Paul Morron who caught Dougie's attention as someone with the commitment and ability to develop the organisation's potential to operate both as a volunteer body providing practical supports like hostels for offenders and travel services for prisoners families and the like and as a pressure group to help bring Community Service Order legislation and related provision to Scotland as had already occurred in England and Wales in 1972. This would be achieved through the Community Service by Offenders (Scotland) Act 1978, and Paul was eventually recruited by Strathclyde to install and manage the new scheme across its breadth, which contained half of Scotland's population. And so, despite Dougie's indefatigable taste for intrigue, a serious initiative emerged with serious people on board, including Lord Mansfield, a Tory Peer, barrister and first President of SACRO.

Dougie and Morrison also brought in a retired admiral, if I remember right, to head up the organisation, who eventually told Dougie to bog off, or words to that effect, as any sensible person would. I recall Dougie and Morrison commiserating once it became clear that the old seadog was going to chart his own course. Morrison said philosophically to Dougie, who sat with the look of a man who had been thrown out of Dante's *Inferno* just before Happy Hour, 'We picked the wrong man for the right reasons'. Thankfully, they had also managed to pick the right man for the right reasons, Paul, SACRO's first full-time Regional Development Officer. He would become Head of Criminal Justice Social Work Services for Strathclyde and Glasgow City, a founder member of Victim Support in Scotland and helped set up Drug Courts in Glasgow all of which brought him an MBE in 1999 for services to Criminal Justice in Scotland. (Did I not say he was a referee?)

At Reorganisation, Paul would leave Falkirk Burgh to take up that post, writing an article published in December 1974 in the first and only issue of an intended Central Regional social work staff magazine entitled *Communicate*. It sets out why an initiative like SACRO was needed at the time and, indeed, why it still is to this day:

Little encouragement can be drawn from our record in After-Care: of the latest figures I've seen, around 30,000 offenders were released from Prison establishments in the year and only 4,000 were subject to statutory after-care with less than 300 being discharged on Parole... It is to tackle these glaring gaps in Scotland that in 1973 the voluntary body was formed called SACRO.

The dark cloud that became Regionalisation crept slowly over the horizon. *Communicate* mentions the departure of Falkirk Burgh Director, Geoff Evans, who had been appointed Deputy Director for Borders Region. Rumour was already rife in Falkirk that John Murphy only got the job over Geoff because Stirling County had the lowest rates and the worst material resources, the worst office provision, the worst equipment levels (phones, desks, vans) and the thriftiest care budgets and staffing ratios of all the constituent authorities that comprised Central Region: Stirling County, Stirling Burgh, Clackmannan and Falkirk Burgh. On such comparisons Falkirk Burgh came out top of the league on every count. Continuing the footballing analogy, it seemed to most of the Falkirk staff as though the hamper-boy had become Scotland's manager instead of Tommy Docherty. These rumours seemed compounded at the next round of appointments when it emerged that every single Senior in Stirling County had been promoted, along with a sprinkling from Stirling Burgh and Clackmannan, despite some obvious discrepancies in experience and ability compared to Falkirk Burgh staff, particularly Danny and Big Alex, a seasoned Senior from Fife who had recently replaced Sheila, the other Falkirk Burgh Senior.

Whether these views were entirely correct or fair soon became irrelevant because, by promoting all those loyal to John Murphy's old regime, a vacuum had been created at frontline management level into which people like myself and Big Tam would soon be promoted, despite our own relative inexperience. I was asked to go to Stirling as a Senior and Big Tam was asked to go somewhere else, but we both refused for our own reasons. For my part, I was quite happy chipping away in Falkirk learning my trade. I told Ian Gilmour I intended to keep a small caseload of the kids I had in long-term care at Redding House even if I became a Senior so I would not be moving anywhere at present. The idea of Big Tam and me moving was dropped.

Another colleague who had trained with us at Regent Road, Davis, was also promoted at this time and so we all joined Danny and Alex as the designated Senior group for the new Falkirk District Office based in Brockville House, Falkirk, on 1 May 1975. All that remained was to appoint a new Area Officer. Danny did not get the job and neither did Big Alex. Instead, Bob got it, an amiable training officer from Stirling Burgh, a rotund wee man who unfortunately wore braces over his shirt and these, also unfortunately, tended to bounce, giving him a rather clownish appearance. This did not help his attempt to establish his professional authority over the Senior group who collectively cringed at his persistence in pretending to know that which he evidently did not but continued to assert, with predictable results.

Alex had arrived in Orchard Street at the end of 1974 as a replacement for Sheila and so Danny moved along to Newmarket Street to take over her team, which allowed Big Alex to supervise us at Orchard Street. I was in fact Big Alex's family social worker for he and his wife happened to be long-term foster parents for several ethnically diverse children placed by a few authorities, including Falkirk, one of whom I inherited from Liz's caseload, a lovely girl who would become a social worker herself in due course. Big Alex was already a Senior with Fife, having come through the ranks as an RSPCC Inspector and so he was a veteran of the childcare scene. He was also a large and genial character, unpretentious and straightforward in manner and outlook and as delighted with us as we were with him. I was particularly delighted because Big Alex did not seem to mind being kissed full on the mouth by one of my cases, Barbara, whenever she met him in reception, which took a lot of pressure off my own lips I do not mind admitting. Indeed, whenever I got the call from Wee Marion that Barbara was downstairs with her husband-to-be, old Willie, I got her to phone Alex immediately to say there was stuff he had to sign urgently waiting for him in reception. Big Alex thus became caught up with Barbara which allowed me to sort out Willie reasonably quickly.

I had inherited Willie from Liz's caseload. I would write a two-and-a-half page poem about the experience of working with Willie and Barbara, 'Care in the Community, 1974', for *Dancing with Big Eunice*. Willie was in his early 50s when we met, which was on the dot at 5.00pm every Thursday after he finished work at Carron Ironworks where he worked as a labourer pushing iron hutches about laden with steel. Liz had managed to get him a job and a flat in Falkirk and out of Larbert Hospital and a long-stay psychiatric ward where he had been placed from an early age. Liz also got him a mortgage for a two-bedroom flat and, ever since, Willie came up faithfully every Thursday (pay-day) to hand the money over to Rita at reception to settle his bills. Willie was then called 'mentally handicapped' or a 'slow learner' but it was difficult to know the part played by being institutionalised for so long in such a setting. When I did get to know him and asked why he had been put into Larbert, he said he had asked a doctor once who told him he had been 'a bad boy'.

There were no medical records to consult and nothing in the file either about Willie's life prior to, or of his stay in, Larbert Hospital. We then moved along to Orchard Street and one night he said he had something to ask. He had met a girl, up at the bus station and she had asked him for a kiss. Well, she had asked his lodger, Big Wull, first but, since he did not fancy it, she asked Willie instead. Now they were going to get married and have kids, which is what he wanted to ask me about: having sex. I knew of Barbara from Danny, who had supervision of one of her several daughters, all of whom had been adopted at birth. Sometimes mother and daughter sat beside each other in reception without knowing of their kinship. This was one of the perils of a relatively small local authority like Falkirk acting as an adoption agency. I knew that Barbara was now living in the Borders and working in the laundry of an old folk's home down there, which supplied her with board and lodgings. She also had 'learning difficulties' and, after the sixth child born to her had been adopted at birth, she had been given 'the operation'. Willie knew nothing of this and waxed lyrical about having always wanted to be a father and how he hoped this might happen with Barbara.

When it became clear that Willie and Barbara did intend to wed, I contacted Barbara's social worker in the Borders, who seemed close to retirement and unmarried herself. She was initially rather sceptical about the whole affair. Since the proposal envisaged Barbara coming to Falkirk with my support rather than Willie going to the Borders with hers, the matter proceeded amicably. Willie already had a flat and Big Wull would remain lodging with the happy couple so all was set fair. My colleague Helen, another Regent Roader, was asked by Barbara to be her Maid of Honour and I, of course, would be the Best Man. The whole Office turned out and the reception was held in a local pub, The Hurlet. The Borders social worker attended, along with her aged mother, who was in her 90s. Big Alex was smothered in kisses by the ever-affectionate Barbara. The only slight wobble occurred during the wedding, a civil-ceremony at the Registrar's, when Willie was asked to repeat the marriage vow. He looked like a dead parrot as he stared uncomprehendingly from the Registrar to me until I said, 'Repeat everything I say, Willie,' which Willie did, like a tin robot.

Afterwards, Danny sidled up and whispered, 'You realise of course that, legally, Barbara really married you?'

I did not care, for Willie was radiant, and the photographs proved it.

What else sticks? Oh, yes, my first week's court duty in Falkirk Burgh Court, which was presided over by a local councillor, a Justice of the Peace, with a legal aide by his side to keep him right as to the law and range of penalties. The District Court was held in the Council Buildings, not far from the old Sheriff Court, and consisted of a large hall with a series of wooden benches and solid wooden floorboards at the end of which, elevated, sat the JP and his trusted legal advisor. Something of their atmosphere on the farcical end of the spectrum was well captured by a young Edinburgh councillor, Drew Meek, who started out on the bench during those years and later became the Tory leader of Lothian Regional Council from 1982 to 1986. He was a journalist and recalled the following experience printed in *The Scotsman* in 2004:

> I told a woman whose husband had failed to make maintenance payments that I was awarding her an extra ten shillings a week. 'That's very good of you, your honour,' declared the man in the dock. 'I will try to chip in something myself.'

That could have been in any District Court in Scotland.

The first day I sat in Falkirk District court as duty social worker, I found myself right at the front, immediately underneath the magistrate's elevated position. The 30 rows of benches directly behind me were absolutely empty except for the very last few at the back where sat those who had been summoned to appear before the dignity of the bench. An usher, who doubled on non-court days as a janitor, shouted out the name of each sinner to come forth. On one occasion, there was the slow, deliberate rumble of someone getting to their feet, clambering past the seats to get to the aisle and then beginning a slow amble – indeed, scuff – all the way down the long walk to the front of the court. With my eyes fixed firmly to the front, wondering what the charge might be and if the Department might receive yet another Fine-Supervision Order for someone peeing up a close, I heard the unmistakable strains of low whistling emanating from the accused. Combined with the syncopated clump of feet it began to resemble a percussion-band waddling unhurriedly towards the Justice that was waiting for him stoically at the foot of the hall. When the ensemble did eventually hove into view, true enough, it was an old vagrant, a tramp, raincoat tied classically in the middle, wearing an old hat. He stood thus, whistling away to himself, a man who had no doubt seen much more in life to worry him than the wheels of Justice grinding slowly that day in Falkirk Burgh Court.

He would not have been out of place in George Orwell's account of tramping life in *Down and Out in London and Paris* in the Thirties, much of it still relevant to the nether world of Falkirk District Court in 1973. The old guy would have got a Fine-Supervision Order, despite being an itinerant and brief resident of the local Working-Men's Hostel, another hang-over going back to the Poor Law, when unemployed workers used to 'tramp' the country looking for work, staying in 'model lodging houses' along the way. Their inhabitants were usually too old to work, many ex-servicemen simply seeking a non-restrictive refuge, a place in which to end their days with minimum fuss. When they died, small packages of their belongings would appear on the duty-desk, sent along from the Hostel to do with as we would. These belongings generally comprised baccy tins and cigarette-making contraptions, rarely anything to identify individuals. You then notified Wee Bill who passed the contents on to Miss M for Big Eunice to arrange a 'pauper's-funeral', paid for by the Parish. The belongings were put in a large envelope and placed in a manila folder and logged as a case file, then 'closed', no doubt never to be opened again before being destroyed after the set number of years such files are legally kept.

At the other end of the Justice scales stood Falkirk Sheriff Court, presided over by Reid Kerr, a brisk, no-nonsense Scottish lawyer and public schoolboy. Monday mornings were the busiest of the week processing those detained in the cells over the weekend for drunkenness, violence, football hooliganism and the like which were dealt with first and in conveyor belt fashion. This lasted about an hour though I believe in Glasgow it could take all day. There were invariably Social Enquiry Reports (SERs) requested and this was the main task of the court duty worker to obtain early notification of since there was only 21 days allowed for us to prepare the reports and 14 days for remands in custody. On one particular Monday morning, the public benches were packed because an infamous local criminal family – one of Big Tam's in fact – had one of their own in the dock being represented by the famous Glasgow criminal barrister, Joe Beltrami. I noticed him immediately when I entered the court, sitting in an elegantly tailored suit, tall and slim with silver hair slicked back and formidable eye-contact. In the middle of the morning's guddle, an old vagrant appeared to answer charges of drunkenness and breaking-and-entering, albeit of an empty building, and he stood looking distracted while Reid Kerr attempted to establish his plea.

After a few minutes, Joe B sprang to his feet and, in the most silken and flowing fashion, begged the court's leave, since the court duty lawyer was obviously overwhelmed with cases, for him to be allowed to speak to the man in private in order to ascertain his plea. Reid-Kerr could have kissed him. Indeed, I could have kissed him myself, especially when he came back a few minutes later, with the old guy once more in the dock still looking bemused.

Joe immediately launched forth: 'Your Honour, my client is rather unclear as to what occurred on the evening in question, for he had been drinking, and although he has no recollection of actually entering the building, he accepts that he was discovered there by the police.'

And so on and so forth, the place ringing with Joe's mellifluous stream of cadenced vocables. The old guy seemed hardly to know he was in court at all, let alone being represented by Scotland's greatest criminal defence lawyer and for nothing, though no doubt paid for by the Falkirk hoodlum whose case Joe was about to plead and for which, alas, I could not stay. Joe Beltrami was pure theatre, a class act, with not a camera in sight in Falkirk Sheriff Court. A lawyer friend of mine, Dick Whyte, who knew Joe well, confirms that he was a lawyer of high principle who believed that crime should not pay. It did pay, however, in a story he told against himself going to watch his beloved Celtic FC when a young Glasgow urchin approached him in the car park with the usual ill-disguised offer to 'watch his car disnae get damaged'. It was an offer Joe declined, saying that he had two Doberman attack dogs in the back. When Joe returned, his car was up on bricks, all the wheels gone. The small urchin was sat on the wall waiting to shout across at him – 'Haw mister, can yer Dobermans pit four wheels back oan?'

Other images remain, less dramatic but still unforgettable, such as Falkirk Burgh social work office's football team, whose 'manager' was Walker Butler, Danny's old Probation boss. He had suffered a stroke which reduced his capacity but Geoff Evans kept him on at a Senior salary to do mostly duty-cases and the like. He also arranged Sunday football games with other local social work offices, social security, the police or housing. His method of team planning was unorthodox in that he invited everyone he met to play and somehow only 11 ever turned up on the day until, one day, all 25 did. We were all milling around Victoria Park dressing rooms waiting for Walker to arrive to announce the team. I can see him now, parking his Honda Civic automatic and walking towards us carrying the ball, his Harold Wilson raincoat blowing in the breeze, until he suddenly caught sight of the large crowd his team had become. He slowed his pace, suddenly booted the ball high into the air and, while we watched it soar, he turned on his heel and drove off. I only learned years later that Walker had gone with the International Brigade to fight Fascism in Spain in the mid-1930s. He had never mentioned it, not even to Danny.

In my mind's eye, I can still remember Big Tam's finest game and the final one for our football team, another Sunday down at Victoria Park, myself playing right-midfield and Big Tam up front on the wing. Big Danny Murphy of the Bog Road Polis and me were in complete control of the middle of the park, so I played a long, diagonal through-ball inside the left-back which Big Tam gamely ran onto, took to the bye-line and crossed it into the penalty-box, which everyone missed. So, a goal-kick, which the goalkeeper booted straight back out to me still standing on the halfway line. To my urgent signal, Big Tam hared back down the wing to collect another 40-yard ball I placed again inside the full-back and he took it once more to the bye-line and crossed it brilliantly into the box, which everyone missed. Another goal-kick. The goalie again booted the ball straight out to me, still standing on the halfway line. I could see that Big Tam had hardly walked past the penalty box and was blowing rather heavily, so I shouted again to him to get ready for another ball, to which he stuck up two fingers and held them up defiantly as he continued his long walk back towards the centre line. Perhaps that gesture may stand for the end of the old Falkirk Burgh, haring down the wing in all its glory but now nearing its end, with only a tired walk back to the centre circle left before beginning a new game on a new pitch with a new team and a new manager, with who knew what results in store.

We had a farewell party in Orchard Street on the eve of Regionalisation, memorable mostly for the antics of one of our trainees, Big George Smith, a Glaswegian who later became a senior manager in Strathclyde and Glasgow. Some of us were sitting talking in the typing-pool room when George threw open the reception hatch and demanded to see the duty social worker. Every now and again, George momentarily halted his client-like rant by addressing an imaginary partner just outside the frame of the hatch with soothing and amorous remarks, before turning back to unleash yet another verbal onslaught in an affectionate caricature of a tipsy but rancorous client, our daily bread. Big George later led a conga out of the office and into the street for a couple of turns, which brought the Bog Road police along, phoned by the neighbours. Big Danny Murphy it was who arrived, our football team's left-midfielder, who detained no one, the party already having long petered out through exhaustion and drink. The *Falkirk Herald* reported the matter briefly and got John Murphy, no relation to Danny, the newly designated Central Region Director of Social Work, to comment. He said that we were just high-spirited but dedicated young professionals letting off some steam in the course of celebrating an historic occasion. And indeed, so we were.

7

Dante's Inferno: Regionalisation

Another incident in the unreported war
of manoeuvre between the establishment

and the underclass
'Mau-Mauing the Flak Catchers', *Dancing With Big Eunice*

*Being an encounter with early managerialism which did not go unchallenged
by those on the Falkirk front line; a depiction of the author's team and their
work; a song he wrote to keep up staff morale through being managed by
serial numpties; the dissection of an internal report on service delivery in
the office which cleared the Seniors of mutiny but does not stop the author's
daring escape to England disguised as an Emergency Duty Senior.*

REGIONALISATION CONVERTED 52 Scottish local authorities of various sizes
into 12 large Regions. The biggest anomaly was Strathclyde Region which
contained about half of Scotland's population, a monster designed to tackle
monster social problems, but a monster administration nonetheless. Surely it
could have been halved or divided into three, if only to make it more humanly
proportional. But no, this was the era of Big Plans and Big Bulldozers, driven
by Labour notions of Municipal Socialism being delivered from Town Halls
in Glasgow, Liverpool, Sheffield and the like. And a lot of it worked, too, for
its time. What it certainly achieved was monumental upheaval throughout
Scottish local Government and a restructuring of social work services into
Departments that might at least vie for resources on an equal footing with
those other budgetary giants like Education and Housing in terms of local
politics and so-called economies of scale.

In defence of Regionalisation, it did pave the way for the Chairs of
more powerful social work committees to work closely with more able
Regional Social Work Directors to create a professional lobby within local
Government that was far less in hock to parish pump politics. If the Regions
became large bureaucracies, then they did so by taking greater account of
wider statutory social work responsibilities and perspectives. Local politics
operated at Directorate level and housing sub-committees etc. Individual

councillors were kept well away from the daily doings of social workers and their cases. At regional level, social work committee Chairs and Directors ran the show, which enabled modern social work legislation to function despite the residual welfare attitudes of previous committees thoroughly committed to keeping the rates down.

Intimations surfaced that the new world of Regional social work might be a tad different in spirit than previously met with in Falkirk Burgh when I dropped in to meet some of the social workers I was due to begin supervising a week or two before the new Regional Authorities opened their doors on 1 May 1975. The workers were based in a nearby office still technically within the jurisdiction of Stirling County, John Murphy's old regime. I phoned one of the workers and called in to meet some of them on my way back from Redding House. I had a cup of tea in the team room and I was on my way out when I was beckoned into the Area Officer's office to be ticked off for not having the 'courtesy' to notify him of my visit beforehand. I told him to stick his courtesy where the monkey stuck its nuts and he reported me to a rather apologetic Ian Gilmour. This was the first hint of managerialism and the first true jobsworth that I had encountered in local authority social work so far, having a disproportionate concern for form over content.

At that moment, I still had a full caseload as a social worker further burdened by the need to write up reports, case notes and transfer summaries and organise transfer visits and the like, while still working with four long-term kids in Redding House. In the midst of this upheaval, this wee twerp had little more to worry about than keeping his tidy desk even tidier. I christened him Little Sport, a newspaper cartoon character of the day, a stick-like creature always wearing a running vest who had a tuft of spiky hair uncannily like that of the officious throwback whose sense of petty-bourgeois propriety I had inadvertently offended. It soon emerged that he was mocked and loathed by many of his own staff, including some I was about to manage. Once a Probation colleague of Danny's, the old Poor Law mentality that used to distinguish the deserving from the undeserving, now seemed recast in this clot's anachronistic impulse to segregate the polite from the impolite. A lay preacher and what Billy Connolly calls 'the beige people', he would leave the increasingly irreverent profession of social work for the doctrinal purity of the ministry, where he could continue to divide the sheep from the goats to his heart's content. Amen to that, I thought, and bloody good riddance.

I have since reread the foregoing passage a few times, wondering about its feeling and tone. There is obviously some element of catharsis involved in revisiting strong emotions no matter how many years may have elapsed since but this incident was the opening salvo of other annoyances, petty and less petty, about to unfold. On 1 May 1975, we moved into Brockville House, Falkirk Area Office, the largest workplace in Central Region, which also had offices based in Stirling, Grangemouth and Clackmannan and a sub-office in Denny. Since all the Seniors were from Falkirk Burgh, I quickly secured their agreement to adopt an Intake-Longterm system, this being widely discussed at the time in professional journals like *Community Care* and *Social Work Today*, the magazine of the professional association (BASW). Intake teams were a response to staffing reductions, a mechanism for identifying the most urgent new cases and enabling long-term social workers a protected 'space' to deal with already identified high-risk cases – mainly children in care or on Hearing supervision. An effective and proactive Intake Team thus enabled pressurised offices to function without becoming engulfed by lower priority cases, the routine chaff which could become dangerously mixed up with the more volatile wheat. That was the theory and I found it to work well especially in large busy offices like Falkirk and then later in Craigmillar in Edinburgh.

Danny became Intake Senior and the anchor man of the Seniors group. Bob, our new Area Officer, cheerfully endorsed the proposal. I became a Long-term Senior for The Braes, a patch ranging from the top side of Falkirk which took in the new housing scheme of Hallglen and also the arc of outlying rural villages from Slamannan and Avonbridge to Redding and West Quarter. For the remainder of 1975, we thus struggled along with 50 per cent establishment level, meaning we had only half the social workers we were entitled to. It was the same all over Scotland, though we held back from employing unqualified staff, probably because experience had shown already that this merely delayed building good professional standards over the long term, if we could just dig in and take the hit now.

My main priority was to supervise the group of social workers assigned to me, none of whom were from Falkirk Burgh. There were five in number initially, comprising an experienced female worker who was leaving in a few weeks; two recently qualified workers, a female and a male who were still finding their feet; an entirely useless unqualified male, for me a middle-class poseur; a loud-mouthed and bumptious middle-aged female, who argued with me about nothing during team meetings but was nice as nine-pence during supervision, which she badly needed, having been trained in England. A late entrant to the profession, I think she felt offended at my relative youth compared to her good self – I was 26 years old at this point. At any rate, this person had some links with the Liberal Party which seemed in her mind to make up for an absence of basic childcare knowledge and practice experience. I was truly joyful when I learned after a few months she had obtained a promoted post somewhere, for which I had given her a cracking reference and would do so again, any day. Likewise with the unqualified who soon moved on to social work training: another good reference supplied. Let them kick him into shape if they could, or counsel him out.

If such attitudes suggest a war zone mentality rather than a meeting of true minds, then welcome to Regionalisation, certainly in Falkirk. The truth is that the massive upheaval involved was endured more than loved by frontline professionals as a huge intrusion and imposition on our working lives, over which no one felt they had any real say, far less control. Those above relied almost entirely on those immediately below them to get the job done. They had rarely chosen the other, either above or below themselves. What happened in Falkirk was replicated to different degrees across Scotland as we heard from a variety of far-flung ex-Regent Roaders: bureaucratic upheaval, personality clashes, professional cultural clashes and in-fighting, all underscored by a lack of staff resources at ground level. I would never have applied to work for John Murphy's Stirling County in a month of Sundays and I very much doubt that it would have welcomed me. Now we were flung together by circumstance and had to get on with it. Professionals who had been appointed and managed under one regime – autocratic, bureaucratic, top-down, ageing, conformist, as I would characterise John Murphy's Stirling County – were forced to embrace those chosen by an often quite opposite mindset – inclusive, non-hierarchic, young, questioning, progressively minded like those in Geoff Evan's Falkirk Burgh.

The issues were not simply personality clashes, though these did exist, but questions of managerial competence and style rooted in differences over a watershed change in professional cultural values: the old school met and drastically misread the new one.

The clash between old professional aspirations meeting the reality of modern cultural and social conditions is clear enough when one reads John Murphy's own history of Scottish social work in *British Social Services: The Scottish Dimension* (Scottish Academic Press, 1992), assisted by his daughter, Gill McMillan. It is the first and still perhaps the only attempt to describe comprehensively the development of Scottish social work from its origins in 1945 down to 1992, and it should be commended for that alone. It is in the main an institutional history, drawn from the major Committees and Reports of the period and in that sense may be classified as what radical historians call 'History from Above', an account of what a group of 1960s politicians, academics and well-placed Scottish Office insiders thought welfare ought to comprise and the legislation required to enact it. John Murphy's narrative in effect shows how the Social Work (Scotland) Act 1968, was the joint product of some Scottish Office mandarins, a few progressive politicians and academics who built on the work of enlightened practitioners and researchers, mostly English – John Bowlby, Clare and Donald Winnicot, Barbara Kahan, Peter Townsend – and Professor Fred Stone, a member of the Kilbrandon Committee and director of child and adolescent psychiatry at Glasgow Hospital for Sick Children (Murphy: 13).

John Murphy's history of the creation of a modern Scottish social work service in 1975 testifies to the general upheaval that also marked the formation prior to that of the new generic social work service in November 1969, staffed by a motley collection of trained and untrained specialist professionals drawn from the disparate fields of criminal justice, mental health, childcare and local Government welfare. They, too, were thrown together and expected to get on with it in 1969 as were we in 1975. No doubt they too had wide personal and cultural clashes to overcome but the necessity of including and integrating these different knowledge bases led to a comprehensive muddling-through attitude being adopted. My own view is that no one, including most of the Directors of the new service, was at all sure what 'social work' itself comprised. It landed amongst them like an alien. The extent of the guddle is clear in the account of Gill Martin, John Murphy's daughter, who wrote about the new departments that opened their doors on 17 November 1969:

> On Friday night there were 305 childcare officers, 281 probation officers, 276 welfare officers and 97 mental health officers. On the Monday morning there were 959 social workers with shuffled caseloads, and naïve assumptions that they had been transmuted into generic workers. Those who doubted the transubstantiation were not infrequently suspected of heresy, and the workers concerned were often hesitant to pretend other than omnicompetence. Older and wiser heads recognised a generic department without necessarily declaring for instant generic workers... It took bad experiences [in England and Scotland], calmer days, and time, almost two decades, before the inevitable importance of specialization was fully recognised.

Of the 1,000 or so basic-graders who manned the barricades of the new social work departments in 1969, only 300 held professional qualifications. By 1975, there would be many more qualified as a proportion of the whole and trained specifically for generic social work. By 1989, there would be 5,000 field staff, all of whom would be qualified. As for the disparate professional backgrounds of the Directors of Social Work appointed in 1969, we have the authoritative summary of John Murphy. He was himself a Home Office Inspector of approved schools in the 1960s, which were then highly custodial and institutional in nature, and their reform he is widely credited as championing. That said, his candid précis of his future fellow Directors suggests a mixed-bag of Scottish local Government internal-appointees and time-servers, some English 'carpet-baggers' some of whom were progressives and a few women (Murphy: 173):

> Of the 52 appointed [Directors], four were women, four came from SWSG and a dozen were from England, Wales and Ireland. The largest single source was former welfare officers, at least 20, appointed mainly internally, and illustrating in some cases the inherent temptation in local authorities to appoint their own men as a reward for long service or other loyalty. Some ten were from probation, but only a handful from child care, the discipline which had fought hardest for a family service. One appointment, for Edinburgh city, was a doctor who had been responsible for the joint health and welfare department there. The proportion of women may now seem small, but was then advanced, when there were no women in education directorates and relatively few holding chairs even in social sciences. The directors from outwith Scotland, particularly those appointed to larger authorities, and this included a few 'carpet baggers', often brought with them the standards of more progressive places, and the capacity to influence committees to provide greater resources. They were a timely and influential transfusion to the more torpid Scottish social work body of the period. The four from central Government [which included John Murphy], and even some probation officers, had to adjust to the very different dimension of local Government, whose jungle quality they had probably underestimated from their previous more sheltered roles. For the welfare officers appointed *in situ* the transition was the least disturbing, and by the same token, their appointing authorities experienced the least disturbance – in every sense. Of the 52 appointed fewer than half had a recognized qualification in any branch of social work. On the whole this great exercise was achieved as fairly as possible in the circumstances, and the results were generally accepted, apart from some desultory press correspondence from interested professional bodies.

John Murphy's administrative and professional history of Scottish social work is not the commentary of a disinterested academic but a participant – someone mired in the 'jungle quality' of professional interest-groups and the skulduggery of Scottish Office politics. The unparliamentary language he occasionally deploys captures a world filled with the petty personal rivalries which drove and drives so much of local council politics. It thus makes crystal clear that the social work departments that opened their doors in 1970 were dominated numerically by the least professionally qualified and trained groups who were often local Government yes-men. The best trained were probation officers, children's officers and medical and psychiatric social workers, people who had fieldwork backgrounds and able to offer professional leadership for new social work departments. Not welfare officers, the kind of clerical council bureaucrats long schooled in the penny-pinching, public-assistance mentality that Lord Wheatley's Report clearly wanted to sweep away and replace with nothing less than a progressive and radical Scottish 'New Deal' through the new Social Work (Scotland) Act 1968.

That a New Deal was needed is suggested by a future colleague of mine who began his career as a trainee welfare officer for a large authority in the Highlands on 10 November 1969, aged 17. A week later he became a trainee generic social worker in the same way as his more experienced colleagues became qualified generic social workers – overnight. The first task he and the other trainee performed was to keep the reception counter stocked with baby products – National Dried Milk, Ostermilk, orange juice, cod-liver oil. These were exchanged for vouchers which mothers were given by health visitors mainly. There were other depots that also had to be supplied and for which purpose they used the office van. The receptionist or they themselves collected the vouchers or money for sales over the counter, for which a nightly tally was made and if the books did not balance they were obliged to make up the missing cash themselves. Their other main job was to drive the Director round several old people's homes every Friday. The Director thus stood and shouted out the names of the residents who came forward individually to collect their weekly 'pocket-money', publicly doled-out in small brown envelopes.

John Murphy clearly had little time for local bureaucratic welfarism, though his own professional background was primarily institutional rather than community-based. Born in the small rural village of Slamannan near Falkirk in 1917, the year his father was killed in the Battle of Ypres, his background is detailed in an obituary, Scotsman, 3 May, 2010. It is not the description of a retiring sort of person but mine and my colleagues' experience of him as the Director of Social Work for Central Region between 1975–77 was certainly of a remote and aloof figure.

I met him only twice in two years – and in public – as a Senior during a period when the stresses and strains of Regionalisation were at their height, and when showing the flag on the frontline would have been welcomed by a beleaguered staff-group in Falkirk. The first time we met he complimented me on an article I had written for the Communicate magazine, the second time being lectured to at a mass meeting of Falkirk office staff for upsetting the new area officer at which no one else was allowed to speak or ask questions. By then I had learned from a colleague who had worked for him as a Senior in Stirling County, before Regionalisation, of the 'distance' he had kept from frontline operational staff even when Director of that relatively small authority. He described how he had had a very difficult case that required the Director's personal approval, and since he was not replying to phone calls or memos, he travelled up to HQ to find the office door locked behind which John stood, refusing entry. The Senior was required to shout the details of the case to him through the letterbox.

When Regionalisation arrived in May 1975, generic social work departments had been operating for over five years and had received an influx of new generically trained qualified social workers with some basic frontline grounding and experience. They had a much more broadly based professional and social outlook than those occupying middle and senior management positions in the main. If John Murphy could be regarded quite sincerely as an advocate of radical childcare and penal policy reform in the 1960s, by 1975 he would come to be seen by the new generation of generic social workers and their Seniors located in Falkirk Office as invisible. He made no effort to meet us and so we were left to judge him, dismally enough, by the standard of the people he appointed as managers over us. Between 1975 and 1977, therefore, Central Region resembled nothing so much as a layer cake with the Director on top, beneath him the former Directors of the former authorities and, below them, the Director's appointees in middle-management posts, mostly from his own ex-authority. Below them came the appointees of the former Directors of the former authorities to frontline management positions, the Seniors, which had to include people like Big Tam and myself, the best of a new lot. And below all, the social workers, the 'poor bloody infantry', who were now professionally reliant on us, their Seniors, who mostly had little direct knowledge of and no loyalty to or relationship with the Director, John Murphy, a name on a chart.

This did not bode well, either for us or for his first appointee in the Area Officer post, Bob, who in a more just universe should have been allowed to fade into retirement in a tertiary post in as benign a way as possible. A former Probation Officer, Bob was a nice man but lacked professional authority. He seemed to feel that he had been appointed to bring 'order' to the Falkirk office, which was now operating at 50 per cent establishment level. Even more critically, he lacked any sound operational knowledge of childcare and the Hearing system. Since 70 per cent of generic social work involved precisely that, this lack was a big handicap for any frontline manager, especially one responsible for the largest and busiest social work office in Central Region. Bob would be gone within 18 months, only to be replaced by an automaton. During both of their tenures, frontline work got done only because the Senior group was both able and supportive of their staff-groups. A good social and professional camaraderie thus evolved as often happens in workplaces under pressure, so long as frontline managers are honest and capable in their dealings with staff as a whole and the diverse individuals within it.

Bob was eventually released from self-inflicted purdah and retired on medical grounds in late 1976. All that the Senior group had seen was a middle manager trying to impress his superiors rather than focusing on the real problems we were trying to deal with daily, some of which required senior managers to take on local councillors and agencies like the DHSS, Education, Health, Police – tasks which Bob could not hack. He returned from senior management meetings mostly empty-handed as regards the most pressing practice and policy matters. He even managed to compound this by asserting to the Senior group that a child could be placed on a de facto fostering basis, a term which Danny and Alex kept requesting he provide legal citations for. One can look back and think perhaps we could have made more allowance for this kind of thing but the times were, to say the least, demanding and we were bailing out constantly just to keep the dingy afloat. There was simply no room for passengers on our leaky craft, especially on the bridge. We had statutory responsibilities to fulfil which seemed to be expanding daily for taking children into care or returning them to fairly iffy parents during the rising iceberg that was child abuse, as well as for the sudden panic, verging on hysteria, which greeted a new craze, solvent abuse – 'glue-sniffing' – amongst Falkirk's rebel youth. No one, certainly not Bob, had any immediate answers to what seemed like a pandemic breaking out all over the UK.

As Bob would admit himself at the end, although he had not worked for John Murphy before, he assumed that he had wanted the somewhat outspoken ex-Falkirk Burgh Seniors to be brought into line. The trouble was that Bob had no basic line to offer anyone back. He managed us in a way he imagined might please the Director – a constantly shifting horizon, a mirage. What that did was expose his own frailty as a manager but, more importantly, he portrayed the Falkirk Seniors as a bunch of malcontent lefties forever questioning authority. What was up for question was not his authority but his competence. In truth, I regarded Bob as a bit of a comic figure. Tam, Davis and I were at the beginning of our professional careers and we got our support from Danny and Alex. They would be the real victims, passed over for the promotion that their abilities would eventually secure for them both, which would include Big Tam as well.

My own mind was less on Bob and Murphy than in finding my own feet as a long-term Senior trying to supervise a diverse group of social workers, all of whom had marginally less frontline experience than me. In the summer of 1975, I found that being a Senior meant making professional judgements based not on one's own first-hand observations of clients and their families but on the information and opinions social workers formed and then reported back on. When supervising a group of workers who vary in age, gender, experience and ability, you discover some you will warm to, some who will warm to you and some who will do neither. No matter, your job is to supervise them irrespective of personal likes and dislikes, just as social workers will find ways to relate professionally to their often widely different clients. You were aiming at creating a working partnership with your workers, each one of which might be different, even if you remained the same.

My Senior's job was to manage between six and nine social workers, support them to manage their own caseloads and workloads while also carrying out other Team and District tasks and responsibilities. I initially inherited five social workers at Regionalisation, three of whom departed over the summer. They would be replaced by social workers who brought less baggage with them, including no sense of loyalty to a now dead regime. Indeed, this was never a problem with the new basic graders in the new Falkirk Office. Conflict remained over professional issues between the Seniors as a group and the Area Officer but workers mostly got on with the job unaffected by occasional 'noises off'. Workers could work out for themselves the competence or otherwise of the Seniors through their dealings with them and could compare this with the performance of the Area Officer.

My own group comprised Mary McKenna and Bobby who I inherited from the previous regime, then would come Sheila Maguire/Taylor, Miriam Heather, Diane Gordon and Raymond Johnston later in the year. I also supervised John Toland, a highly experienced social worker for the blind on a District basis and he was almost entirely self-functioning, as was Craig Robertson, now Community worker for the new housing estate on the top side of Falkirk, Hallglen. Craig did mega welfare-related work with the DHSS and the Fuel Boards over gas and electricity disconnections and poverty-related matters. The point was to stop avoidable disconnections, evictions and abrupt benefit stoppages which left vulnerable families destitute, hungry, heatless and often homeless. This inevitably forced them along to our door, the local authority, for discretionary Section 12 grants to tide them over and so prevent children and vulnerable people being taken into care. Our generation thus fully supported the development of Claimants Rights Groups and the appointment of Welfare Rights workers by local authorities and voluntary agencies, which we saw as part of the local authority's general Section 12 'duty to promote social welfare' under the Social Work (Scotland)

Act.

This meant that local authorities were increasingly brought into conflict with central Government agencies responsible for social security and sometimes with their own rent and housing department policies. This meant a conflict between the council's duty to effectively manage housing and their duty to care for the vulnerable, the very people they were obliged to evict or place in sub-standard housing – the young, the elderly and the sick for whom we had responsibilities through the Children's Hearings and other care legislation. This more proactive claimant's rights approach fed a further media backlash about leftie social workers to add to the mini skirts and sandals rhetoric of a few years earlier. But it was all part of social care legislation, paid for through the rates, and so, for us, we were simply doing what it said on the tin – helping people, professionally.

As Intake Senior, Danny was more involved in this kind of work than I was, a long-term Senior for the Braes. I began to see that, when supervising individual social workers, one had to avoid the twin perils of either case-working the cases for them or, indeed, case-working them. Given my experience with Danny, I was crystal clear that cases were the responsibility of the social workers to engage with and manage. My role was to form trustful supervisory relationships by providing reliable information regarding legislation, resources and processes to enable workers to deal with a range of individuals who could be on anything from Children's Hearing supervision to needing placed in an 'old people's home' (OPH). We were, after all, a generic one-door service, the first ever. The fact that my team dealt with long-term cases meant that we were dealing with cases that already had extensive care-assessment histories. This meant that new or inexperienced workers had something quite tangible to start from – a narrative, a history, no matter how complex or incomplete – which provided a base from which workers could begin working with them as individuals. It also propelled me as their supervisor into making sense of these histories too and how the workers might relate to and deal with them in the present – here, now, today.

All my team had had a previous supervisor except Miriam. Indeed, I learned later that Raymond had married his first Senior, Liz, which I always thought was a lucky break given the rapport we established. The parallel, of course, is that just as cases may have had a social worker before you, a worker may also have had a Senior and this may be a factor you have to deal with when managing them. New Seniors have to manage the expectations of their new supervisees just as new social workers have to learn to manage those of their clients who compare them to their previous social workers. In the case of Miriam, who was Swiss and had been a health visitor before training as a social worker, she thought I was brilliant. I learned this from my successor, Alex, who, pulling a face, had inherited Miriam from me when I left Falkirk a couple of years later. It was similarly conveyed to me some 14 years after that by Miriam's then Senior, Big Ronnie, when I went to work in the Broxburn Office in 1991. Miriam was still burning his ears as to what Alistair Findlay used to say and demanding the same from him. Big Ronnie caught perfectly Miriam's unaltered Swiss accent and perennial query, 'Vot about the veans?'

Miriam was a great worker for me. Schooled already in health visiting and the mother of two children herself, she was completely open and honest with everyone – clients, other professionals, Seniors, Sheriffs, it didn't matter. This fearless honesty with people is very important in social work, mixed with integrity and warmth. Miriam had all of that, so there was no need for me to develop those aspects and so I went to the most obvious area regarding her professional self. This was related to Miriam's love of and reliance on psychology, which she had come across during her training. Now in the field, she tended to analyse cases in terms of their 'psychology'. I saw my job as reducing this tendency by helping her put her concerns into the context of specific casework tasks. That is all I did. I listened and listened and then we agreed what to focus on in the immediate term. Miriam went back out the door happy with a plan, for, once Miriam got a plan, any plan almost, she relaxed and all her other attributes as a worker could kick in.

Bobby had some previous social work experience in the area and had just returned from a two-year training course at Robert Gordon's College, Aberdeen. He had been supervised as an unqualified worker by an experienced Senior and former children's officer, Janet Wilson, who was appointed as Central Region's first Child Protection manager. She was thus responsible for chairing inter-agency case conferences which put children on the Child Protection Register, set up nationally after the Maria Colwell Enquiry in England and further reinforced in Scotland by the Richard Clark Inquiry as already mentioned. Janet was clear and informed. I learned much from her calm and thorough approach about the need for inter-agency collaboration and joint-working, which the CP Register system pioneered and built from this point onwards. As for Bobby, he was a fairly unflappable character and seemed clued up on his cases. He seemed quite pleased with the move to a larger office and bigger staff group. Bobby did not exactly emote over his cases and so I kept an eye on this until the social side of his personality was revealed. In future years, he became a Senior social work manager up north.

Mary had several complicated childcare cases and liked to be clear about things. She seemed slightly anxious about some of them and my initial impression was that she may have gone to her previous supervisor for answers and, on getting them, her anxiety did not diminish that much. This often relates to over-conscientiousness in some workers. If this seems edging towards 'case-working the caseworker' referred to earlier, it is simply the initial evaluation every Senior will make of the individuals they are responsible for supporting in their professional work and development. My professional development was still proceeding apace and was not that much further along the road than those I was now presuming to lead. With Mary, it was more about her learning to trust her emotional intelligence as well as her rational analysis of cases and people.

One case I recall in particular perhaps pushed Mary and me along our respective paths, a protracted and convoluted Children's Hearing case that involved collaborative work with Pilton area office in Edinburgh. The Edinburgh worker had left and there was a delay in reallocating it until a new Area Officer for the team, Gus Campbell, took it on himself. I thus had the experience of Mary and Gus reporting to me periodically on the whole mechanics of a 'heavy-end' childcare case with inter-authority complications and collaborations whose satisfactory conclusion helped give Mary and myself that important confidence in our respective roles. I also remember being staggered to learn that Gus, who had the same managerial responsibility as our Area Officer, was getting paid the same salary as me for a modicum of his responsibility. It showed me how smaller authorities like Central Region paid generous salaries to recruit and retain experienced social work staff compared to Edinburgh, which could rely on its attractions as a city for this purpose.

As for the rest of my team, Sheila was a striking-looking young woman but comfortable with it and she proved well able to muck in and learn. Sheila is one of the more obvious examples of what this new generation brought to the welfare scene – youth, vitality and good looks. Textbooks and academic studies may steer clear of such things but the impact of large cohorts of committed, idealistic and modern young people, often sporting the latest fashion and hairstyles and spending time and effort on often ill-kempt, illiterate, vilified, inarticulate and discounted individuals should not go unconsidered. This was part of my experience, too, in Craigmillar in the 1980s and Livingston in the 1990s, a good third or so of teams comprising young people in their mid- to late 20s. New blood, just as we were the new blood of the 1970s, comprised perhaps three quarters of the staff group. All of my team, apart from Miriam, were in our 20s, including me.

Diane had a couple of years' experience and was slightly older than me. We also had gone to the same secondary school, Bathgate Academy, so we fitted well culturally and I think she also trained at Moray House. Diane could be quite serious discussing cases, with her brows severely knitted together, and I sometimes found myself cracking jokes to lift her out of the gravity of some of the decisions we were faced with. Diane was very pleased to be amused and had a lovely broad grin that I wanted her to use much more in her work. Workers have to relate on the basis of who and what they are as people themselves – real people, not some phony notion of what an ideal caseworker might do or say in specific situations. This is the attitude I was trying to create generally within my team as I would every other team I managed, some needing or appreciating it more than others. I wanted workers to think for themselves, not simply do what I told them to do.

Which brings me to Raymond. Raymond came to us from Greenock social work department where his fiancée, Liz, had been his Senior. He had trained with Mary at Robert Gordon's College and she could never quite see what people saw in him. What I saw was someone with a special manner that seemed to engage clients very quickly. In retrospect, I would say that he combined animation with stillness: he could listen very quietly and patiently to people until you thought he had maybe dozed off and then he'd be very enthused when he gave them back a brief potted summary of what they had just told him. He would then ponder it for a wee while, saying 'right' a few times, then come straight along to my office for authorisation of a Section 12 loan, which was really a grant. I am sure Raymond will deny this depiction but, over the years, I would have it confirmed by some of his future colleagues and managers in Leith in Edinburgh, such as Joyce Wood, where he moved to after Falkirk. It is now impossible to do full justice to the historical truth of Raymond as a worker given the time I have known him. What is beyond doubt is that he gave 100 per cent backing to all his clients, especially those down on their luck, which seemed to be all of them and all of the time.

Raymond was basically 'for' everybody and you could tell this from the long queues of clients forming outside the duty-social worker door when news filtered out that he was inside. He managed about as big a caseload on the duty-desk as were allocated to him officially by me – old guys in hostels, ex-veterans, alcoholics, individual adults who had no priority compared to children. In the end, everyone had a story to tell about Raymond, who was one of those beloved characters and who his clients could see going to massive lengths on their behalf. With Raymond there would be no 'fancy footwork', as he would say, or theorising over particular case scenarios. Raymond had only one theory – unconditional positive regard – a total commitment to doing the best he could for every person who walked through the door. I never saw Raymond crestfallen, despairing, pissed off or worried, except when I told him I was leaving Falkirk. His face ran the full gamut of emotions until he gasped, 'Who'll authorise the Section 12s, Alistair?' Indeed.

My own Raymond story started simply enough, late on a Friday afternoon when the office was near to closing. I got a phone call from a local GP 'up the Braes' who said he had forgotten to book a bed in an old folks home for 'an old dear' whose family was going on holiday, tonight, and needed 'a break' from looking after her. Could we help? I checked and there was an emergency bed and another one being freed up on Monday in the local Old Persons Home, so yes. Raymond was the duty worker over the weekend so I asked him to go up, collect her, and take her to the home. No problemo. I got the rest of the tale when I came back on the Monday morning. Raymond had indeed gone to the house and the couple had already left for a week in Spain, leaving their 17-year-old son to 'granny-sit'. The old wife's suitcase was sitting in the hall while she was sitting in the living room refusing to budge. Her grandson was pleading with her to go and Raymond took over and after half an hour persuaded her to visit the 'home' and if she did not like it, he'd bring her back again. The grandson waved them off. His granny spent two hours being shown round the place, meeting the staff, other residents and having a grand high-tea, but decided she did not want to stay. So Raymond ran her back up to the Braes to the family abode, where the grandson refused to open the door. Raymond spent a long time speaking to him through the letterbox, while the old wife sat in his car. No deal, so he ran her back to the care-home promising to come back for her tomorrow and try again, which he did, and again the next day, all to no avail. Raymond had just been up to the place to see her first thing that morning and she had decided she wanted to stay there for good. It could not happen now, of course, but this was when 'elderly people', meaning those of pension age, could simply ask to go into old folks homes even when perfectly fit to look after themselves – and got in!

* * *

The office had its first golf outing to Crail that first summer of Regionalisation, which would continue for the next 35 years on a biannual or triannual basis. We played mostly at Tullyallen and Gleneagles through the 1970s and 1980s and brought an expanding group of new work colleagues from wherever people moved on to in the course of their evolving careers. Danny, Big Tam and I played together regularly and these outings built a camaraderie which permeated working relationships right across Central Region social work, for it included numerous residential care workers and foster parents, too. Newmarket Bar in the centre of Falkirk likewise became a social hub for the workplace on Friday evenings after work from about 5.00pm till late. A closing time 'cairrie-out', a brown paper bag with the drink, would be collectively purchased and those still standing would pile down to Danny and Jeanette's, indoors with the kids, for a sing-song and a laugh till the wee-small hours. They must have had tolerant neighbours. Danny and Jeanette sang Bread's 'Diary'; Big Tam and Anne sang Leonard Cohen's 'Suzanne'; my wife Helen sang Joan Baez's 'Plaisir D'Amour'; and I sang 'A Man's a Man'. Big Tam was always pressed to attempt the Irish Rebel song, 'Shall My Soul Pass Through Old Ireland', but he never got beyond the opening line because I could never quite prevent myself from hooting at it, which, of course, Tam was always waiting for.

My final days in Central Region were now drawing closer. In the early months of 1977, Helen, who had given up teaching to undertake a social work course at Moray House, and we decided that, when she qualified that summer, we would move south as a prelude to emigrating to Australia or New Zealand. The trouble was that these countries required social workers to have a university degree, which I did not and so I applied for a Masters degree in Social Policy at Bradford University as a first step. Until Bob was replaced, Falkirk office enjoyed a mellow interregnum by having Tom Coll coming down from Langgarth HQ for a couple of days a week to help the Senior group manage the office from about November 1976 until April 1977. Tom was a shrewd former Director of social work for Stirling Burgh and the workplace buzzed along harmoniously. Danny and Big Alex threw their hats into the ring for the Area Officer post but, alas, neither was appointed. Danny would learn later that the Labour councillors in Falkirk had thought he was 'an SNP man'. He now wonders where they got that impression. In any case, both he and Big Alex were beaten to the job by a young suit from England with perhaps a background in prison social work. No one was quite sure what managerial social work experience he had but it surely did not include any gained in Scotland.

I am quite tempted to stop here, for it soon appeared that this time the Director had gone to great lengths to specially fly in an alien from Planet X just to punish us. I shall call him Queeg – Q for short – from the 1950s film, *The Caine Mutiny*, in which Humphrey Bogart plays a psychotic commander of an American minesweeper during the Second World War, whose paranoia becomes more and more obvious to his war-weary crew the more he throws up those wee metal balls in the air while talking to himself obsessively about a few missing strawberries. In Q's case, it was mostly his own screws that were missing. A few weeks into the job, which Q had spent asking questions about systems and the like, we had a Seniors' meeting at 9.00am on the Friday morning for which I was about five minutes late, having decided to walk up the road since it was a very sunny day. All the Seniors were seated quietly round the table when I entered and gave my breezy apology. Nobody said anything, just looked straight ahead. Then Q started a cool rant about the sloppy ship being run. I heard later that Danny had already got it in the neck for leaving the meeting just as it was starting in order to deal with a duty matter, him being both Duty and Intake Senior.

The next scene took place a few weeks later when Q presented 'a plan' that involved some changes which made no evident sense from a practice or management point of view and all the Seniors said so. Q then took it to a team meeting and I criticised it openly, as did most of the others. The following week, Danny, Big Tam and I were invited for interviews with Ian Gilmour and Ian Ross over complaints the Area Officer had made to the Director: Danny was accused of 'obstructive behaviour' related to taking that duty phone call and Big Tam for not wearing a tie when attending a Housing sub-committee meeting which had local councillors present. Big Tam explained that it was a sweltering hot day and the councillors were not wearing ties either, neither at the meeting nor in the pub afterwards because Big Tam knew them all from being in the local Labour Party. I was accused of saying at a team meeting with junior staff present that the Area Officer was 'talking shit' and repeating it when asked to do so. I denied it. I said there was a translation problem, I probably said 'whit', it wasn't in the minute, and they could interview the whole office and find that was the case. And while they were at it, perhaps they could ask people what they thought of Q and his 'plan'. I could see it in their eyes: 'Houston, we have a problem', and it wasn't with me.

I gave them chapter and verse of what I thought of Q, Murphy and, indeed, them for not anticipating the whole sorry mess. Had the office not run like clockwork for months while Bob was off and Tom Coll only popping in a couple of days a week? Had a light hand on the tiller not been deemed sufficient then? Had the place fallen apart although short-staffed and 'leaderless' except for the Senior group? Was it falling apart now with court reports and hearing reports rolling off the press and no major cases waiting for allocation as in most other authorities? Did they actually want the union brought in? Oh no, there was no question of disciplinary action. I told them I was offski anyway and so it would not be my problem. Some workers were already seeking new jobs which were ten-a-penny all over the country.

As for Big Tam's interview, him being a shop steward meant he had to be accompanied by a union rep. As soon as it was clear it was not a disciplinary matter, Big Tam said, 'right, I'm off'. He was prevailed upon to stay to 'share his views'. Big Tam and Ian Gilmour then agreed to disagree over Tam's view that he considered he was a professional employed by the Council to carry out responsibilities according to statute and not 'pee-hee to councillors' or to operate as a local Government yes-man in the same way Gilmour was interpreting his own role. The two Ians then interviewed the other Seniors and some other staff which pointed to the need for further measures to turn the workplace round.

One can, of course, surmise that replacing the Area Officer after a few months would not have reflected very well on those who had appointed him or advised the Committee to do so. What to do? What John Murphy did was come down to Brockville to address a team meeting on 29 June 1977, his first ever foray into the office in over two years. His speech was preserved for posterity in the Appendices of a Report on Service Delivery in the Falkirk Area Office produced by Ian Ross and Ian Gilmour in January 1978. It was made clear at the outset that this 'talk' was not open for questions and so it was recorded verbatim by Craig Robertson, a former journalist, and gathered into 14 'notes', of which I give the opening 1–3 and then 6–7 for the flavour of the whole:

> You are employed by the agency, paid a salary and get the tools of the job, not to act as free-lancers... You are servants of the agency. You are not like doctors... There's a lot I could criticise about doctors... Education... bloody hierarchical... You have certain duties to carry out, in the most efficient manner... Section 2 of the Social Work Act says there shall be a Director of Social Work and it is my job to see that these things are done. There is no escape from these things.
>
> I'm getting nervous because I see a man taking down every word I say... ah, well, we'll just have to thole that as we have to thole a lot of other things he writes.
>
> I must delegate complete authority... For 'Area Officer' read 'Director of Social Work'. I place responsibility on the Area Officer and he does it in his own style. The Area Officer will be responsible for the delivery of service in the Falkirk area. I trust that will get your full cooperation... We have not really fully tapped the consultation methods in modern management.
>
> Your roles are important.. the important role of the senior social worker... in hearing what the team is thinking, in guiding the team and maybe in seeing what the team are doing. These senior social workers don't get £1,500 a year extra just to be super professionals and a super career grade.
>
> The fault does not lie entirely with one side. You may ask what is the directorate doing about this? I have not seen enough of you... but Tom and Ian have kept in touch with you... It's easy to make Langgarth the whipping boy... and the less I say about members [presumably councillors?]... I will say nothing more about members.

The image of a man shouting through a letterbox comes over readily to mind, but unlike the haunted Dr MacKintosh in Moray House some five years earlier, Mr Murphy sadly did not tear up his pre-prepared and fluently delivered remarks to sniff the air. He seemed not to recognise that what he was dealing with were not a few lefty agitators but the shift of a new generation into a whole new profession, and so a whole new ball-game.

The Report contains some interesting indicators of service delivery at that time, though all was buried under a bewildering miasma of unsubstantiated observations and innuendo about the need for everyone to improve and pursue that winsome thing – a fresh start. Two tables show that Falkirk's social worker staffing on 1 April 1977, a few weeks before Q arrived, was 20 per cent below Establishment level (22/27) but then fell to 40 per cent below Establishment level (16/27) on 6 January 1978, the month the Report appeared. In other words, people were making their own fresh start by voting with their feet. Another table shows that caseloads stood at an average of 25 cases per worker (508/20) but, since two workers were on secondment, this would have been more like 28 cases. The Seniors were each carrying an average of eight cases held until they could be allocated to workers, which puts in better perspective the criticism implied by John Murphy that Seniors might not be fulfilling the whole width of management responsibilities the post demanded. We were still struggling to maintain direct frontline services like the rest of Scotland and far more successfully than most according to our extensive anecdotal professional grapevine.

Positive mention was made in the Report of the excellent work done by the Regional Adoption Panel but not that it was run by two of Falkirk's 'rebel' Seniors, Danny and me. Nothing much was made either about the fact that Court reports were 'almost exclusively on time' and 'almost without exception well-written, concise professional assessments of which the office can be justifiably satisfied', nor that the tie-less Big Tam had responsibility for Court matters. Reports for the Hearing system were described as 'more varied in quality, but were in the main satisfactory' but not that this was so despite the volume of reports being requested. Indeed, this formed one of the few concrete things the Report came up with as regards service delivery: that the Department should discuss with the Reporter the over-provision of reports for Children's Hearings. This was what the Senior group was actually about and we did not need a half-baked Report to tell us what was already obvious: the team needed an able, supportive Area Officer attuned to practice issues and community-based services consolidation and, if possible, even expansion.

The Report in fact began with an admission by its writers that perhaps it should have been undertaken by properly independent researchers, not those managerially responsible for the Area Officer's performance. There was a concession allegedly made by Q that he might have gone at the Senior group 'too negatively' and 'too early' which is clearly at odds with his own statement in the Appendix which never comes close to voicing such an idea but says instead that not only was Q disappointed by the lack of loyalty shown to him by the Senior group but also by the Directorate! There is thus the surreal spectacle of Q ruminating away in his statement as though he was a kind of interested bystander to the whole affair instead of the prime instigator of what amounted to a fatal accident inquiry into his own adversarial management style and conduct. His three-page statement ends with the following, which may serve for the whole:

> Much of what I have said I have said before to various Groups or individuals, but I agree it is helpful to draw it together as a consolidating piece of communication so that you are clear what my expectations are. Maybe I expect too much of myself, and others. Maybe the directorate do not expect enough of us, and opt out of their responsibilities. That is no excuse for us not to want to move forward positively. I suspect we could easily teach them a thing or two, if we work together in concert. We could make them raise their own standards and expectations, and that would help the Department be a healthier place to work in. My hope is that you want to endure the pain of growing still further.

Oh dear me, no. Our hope had been not to have to endure any further pain at all, certainly after Bob, never mind more of it. The Report included the following recommendation:

> In view of the weight of information offered to us we recommend that the Area Officer needs to make certain adjustments in his style of management while not operating a policy of appeasement or adopting a false persona. This should be subject to discussion between him and us.

It should be noted that the word 'appeasement' is lifted from an earlier part of Q's statement that 'there will be no appeasement policies pursued here'. The wooden way that recommendation reads makes one suspect Q may have insisted it be phrased like that, since he thought it made such a telling point. I think it does too.

Something stirs in the back of my mind that Q was a highly religious person in a kind of Salvationist way. But in any case, he would be gone quite soon, possibly back to prison, a closed community where no one spoke up or back. Big Tam later reflected that he could never warm towards a man whose wife bred rabbits for his children to play with and then eat. Other incidents stick with Tam, too, such as the day Q came into his office demanding where Russ, the adoptions worker and office shop steward, had been on the 16th and 17th of the month a few weeks ago. Russ was actually sitting at his desk across the corridor trying not to look too interested in this conversation and one might think a more normal manager would simply ask him this himself. So Big Tam asked why he wanted to know and Q said that he had been checking mileage returns and Russ had not claimed anything for those days. Tam opined that maybe he'd be better checking folk who were claiming 200 miles a day rather than those who were claiming nothing but he went across to check Russ' diary. Sure enough, Russ had been on Court and office duty on both of those days.

Q's own days in Falkirk would end not long after a new Director, Harry Garland, arrived in Central in 1978. On Harry's first visit to the Falkirk office, Q introduced him to the office junior who had just brought in their tea: 'And this is Mary, the least important person in the office'. Upset, Mary told her colleagues and this, too, would go down in the folklore of Falkirk social work office 1975–8. This was also part of local authority generic social work history and legend. It was not the boss-class, this says, who made the Regional departments tick, although there were exceptional figures amongst them, but the workers and frontline managers who held the ring, doing what we were trained to do – seeing for ourselves what needed done. Indeed, one of the reasons I am writing this memoir is not to contradict John Murphy's history from above but set it alongside the frontline realities we encountered along the way, history from below.

One of my old Falkirk office colleagues dug up the letter cited below, dated September 1977, the month I left Falkirk. It was written by John Murphy to the Admin and Legal Services Director of Central Region telling him to convey to a Sheriff and a parent where to get off, that social workers were not some kind of magicians able to banish truancy overnight. This was the kind of professional matter that John Murphy knew something about, and it shows, but it was also exactly the kind of backing that was never made evident or offered to the Senior group in Falkirk in any way when it was needed most:

> Further to your letter of 23rd September, it amazes me that anyone could be quite so naïve as to be 'concerned' that a girl, while supervised by a social worker, was still not attending school. Anyone with the most vestigial knowledge of the problems of truancy, especially those of the adolescent girl, must know that even a posse of police cannot get such a girl to school, if she has decided to the contrary. If the parents have

consistently failed over the years to get her to school; if the school itself has failed for considerable periods to entice her there; how in heaven's name does anyone expect any professional – even as experienced as a good social worker, to perform the act of ritual magic by ensuring the metamorphosis from truancy to good attendance. If you or the Sheriff or the parent genuinely think that such an *obiter dictum* in the form of a will of the wisp need consume scarce time the matter will be investigated. Please advise me accordingly.

John Murphy can certainly be counted amongst those who helped push the door of Scottish social welfare reform open but it would take a new generation of Regional Social Work Directors to take it off its hinges and allow fresh breezes to blow through its fusty corridors. Scottish culture had changed through the late 1960s and early 1970s and would change further, as would the whole social work profession created to meet rapidly changing social needs and requirements. Our generation created the modern profession, not 'the oldies' like Bob and certainly not the 'new oldies' like Q, to use Iain Morrison's favoured terminology. John Murphy is referring to us, therefore, in the final paragraph of his own history of Scottish social work, *The Scottish Dimension* (1992: 183): 'Local Government re-organisation was the dawn of a new and richer era for social work.'

I think it fair to say that, while Q was universally condemned by the Falkirk staff group and John Murphy found guilty by association, Ian Gilmour got handed the not proven verdict. Ian died tragically young at the age of 57 from cancer of the throat in 2001, having retired in 1999 as acting Director of Social Work for Glasgow City. He would move to Strathclyde as a Divisional Director in the early 1980s then become its Deputy Director for Childcare. By then, Big Tam was an Assistant Principle Officer Children's Services there. When he arrived, Ian gathered all the staff together and said that no matter what they had heard about him (for he had acquired by then a reputation as a hard-nosed senior manager), he was fair-minded and everyone would start with a clean sheet, before quietly adding, 'even Big Tam'. Hard-nosed senior managers never bothered me, of course, or Tam or Danny, so long as they were telling the right people to fuck off.

Ian Gilmour also served the Association of Directors of Social Work (ADSW) with distinction as Secretary and President. He was no stuffed-shirt but a young modern manager that the Regional social work departments arguably needed to produce over the coming decades. But he also liked a laugh and a joke and, indeed, this was central to the culture of local authority social work at the time. In his youth he played for a band, The Moonbeats, and combined a serious commitment to the nuances of social work practice with a relaxed manner and quietly astute temperament. Of course, none of this stopped me from taking him and the other members of the Directorate to task in a song I wrote around this time which became a minor hit on Friday nights down at Danny's when the drink was flowing and the spirits needed lifting. It was called 'Clowns' and not a hundred miles away from Joni Mitchell's 'Both Sides Now'. There was certainly no need to explain its lyrics to anyone present:

> Meals-on-wheels and home-helps too, they're all available to you,
> Luncheon-clubs and gardens too, we've looked at life that way.
> But now they say we're acting strange, what's all this talk of social change,
> Falkirk Office is deranged, the punters want a say.
> We've looked at Life from both sides now,
> From 'up' and 'down', and still somehow,
> It's Clowns in Stirling we recall,
> That's Murphy, Gilmour, Ross, and Coll.
> Building castles in the air, creating non-posts everywhere,
> We are here, Langgarth is there, that's all there is to say,
> And now you're just a bureaucrat, you fill in forms and the Martin Stat,
> Somewhere up there you smell a rat, John Murphy's on his way.
> And now it's just another show,
> You hear them laughing as you go,
> And if you care, just let them know,
> They'll file it all away.

Ian Gilmour would have got the humour of that, for he liked a joke. He told me one that reflects the rumbustious culture of local Government during this period, what John Murphy had in fact referred to as its 'jungle quality'. So, a group of Central Regional councillors are flying across Africa when their aircraft makes a forced landing. They are captured by the locals and put in a pot which is slowly boiling away. Suddenly a huge Chief appears and the Convener shouts out, 'Hey Chief! We come in peace, big bird in sky, all the way from Central Region Council. We want to help you and your people. Anything we can do?' And the Chief replies, 'Oor Jean got a new hoose yet?' For me, the two Ians' Report would have been better addressing the cultural realities which produced that joke and provided the social context in which we as a professional group worked.

I was now nearing the end of my time at Falkirk. Helen and I spent the summer touring round the Highlands. I had obtained a place on a Social Work Masters degree course at Bradford University and so we began looking for jobs within commuting distance. We eventually settled on Nottingham, which was starting a new Emergency Duty Service to which I was appointed as a Senior, one of four. Helen got a job as the deputy officer-in-charge of a children's residential unit, Orchard House, which had the extra bonus of coming with staff accommodation – a good-sized flat attached to the unit.

I was well pleased to take the Nottingham Emergency Duty job because working out of normal office hours enabled me to attend university and to study almost full-time, as well as giving me 15 per cent on top of my salary for working 'unsocial hours'. I now told everyone in Falkirk I was leaving. Danny was morose, Big Tam philosophic and Raymond panic-stricken. I said that he did not need to worry about those I had signed, just the ones he had authorised himself once Q got round to looking up the stats, his main occupation in life. Big Eunice and Wee Marion took it pretty well on the chin – 'Whaur's the leaving-do?' The leaving-do was a big and noisy shindig which ended, I vaguely recall, with myself and Big Tam, who had his tie (the one he was allegedly not wearing at the Housing-sub) looped round his head like a bandana, waltzing slowly together round the centre of the floor while Perry Como sang 'For the Good Times' – the soundtrack which sent us off to England for the next three years, to a fresh start and with no one's expectations to meet but our own.

Before getting these posts, I had explored the possibility of becoming Adoptions Officer for Doncaster Council and visited the Director of Social Services, Roger Kent, a rather large, no-nonsense, rather 'clipped' and concise character, who showed me round and 'interrogated' me forensically about the childcare work I had been doing in Falkirk for the last four years. This was in fact a preliminary visit to discuss the job and when I went for interview I sat in the reception area waiting to be called beside a young affable and talkative young man who I learned was the 'acting' District Adoptions Officer. He affably told me that this interview was a formality for me. Big Roger had been raving about the new young Scotsman who was going to sort this effing place out good style. Basically I was a shoo-in. Then I got taken for interview. Instead of Big Roger and a couple of his buddies, I was faced with what seemed like the whole of Doncaster council, about 20 of them sitting in serried ranks behind a long trestle table in front of which was placed a solitary chair – mine. A nightmare ensued. I did not understand them and they did not understand me because, thankfully, I was not offered the job. The next time I saw Big Roger was in Edinburgh four years later, by which time he was Director of Social Work for Lothian Region and I was Convener of its Social Work Shop Stewards Committee.

8

The Social Work Bubble

A Noddy view of the world.
Geoff Pearson, Bradford University,1977

The author and his wife travel to England, he to study Marxism under the pretext of its being an advanced social work qualification which would allow them to be smuggled into the Antipodes. He works nights and weekends in newly established Emergency Duty Teams in Nottingham and Derbyshire for which he is grossly overpaid. Intelligent and charming English people are met, an old face visits, amateur football gets played, essays are written and letters from his father laughed at. When Mrs Thatcher surfaces, author and wife hail a passing frigate to sail them back to Scotland to await the on-ding (sudden storm of rain or snow) on home turf.

I HAVE ABSOLUTELY no recollection of being interviewed for the Emergency Duty Senior job or, indeed, who my boss was in Nottingham. I do remember meeting someone at HQ who looked a bit like Ronnie Barker, chubby, silver haired and with a pin-stripe suit, who kept saying to Helen and me how healthy and young we looked. This kindly old buffer might well have been the Deputy Director of Social Services. From what I had read, Nottingham did have a reputation as a forward-thinking authority and thus amongst the first to set up a full-time Emergency Duty service. The demands of the job, compared to my last four years, would call on a tenth of my professional capacity so I was perfectly able to study virtually full-time.

In Nottingham in early October 1977, the opening week was taken up with Induction, the only part of which I remember was a meeting with a local police inspector in the centre of Nottingham with me and my two new colleagues, Jim and Gwyn. He told us there were certain areas, what he called 'the black ones', that were completely no-go unless they loaded up a van with a snatch-squad, went in, arrested someone and took them back out for questioning. Even Wee Jim, one of my new colleagues who had just come from working in London, seemed taken aback. The other notable feature of our Induction was being told we would have no social workers for the first week because the union, NALGO, was disputing the level of payments offered to the workers covering for the as yet unfilled Emergency social worker posts. Indeed, there were only three of the four Senior posts filled so far by a

Scotsman, an Englishman and a Welshman, with everyone hoping we would end up with an Irishman, the full set. Local Area Seniors were being drafted in to cover for the fourth post. This would last for as long as it took Gwyn, a silver-haired, silver-tongued 'no-good-boyo' from Anglesey with a decided twinkle in his eye, to negotiate for the three of us to cover the fourth Senior post – so more dosh for us. Gwyn had once been a shop steward and, if not, he should have been.

We were based in a large Assessment Centre for teenagers in Mapperley in a large staff flat separated from the kids and staff by its own entrance. It had a large kitchen, lounge, bathroom, couple of bedrooms, all furnished and with a phone, our only contact with the outside world. Helen and I lived in similar accommodation in the leafy suburb of Sherwood, not far from my base. All our work was done from this base by phone which included taking referrals, sending out workers and notifying Area Teams of work done the next working morning. The first week we sat in the base with no social workers to send out. We relied on the police, health staff, voluntary organisations, families, neighbours, friends and the like to tide people over until Area offices opened the next day or the Monday morning. It worked, at least for that limited period, probably because the police just dealt with stuff themselves or held it till the next morning or ignored it entirely or left it with the families. Compared to generic casework, Emergency Duty work required no casework, merely patching up work, until the local offices opened in a few hours' time. My perception of the support offered shrunk from almost infinity to the end of the current shift or the width of the weekend. Professionally, it was a bit like switching from driving a Rolls-Royce to riding a bike and getting paid 15 per cent extra for the privilege. I could not believe my luck. I was getting respite after four arduous years of professional mayhem and now looking forward to two and a half years' full-time study that would give me further academic advanced professional qualification via an MA in Social Policy.

One of the differences immediately noticeable to me was the lack of resources in Nottingham compared to Falkirk, especially in health and local authority care and support services like home-helps and care services for the mentally ill and elderly. I remember constant phone calls from relatives seeking help with demented old people, which I simply passed over to day time Area offices and health professionals with no obvious effect. Some of the situations I was passing over I could not but think would have been responded to far more quickly and fully in Falkirk. Impressionistic, certainly, but such perceptions have stuck with me for 40 years and were confirmed by subsequent comparisons I would make regarding the responsiveness and standards of Scottish childcare and child-protection services compared to English ones. This had something to do not only with the quality or availability of resources but the more proactive role that Children's Panels played in monitoring case transfers between the countries as well as higher qualification levels social workers possessed on this side of the border.

Spoken language – mine and the local dialects of Nottingham and then North Derbyshire – leapt out, none of them Queen's English. My work entailed living on the phone and my Scottish accent was frequently remarked on favourably – 'Yew 'ave ae loovely voice, me doock' – the sort of 'eh-oop-me-dook' accent I had previously heard only on the radio from people like Jimmy Clitheroe, the erstwhile 'Clitheroe Kid'. One of the Nottingham Area Seniors did occasional shifts in the early days and chatted away during the hand-over periods. Pete. A bluff Yorkshireman, he told me about his wife trying to get into a size-10 pair of jeans but with a 'size-14 boom'.

Not easily forgotten either were my fellow Emergency Seniors, Gwyn and Jim, who were dead-ringers for *The Odd Couple*, the film starring Jack Lemmon and Walter Matthau. Neither of them had previous Senior experience and Gwyn was also much longer in the tooth than me and Jim, possibly a late entrant to the profession. A chain-smoker and streetwise, Gwyn would not have been left standing behind the door if the bread rations had ever run out. Jim soon became the bane of Gwyn's working life, both of them polar opposites. He looked like Dora Hird's son-in-law in *Last of the Summer Wine*, having bottle-glasses, red hair, pullovers, the face of a 13-year-old and a highly apologetic manner. Gwyn could live with this but what drove him mad were the change-overs between them when working weekend shifts.

The system ingeniously devised by Gwyn meant that we got every third weekend off if we worked in pairs covering the other two weekends doing 12-hour shifts between us.

The trouble was that, during his shift, Jim would endlessly roam around the flat, our base, possibly to relieve the tension of waiting for the phone to ring with new referrals from the police or hospital or the public or social workers reporting back and so on. For whatever reason, every time you took over from Jim, the flat looked like a bomb had exploded in every room. Every kitchen cabinet door hung open, every drawer, all the dishes out of the cupboards, the bedrooms dishevelled and the lounge covered in newspapers, pages scattered around, papers piled, cups of cold tea, cushions strewn about and Jim, standing there blinking, overjoyed to see you, a few garbled messages about what cases were on the go, and then he was off in a cloud of apologetic nods and grimaces. Gwyn, of course, was a fastidious tidier, everything neat and in its place, organised, in control.

'I'll tell you this, Ali, I'm going to strangle that little fucker one day,'

Gwyn would confide, but we both knew he would not. The money was too good.

One thing I did learn from Emergency duty overnight shift work was how to stay awake until about 1.00am before trying to get some shut-eye. After that time, unless there was a definite case to be dealt with, usually from the police, then you could probably sleep through until 7.00am or so. It effectively changed my body-clock, as parenthood does. Any time I wakened up for years afterwards, day or night, I knew instantly what time it was, to within five minutes accuracy.

The time soon came when I left Nottingham in February 1979 for a similar job in a new Emergency duty service starting up in North Derbyshire, based at Chesterfield, the largest town in Derbyshire after Derby. Helen had wanted to move to a bigger post as Deputy in a large residential school for teenage boys, Todwick Grange near Sheffield, within sight of an M1 motorway slip-road which meant an hour's less travel for me to commute to Bradford University and for us to drive back to Scotland to see family and friends. We also got staff accommodation and Todwick was only about 30 minutes' drive to my base in Chesterfield. I cannot remember anybody I worked with there except my boss, called Dave, a tall, thin chap based in Derby.

That is essentially all that remains for me of my professional sojourn into England's social services. I can only remember three fellow students on the Bradford University course: Jude Stoddart, Luise Nandy and a guy who was a local training officer called Richard James Ancrum Metcalfe. Jude and Luise were memorable for their questing brilliance, articulacy and feminism, Richard because he was a hoot, especially when we found ourselves equally petrified by a particularly combative academic called Ron Weiner, later Professor of Criminology at the LSE and the author of several books on policing. I remember him as a curly black-haired American(?), short but powerful, with a ferocious intellect that forbade the taking of prisoners. Richard and I would terrify each other going up in the lift to Ron's classes by speculating who was going to get pummelled first for some sloppy argument, either those you actually offered or those you had failed to offer but should have. By the time the lift arrived, we were totally overcome by mildly hysterical laughter and a paralysing sense of foreboding.

My main focus throughout was the MA course, the final part of which entailed a dissertation to be submitted by December 1979. The intellectual and analytic nature of the course was paramount. There was no iffy-feely stuff about social work practice, more a rigorous and critical examination of the political and institutional contexts in which social work and other services like health, education and law are integral to the functioning of the social democratic welfare state. The course basically invited students to study and critique the mainly liberal precepts of the welfare state especially where it failed to live up to its own rhetoric. Much ink would be spilled during the 1970s and '80s by a huge range of Left academics and practitioners over the development of a notion called 'radical social work', much of it unspecific and vague until Mrs Thatcher unleashed her full-frontal attack on public services. This brought both the reformist and radical wings of the Left movement together in the face of the common threat she posed not just to the 'poor' but the wider working-class and its organisations, the trade unions and the Labour Party.

At Bradford between 1977 and '79, therefore, I was introduced to the radical intellectual discourses surrounding the liberal welfare state and its antimonies – meaning the discrepancies between its rhetoric and practices. An acute critical faculty was displayed by all the lecturers I encountered there and collectively they offered me a different level of analysis entirely as regards social policy and the provision of services to the poor and deprived. I read recent social research studies of contemporary British social conditions, not sociological generalisations derived from 1960s American theorists such as Irving Goffman and Howard Becker, the standard texts available on the Regent Road course. The applicability of that American research to British social and cultural conditions was being questioned by the University of Birmingham's Centre for Contemporary Cultural Studies (BCCCS) led by Stuart Hall. The head of the Bradford MA course, Geoff Pearson, was linked to BCCCS and he was amongst the first British academics and cultural theorists to question American sociological research and the need to test its premises and findings against current British cultural-social conditions. He would apply a similarly sceptical approach to the kind of moral panics the mainstream media routinely deployed to stigmatise the young, the mentally ill and the poor – along with any other group that tried to assist them, such as social workers.

Geoff Pearson, who died in 2013, later became a Professor of Social Work and then of Criminology at Goldsmith's College, London, and editor-in-chief of the *British Journal of Criminology*. He trained as a psychiatric social worker and was a life-long Manchester United supporter and a talented jazz pianist. He did not appear to me a political Marxist being professionally sceptical about all belief systems. Indeed, it was Geoff who described much social work theory as lending itself to 'a Noddy view of the world'. He was a rather cool-looking dude in his early 30s, with a kind of retro 'rocker' haircut brushed back at the sides, which seemed odd, I often thought, when he took out an old pipe and started puffing away while slicing and dicing the sacred cows of the liberal imagination, the discourse that then dominated critical debate on the welfare state.

The Bradford course pointed me towards studies on youth cultures pioneered by the BCCCS, which I found relevant and intriguing, unlike some of the radical social work literature, which I saw as deluded or naïve. Rather than postulating 'radical social work' as a distinct form of 'practice', the title of Daphne Statham's *Radicals in Social Work* (1978) seemed to me to be much nearer the mark.

Being 'radical' within statutory local authority social work still meant that you were still a professional social worker, bound by casework principles and practice circumscribed by legality. Being a 'radical caseworker' meant the same as being a 'radical GP' or 'radical teacher' – a good professional, conscientious, competent and well able to explain the intricacies and options available in clear terms in the context of a person's current circumstances but also with an obligation to lobby the wider political system, those responsible for framing and implementing social welfare legislation and funding. This was primarily done through professional organisations such as the British Association of Social Workers (BASW) and Association of Directors of Social Work (ADSW), voluntary organisations (Shelter, Women's Aid, Cyrenians, Claimants Unions, War on Want), public sector trade unions (NALGO, NUPE, TGWU) and those Centre-Left political parties who stood for parliament (Labour, Liberal, Communist). Some of the earlier Libertarian/Anarchist exponents of radical social work practice who had in the 1970s condemned traditional caseworkers as serving the needs of the ruling-class found themselves in the 1980s marching to defend all public sector jobs, including their own, against Mrs Thatcher's generalised attack on the welfare state. We all seemed to qualify as 'radical' then, rather than being that eponymous Ultra-Left catch-all – 'agents of the state'.

What I obtained from the Bradford course was how social work's view of itself as a professional activity standing above or outside the class-struggle history of the welfare state rather than being the product of opposing political and cultural forces and discourses was not only too narrow but self-deluded. What distinguished the writing of the BCCCS for me was the quality of the thick description it supplied in its analysis of the social and cultural factors which produced youth culture in general and its 'underclass' in particular. It focused on the generation gap that emerged between parents and youngsters in the 1960s, mostly seen in diverging tastes in clothing and music. Until then, lads had dressed like their fathers – the cloth-cap generations – and daughters like their mothers. A new social category emerged – teenagers – with money to spend on records, clothes and increased leisure activities. This was soon noticed by the leisure industries in fashion, music, drink, travel and food. Pretty soon, virtually two nations had appeared, culturally, between young and old, which commercial interests catered for differently: they targeted the younger generation for whom full employment, even in dead-end factory work, meant more disposable income for personal consumption. The era of consumer capitalism was launched. Pretty soon, lounges began to appear alongside bars in pubs, older men in the former, young men and women and couples in the latter drinking lager rather than beer. Mothers now began to dress like their daughters even when hem-lines rose to alarming heights. Youth culture itself began to be artificially separated into contrasting camps or fans, which helped market contrasting products as 'styles'. One either had to be a Mod or a Rocker, a Stones or a Beatles fan, and so on. I was a Beatles fan; well, a John Lennon fan, really.

I was thus introduced to the new Left political discourses that took feminism, equality, race and gay rights seriously as a means of democratising a class-ridden social structure by challenging the political and cultural status quo. After a couple of years chewing this kind of stuff over, I submitted my thesis to Geoff Pearson in December 1979, entitled 'The Social Work Bubble'. It was a rather heavy-handed effort to marshal a Marxist informed critique of the welfare state in line with Geoff's own acerbic take on social work theory as 'a de-politicised and de-moralised phenomenological never-never land'. The nearest I ever came to defining or grounding what I actually meant by 'the social work bubble' was that 'the social work bubble rises up and floats on above the infrastructure somewhere beyond Level 3'. In fact, Level 3 was code for the different grading levels recently agreed across England and Wales on the back of national social work strikes organised through the public sector unions, particularly NALGO. These strikes provided the context of my thesis: social work had become inescapably political along with whatever else social workers also thought it was. And the coming decade would make that perfectly clear to anyone who bothered to read a newspaper. Indeed, between August 1978 and May 1979, of the 100,000 social workers in England and Wales, 2,600 went on strike in 15 different local authorities over various matters including pay and re-grading. By 1985, NALGO would acquire a UK membership of 20,000 field social workers (having a trade union density of 75 per cent) and 25,000 residential workers (having a trade union density of 65 per cent).

Back in Falkirk, Russ Paterson, the social work shop steward in Brockville, had not needed to read a single book to come to much the same conclusions about the changing political climate and the need for trade union organisation in the public sector to protect jobs and services. Russ instead looked to the inspiration of Bob Dylan to riff on Big Tam's departure from Falkirk to Langgarth, the social work HQ in Stirling. Big Tam was finally getting promoted – to assistant principle officer (APO) for residential childcare. Russ had loathed Q and his regime with a venom impossible to convey in a family newspaper, so readers of a nervous disposition may wish to look away now:

> They're wearing black ties at the bookies, the Burns Bar's closing down,
> The Labour Club's in mourning, Big Tam is leaving town,
> He's only been here fifteen years, it's time for him to go,
> Fourteen years in Brockville House, one on *Desolation Row*.
> Q is still in prison (working), but his ghost will never die,
> It still screams 'Mr Wallace, please put on a tie,
> And tell your old friend Findlay to cut the swearing out,
> Or I'll bring in John Murphy who really has some clout.'
> And Danny is still puzzled, he really ran the show,
> But the bastards wouldn't let him into *Desolation Row*.
> The Chief Exec's out shooting budgies, he loves to hear them roar,
> The blue ones make it most fun, the green ones are a bore,
> He used to find it difficult, but now he's come of age,
> He doesn't let them fly around, he shoots them in their cage.
> He likes to write about this sport, it's great to hear him blow,
> But the POs never fly about on *Desolation Row*.

I became friendly with Dave Wright, a residential care worker in Todwick Grange and later a Service manager in Fife social work department, then a young Londoner who played football for a local amateur team near Sheffield, called Battley United. Dave spotted my potential when the staff played the kids at football on the field outside our back door and I was persuaded to help out the kids. This consisted of me ambling onto the pitch in old jeans and trainers, flicking the ball up, and sending a 30-yard drive into the roof of the staff net to the great jubilation of my own side. I then limped off, an old ankle injury flaring up after not having kicked a ball for the last 18 months.

When recovered, I started playing football with Dave for Battley United every Sunday. Dave was the only decent player they had apart from a local punk, called Jasper, who was as reliable at turning up as his name might suggest. I started scoring whenever Dave or Jasper managed to get the ball through to me, simply because the opposing teams were as dire as us. At the end of the season, Pete, our young enthusiastic manager, handed me a little shield, a trophy with 'player of the year' scratched on it, and I was very touched until going back in the car Dave pulled out the exact same trophy with the exact same inscription. Every player in the team had been handed one, and we laughed our heads off. But it was a wonderful levelling gesture all the same. Aye, Battley United.

One day a legendary Falkirk character drove, or rather, rolled up to our door at Todwick: Raymond. No, make that pushed his car slowly up to it. He had phoned saying he and Liz were driving back to Scotland from London and would pop in on the way. We waited all day but there was no sign until about dusk when his beat-up old maroon Allegro crept slowly up the drive. The story was that shortly after leaving London, a spring had gone in the suspension and the car's body was rubbing against one of the wheels. What to do? Rather like Big Tam's Tasty-Toaster tins, Raymond's lateral thinking suggested that if he slid a bike's brake-pad between the car's wheel and the body then he could travel a few miles up the hard shoulder of the M1 by changing the rubber brake-blocks as they went. Ingenuity personified; a habit possibly acquired from 'patching up' all kinds of stuff after five years of generic social work. The next morning, Raymond purchased another pile of brake-blocks so that he and Liz could continue their lop-sided journey back to Scotland, sure in the knowledge that they would not get stopped for speeding. Aye, Raymond and the brake-blocks, lead singer of a 1980s punk-band.

A more sombre note intervened when my father died in October 1978 just a week before his 67th birthday. He had been in a coma for a few weeks and we lived on tenterhooks, wondering whether to visit or wait for him to come round and help aid his recovery. Finally, we got the call that he did not have long to live and we raced home just in time to witness the final hours with my brothers and mother. He had started to write letters to us a few months after we settled in Nottingham, his first letter dated 14 December 1977, typed on the 5x4 inch copy paper he had used to tap out his articles and news reports for the *West Lothian Courier*. His stroke had impaired his vision but not his mind or memory, and so, complete with typos and the editorial traces of his trade – 'picture held over till next week' – we had become his readers for the next year or so. I still treasure them, those reports and news bulletins written about the family, his grandchildren, my mother and the bingo, local gossip and anecdotes from his glory days in the mines, his past sporting prowess and, above all, how the paper, the old *Courier*, had gone downhill badly since his departure from it, all of which was true.

Our decision to return to Scotland was perhaps fed by some of the contents of some of those letters. Mrs Thatcher had also made her obnoxious appearance in May 1979 and that would not have been much of an incentive to extend our stay. I think my father's death and the contacts we had maintained with family and friends suggested these would not be easy to replicate or replace either in England or 'Down Under'. I also had to consider my professional career since starting Emergency Duty work. I did not fancy working in the English Social Services given some of the factors already described. There was definitely a strong sense of cultural pull in my case, a kind of unfinished business feeling that I could not quite name but made me want to return to Scotland to assuage in some way. Our sojourn to England had enabled us to examine and experience a different culture and to discover – miraculously – how much we missed our own. And as luck would have it, by January 1980 an Intake Senior's post fell vacant in Craigmillar, a large working-class housing scheme in Edinburgh, where Danny had become the Area Officer a year or so earlier. So I applied and got it. Little did I suspect at the time that the political and cultural critique of the liberal welfare state which I had just been studying would prove a rehearsal, not for how to strengthen it from the broad Left but how it could be attacked from the neo-liberal Right. And thus we loaded up the car and followed the removal van to the environs of quiet, sedate and peaceful Edinburgh.

9

In the Memo

The strike was on, or rather, this
being social work,the work-to-rule

which the bosses and the council were
bending over backwards to ignore
'Work to Rule!', *Dancing with Big Eunice*

*The author is reunited with Danny as his Area Officer, and becomes
NALGO's Social Work Shop Stewards Convener for Lothian Region. His
Intake Team turns into the People's Front of Craigmillar when a vacant
social worker post is left unfilled. In his spare time the author brings the
office's child protection work up to a credible 19th century standard. The
inner politics of BASW, NALGO and Lothian Regional Council are vividly
detailed. The author's record collection is ridiculed by a man wearing a
wedding dress and a vest.*

IN THE COMING period, I would learn that doing your job as a state-
professional could make you not just political but an 'enemy within' – within
Mrs Thatcher's state at any rate. Life as Intake Senior in Craigmillar, a large
working-class housing estate on the south-side of the city, would have been
hectic anyway compared to the undemanding Emergency Duty work and
full-time academic life I enjoyed while in England. My intro to Craigmillar
Area social work office was a three-page outline written by Danny detailing
the team's evolution and restructuring since 1978, him having been there for
a year or so. He began by listing why it was considered an 'area of multi-
deprivation':

High incidence of unemployed, dependant on State Benefits
High incidence of illegitimate births
High incidence of single parent families
High incidence of children on supervision
High incidence of children at risk, emotionally and physically
High incidence of children in care
High incidence of 16–21-year-olds in penal institutions

High incidence of housing/homeless problems
High incidence of fuel supply disconnections
Higher than average incidence of mentally handicapped resident in area
(10.8 per 1,000)

Looking at this now, one wonders what Mrs Thatcher could possibly have done to make it any worse. In recognition of such data, the new Labour Council had allocated a relatively high staffing ratio (21 social workers for a population of 26,000). This was twice the staffing ratio set a decade earlier for Scotland as a whole (10 social workers per 50,000 population). The social workers in Craigmillar were arranged in four interest groups comprising Intake, Childcare, Court and Penal and Mental Health and Elderly which, apart from Intake, had caseloads weighted 75 per cent towards these specialist areas with the remaining 25 per cent drawn from the other disciplines, thereby encouraging an ongoing generic social work practice and experience. In effect, Danny had inherited an Area Team that had remained virtually untouched by generic social work practice in the eight or nine years since its inception. This had also happened in other pockets and places or whole Regions, such as Grampian, which would retain a largely specialist team structure throughout the 20-odd years of its existence.

The Intake team in Craigmillar would therefore operate as a generic assessment unit for work coming into the office, which could then be referred on to the specialist long-term teams that completed the operational structure. Most of the specialist Seniors, bar one, had retired and been replaced since Danny's appointment by younger and generically trained Seniors, many in their first posts as Seniors, and all were very keen and competent. Indeed, three of the six Senior posts were already filled by ex-Falkirk social workers whom I had once supervised, including Diane the Offenders Senior, Mary the Home-finding Senior, and Craig Robertson, now the Research and Development Senior.

The tenor of the times required that my interview had two components – an informal interview of candidates by some of the social workers currently in the group, who then fed back questions or queries to the formal interview panel to raise with the candidates. During my informal interview, I remember that I inexplicably began choking up. I sensed it was a kind of belated grief reaction to my father's death. The reality of his loss may have been masked for me by being away in England when he died which may have delayed the full impact of it and now I was faced with a realisation that I was about to return home and that he would not be there. Whatever it was, by some supreme effort I managed to hold myself together and the group showed no signs of having noticed. The official interview was conducted by Danny and Gus Campbell, who had become Danny's Divisional Officer, all of us squeezed into Danny's cramped office. Gus was famed as old stone-face during interviews, looking entirely blank and expressionless but with a droll sense of humour nonetheless. I was also told later he was famed for possessing a fiery temper on the five-a-side football pitch, which I was fortunate enough never to experience.

Gus and I got entangled in one part of the discussion about pragmatism: to what extent would it influence my decision-making? I said 'intelligently' and Gus queried this very strenuously. I was probably thinking about another of Iain Morrison's phrases – 'who am I to judge?' – and one of my brother Alan's expressions often deployed during political discussions – 'leave that sticking to the wall'. In the nether and murky world of casework principles butting against street-wise value systems and the 'balance of probabilities' evidential requirements of civil law (applicable to Hearings) contrasting with the 'beyond reasonable doubt' standards of criminal law, there was in social work plenty of scope for doubt and uncertainty regarding the complexity of human behaviour and, therefore, of the judgement calls one is required to make in critical situations. I did not then (as I do not now) believe in absolute truth, absolute knowledge or absolute authority and neither did (or do) the bulk of social workers nor, I suspect, did Gus himself. As it was, I got the job, whatever doubts Gus may have had, and I took it, despite being not all that certain how much I really wanted it anyway. In social work, doubt is rarely, if ever, what you might hope it might be: all on one side.

Craigmillar Area team re-energised my professional life. After two and a half years of sitting at the end of a phone speaking to disembodied voices, I was thrust back into the pell-mell of a busy, almost besieged inner-city workplace. Danny would describe it as like stepping onto a merry-go-round on Monday morning which flung you off again on Friday night. The office was a warren of rooms on the upper and lower floors, with a bit built on at the front for interview rooms and reception and a couple of Portakabins round either side, the whole being fenced off by iron railings.

I arrived in May 1980 and spent four years there, hectic not even beginning to describe the experience. The duty system was mostly operated by the Intake group, supplemented by long-term workers, most of whom could have seen their occasional half-day duty-slots far enough. The volume of new court reports which often arrived in splurges also required long-term social workers to undertake some of these and I devised a rota to share the work across the team. One can perhaps imagine how rigorously this had to be enforced, especially regarding a few Criminal Justice workers who felt they had enough reports to do already. I never had much problem exercising personal authority, on the park or off it, and set the standard that unless accompanied by a sworn affidavit from their Senior and two doctor's lines, I was implacable in the face of reasons put forward by those wishing to miss their turn on the rota. Everybody felt equally hard done by, which I was never slow to eulogise as being the outcome of equity and bureaucratic even-handedness. Even Mike Marshall eventually got the point that he could have done two reports while standing arguing the toss with me. The truth is that I always enjoyed a clash of verbals, as did Mike, especially in public, something that sparked debate and maybe even thought.

I would pronounce in team and allocation meetings that this was local Government, not a democracy, but I was willing to listen to any better professional arguments even though, as I also stressed, rather like a trade union baron, I carried the 'card vote' about with me on my own person. At one point, when I was office shop steward, Regional Shop Stewards Convener and Intake Senior, some unnamed person, undoubtedly Charlie Smith, chalked up on the staff room board, 'Stalin was a Democrat, Alistair'. This, of course, was part of the boundary disputes going on between the functions of Intake and long-term groups which exercised the zealots on either side but the Seniors rarely got drawn into these and so we resolved matters sensibly between ourselves as a management group. Pressure of workload was the main driver rather than competing professional visions of the work. After a year or so, we expanded Intake to include two groups and two Seniors, partly through members of one of the long-term groups being dissatisfied with their Senior's supervision style, or lack of it, having come from a specialist rather than generic background. By that time, I had become the Social Work Shop Stewards Committee Convener, which meant I was often being called at short notice to meetings with union officials and senior managers, so having a second Intake Senior in the workplace helped with that. By effectively expanding Intake resources, we were aiming towards short-term and the more focused interventions that Danny and myself felt the area needed to develop given the constant demand and shifting nature of the population we catered for. It also demanded that long-term groups rigorously review and close cases rather than holding them open extensively without continuing priority need being made evident.

Social work was definitely moving towards more realistic case-plans and the closure of cases as soon as identified objectives were met, even if some of them might bounce back. This was preferable to stagnant caseloads rife with over-dependent clients that liked the social work support they received and the workers they had. Expanding the Intake group meant that I took a strategic overview of the Intake system both within the group and across the wider team. I chaired weekly allocation meetings with all the workers present and the discussion of cases which provided some elementary guidelines for action – especially for disgruntled workers and their Senior to take away and progress. I was also positioned to shape the overall policy and practice direction of the Intake remit, which was also important given the various bouts of trade union industrial action that broke out over the next couple of years in relation to the non-covering of unfilled social worker posts.

This had a rather Kafkaesque quality for me since as workplace shop steward I ensured certain referrals were 'blacked' (embargoed by the union) but as Intake Senior, I wanted priority cases allocated. I suppose it was a bit like Lenin ordering the storming of the Winter Palace but not wanting yon big window in the corner smashed. The Intake group was mostly in their mid- to late 20s with a few in their late 30s to early 40s, mostly female. We had a weekly allocation meeting which I chaired and where we discussed all the cases received through the mail, including Hearing reports and Court reports, and that duty workers had put through for allocation or duty appointment or for closure. Initially, I think we looked at all duty referrals, even the 'no further action' ones, because the group did not trust all the recommendations of the non-Intake duty workers but this fell by the wayside once the Intake group had virtually doubled. The meeting thus had quality control, practice and information sharing aspects so workers and Seniors could brain storm ideas about resources, other agencies and possible lines of approach and so on. It also enabled me to identify and take up managerial problems regarding the frontline practices of other agencies, Reporters, Panels, health, schools, DHSS, fuel boards and the like. It fuelled the idea of collaborative practice across the group so that all workers could be seen as a resource, not just everything going through myself.

As Senior, I was able to convey directly what kind of information I needed to do my job and to help workers do theirs, which was effectively to assess and manage risk, not as something conceptual and vague but detectable in specific cases. The Young Turks of the Intake group, inexperienced in long-term casework, were pretty inspiring all the same in their commitment and energy not only as regards the welfare-related issues which routinely flowed through Intake's duty door – poverty, rent, fuel, housing, evictions – but also the short-term cases they sometimes held for three to six months, mostly Hearing supervision orders in respect of children taken into care and placed in assessment centres or foster homes. The Intake team comprised Wee Jan Aitchison/McClory, Sheila Wood and Gary Pinnons in the Young Turk category, Charlie Smith in the Big Turk category, Ann in the steadfastly quiet but determined category, Rita Sharp in the Slightly Scatty But Kind category, Mary in the Slightly Disapproving category – not forgetting Big Evelyn in the Big Evelyn category, for who could? There were also two specialist workers who gravitated round the Intake group in terms of new assessments: Anne Flynn, a detached school social worker at Castlebrae, and Jimmy Johnstone, the Mental Disabilities social worker, and you could read that either way since Jimmy was the workplace shop steward. He was also in the Very Loud Quite Shouty and Often Angry category, which Intake loved to provoke at the slightest opportunity.

The first time I chaired the Intake Allocation meeting, it kind of set the tone for the duration. Gary, who hailed from Belfast and you could tell this by his Beatles haircut, was speaking about a case he had brought to the meeting which he said concerned a person from 'Lonton'. I said 'Lonton?' and Gary said, 'Yes, Lonton,' and I said, 'Lonton?' and he said 'Yes, Lonton,' and I said, 'You mean London?' and Gary said, 'Yes, that's what I said, Lonton.' By this time, the Intake team was screaming its collective head off. This would rarely stop for the next four years.

Despite the wide range of personalities, the workers all pitched in and helped each other and me out. We worked at a frenetic pace punctuated by bouts of mayhem and quite possibly madness, probably as a counterpoint to the constant flow of human misery and degradation that lapped round the duty-desk. Craigmillar as an area had seen much more settled and respectable days through the 1950s and '60s when people had striven to be housed there but now it was becoming a 'dumping-ground' for large families (it had a large number of five-apartments) and also for temporary homeless families and persons, often rootless, placed alongside the long-term residents. Much of our work came from the former rather than the latter, of course.

Welfare rights and clients as claimants were the predominant perspectives of Intake's Young Turks and they were ever-hopeful and ever-disappointed that this approach rarely seemed to catch on amongst the more traditional long-term caseworkers who supported the duty system. The referral write-ups of the long-term caseworkers were ripped to shreds at allocation meetings and a list of to-do pointers drawn up for the next duty session or sent back to the errant duty worker for follow-up. This was seen as an educative function by the Intake group but was not always well-received by long-term workers who often had other complex cases and caseloads on their minds.

This low-level guerrilla warfare between Intake and other groups and segments suddenly turned hot in the case of Old Peggy, the formidable Admin boss, who had been ensconced in the office since nineteen-canteen. Peggy largely continued to march to the beat of the old welfare drum that she had been marching to since the mid-1960s. This meant she persisted in leaving black bin liners stuffed with second-hand clothes that had been handed in lying around in the reception area for clients to rummage through while sitting waiting to be seen by their social workers. Reception sometimes resembled the Winter of Discontent, when striking refuse workers created huge mountains of rubbish which Mrs Thatcher used to beat Jim Callaghan's Labour Government about the head with, so to speak, in 1978. Pleas to desist by the Intake Team, the Intake Senior and even the Area Officer fell on Peggy's belligerently deaf ears, so the Young Turks decided on Direct-Action, and began taking the bags into the big Intake room, one corner of which soon came to resemble, yes, a street scene from the Winter of Discontent. The struggle in that form finally came to a halt the day I walked into the Intake room to find Big Charlie entertaining the troops by pulling on an old wedding dress he had found in one of the bin bags. He had removed his shirt to reveal a rather fetching string vest and had managed to pull one strap of the dress over one shoulder and was busy looking in another bag for a suitable hat to go with the ensemble, much to the amusement of the rest of the group.

The serious point behind the Intake workers' attitude was a desire to reposition clients from being viewed as objects of charity to one of claimants with legal entitlements to state benefits and the like, as well as the dignity that ought to bring with it. This was why the Intake group was pretty miserly in issuing Section 12 grants, preferring to spend the time negotiating with DHSS and the fuel boards to make them fulfil their proper obligations under statute as regards benefits and allowances. Other busy Area offices in Edinburgh which took a more traditional route of handing out Section 12s without much challenge were rewarded, once word got round the local grapevine that the welfare was a soft touch, with busier waiting rooms looking for hand-outs. The claimants' rights approach was adopted by the Regional council which then established a Welfare Rights Team in Edinburgh, one of whom came to us, Jon Laffan, who helped train clients and workers in the arcane workings of the state benefits system. I am pretty sure that is what Big Charlie was trying to explain to his colleagues in the Intake room and using the wedding dress for illustrative purposes.

I enjoyed but did not find the Intake Senior's role particularly stretching as regards my own professional development. Indeed, after about six or seven months, I considered applying for a training-lecturer post and I spoke to Danny about it, saying I would not apply if he had any problem with it. Danny said he would be very disappointed if I left, with a few more expletives undeleted that need not detain the reader here.

I did make a point of attending every new child protection case conference that involved Craigmillar children organised by Susan Brown, who was the Senior up at Edinburgh Sick Kids. The hospital was the most obvious locus for children with dubious injuries to be noticed by medical staff and so referred to the small team of hospital social workers based there. The protocol was that Susan's team should organise inter-agency case conferences at the hospital and invite local practitioners, health visitors, GPs, nursery staff, education and the local Area Team to attend. Most Area Seniors did not attend these, although some may sometimes have sent a social worker along to get information, just in case the child needed to be allocated at some point in the Area Team. Most teams simply filed the case-conference minutes sent to them for information purposes and got on with other work. I thought this a ridiculously perilous procedure because I felt it was vital to discuss concerns about vulnerable children from an Area Team's perspective and shape critical assessment decisions from the very outset. I thus made a point of proactively attending every new case conference, therefore building up a local network of contacts with inter-agency practitioners in the Craigmillar area who were crucial to the ongoing management of child protection work in every case we managed, not just those that came through the hospitals.

I also formed a good working relationship with schools and the local children's centre and nursery in Craigmillar, which had a crucial role in monitoring the attendance of at risk children and their health and appearance – their clothing, appetite and emotional and physical well-being and how they related to their parents and vice-versa. The registration of children on the Protection Register often required that parents agree to sending their children to the Children's Centre, places for which were always found whatever the actual waiting list might be. That was just how it was, how it had to be. Non-cooperation would have resulted in referral to the Reporter, who received all case conference minutes in any case and he could have acted if he felt the need. But the care and protection system was and still is based on voluntary approaches being tried first, and failing, before moving on to compulsory measures, unless the risks are so obvious and well-evidenced from the start.

A step change in my working life emerged towards the end of my first year in Edinburgh as regards the political stance that Lothian Regional Council took against rate-capping introduced by the Thatcher Government in 1980–2. Elected in 1980, a younger generation of radical Labour activists who led the Council refused to implement the cuts necessitated by a reduction in central Government funding. In the Scottish local elections of May 1980, Labour won 49.5 per cent of the vote to the Tories' 26.5 per cent. Some authorities, including Lothian, Stirling and Dundee, claimed they had a popular mandate to protect jobs and services by increasing local expenditure. In 1980–1, Lothian Council raised the rates by 41 per cent and, in 1981–2, planned to raise them again by 24.7 per cent. In July 1981, this incurred a reduced Rate Support Grant from the Scottish Office, led by the

Secretary of State, George Younger, and his Deputy, Malcolm Rifkind. This amounted to £47 million being deducted from Lothian Regional Council, many of whose Senior group of Left councillors had undergone community work training at Moray House. They included the future Leader (following Phyllis Herriot in 1982), John Mulvey; the Group Secretary, Jimmy Burnett; Paul Nolan, who was a councillor in Craigmillar and a member of the Social Work Committee; and Big Davy Brown, the Housing Convener, who was the local District councillor for Niddrie – the very man whom Iain Morrison had tried to set on the path to virtue in that P and P group-work session at Regent Road a decade earlier.

In an interview for the *Edinburgh Evening News* (8 April 2014), Jimmy Burnett recalled their own surprise at winning the Council election and the shock and despair of 'one of the more patrician Tory councillors commenting as we enthusiastically celebrated taking the Stockbridge seat, "this is the sort of scum that will be running our town".' Jimmy accurately put their victory down to the unpopularity of the Conservative Government and outlined some of the big changes in the way the council was run:

> We froze council house rents, which were the highest in Scotland, made vast improvements to our library stocks and significant improvements in our cleansing and litter services. We made higher staffing levels in key areas and greater levels of investment in our housing and recreation services and overall created around 1,000 new jobs.

Written some three decades after the events, Jimmy Burnett hails these credible efforts but the Conservative-SDP Council that replaced them between 1982 and 1986 still cut 4,500 local Government jobs. Lothian Council was part of Scottish Labour's initial response to Thatcherism and, through the 1980s and '90s, the Labour Group was populist and serious about improving local housing, transport and employment towards which they poured as much local Government funding as they could. Lothian Council bears some comparison to Ken Livingstone's GLC which sought to outwit the Thatcher Government's effort to curb local authority powers more through bare-faced cheek than bare-arsed confrontation. It campaigned to win public understanding and support and devised ingenious ways to delay Tory attempts to restrict not simply local Government spending but any democratic force standing between it and their ultimate objective of disciplining the trade unions. At the next council elections in May 1982, Labour lost Regional control of Lothian (but not at District level), tying with the Conservatives at 22 seats apiece. A Tory Administration led by Brian Meek took over with the support of three SDP-Lib councillors but was swept away in May 1986 when Labour won 30 seats to the Tories' 13. Labour was returned, too, in May 1990, winning 34 seats to the Tories' 12.

The political battle in Edinburgh Council chamber was being watched like a hawk by every ratepayer and local Government employee in Lothian Region. Labour had figured that every year Council budgets were never fully spent. This was certainly the case regarding the annual staffing budget because there was always a turnover of jobs so that the gap period between posts being vacated and then filled incurred saving salaries for that time, often a few months. The Council began creating posts using the money they had assigned for staffing which they knew under normal circumstances would never be fully deployed. This funded many of the 1,000 extra posts Jimmy Burnett refers to in his reminiscences. Even when the Labour Group lost council control between 1982 and '86 and the Tory-SDP-Liberal administration tried to cut back to former staffing levels, they were often tied in knots trying to untangle what the original establishment levels had been before the new posts were created and absorbed – which the trade unions constantly disputed thereafter.

The Tory-led administration found that the Labour Group and trade unions hunkered down to defend the jobs which supplied the local services that the community needed and wanted – low bus fares, low council rents and better schools. This initiated a politicised budget procedure carried out in the full glare of the local press. Senior managers in the major departments – social work, education, transport – began drawing up provisional and costed lists of savings. The Council then went through these, item by item and line by line, voting on which council service was to be either reduced or chopped – home-helps, children's centre places, foster carers, old people's homes – which was reported in loving detail in the *Edinburgh Evening News* and *The Scotsman*. Over his four years in office Brian Meek, despite being that rare thing – an intelligent Tory who despised Margaret Thatcher – would discover that he could only hold political sway by using his casting vote no fewer than 486 times. As for any Lothian Region social worker still holding onto the notion that their work was somehow non-political – well, they only had to read the papers. Thatcherism thus served to activate not only odd lefties like myself but it also politicised a whole generation of social workers into defending their jobs and the services these jobs provided for the community in general, and for its poorest and most vulnerable members in particular. Well done, Margaret.

My own political participation began in earnest in May 1982 with the election of this Tory-led Regional Council. The local Government trade unions were fully behind the Labour Group's stance against cuts to jobs and services and so the political battle was joined by NALGO. At a large gathering held for Edinburgh social work staff to explain the job and service implications, I made a contribution from the floor which was pretty well-received. The size of our workplace entitled us to two shop stewards and Jimmy was going round looking for someone else to help carry the burden with no success until I stepped up, otherwise Jimmy was going to resign. So I became a NALGO shop steward and, after a few meetings held on Monday mornings at the Trades Council in Picardy Place, I became Convener of Lothian Region's Social Work Shop Stewards Committee. This occurred on much the same basis as Jeremy Corbyn became the Left's candidate for the Labour leadership in 2015 – nobody else wanted the bloody job!

Although the Labour Council had created many temporary – 'supernumerary' – posts there was a large measure of serendipity over the kind of vacancies that arose and in which departments – anything from admin to manual, housing or social work or roads and so on. National NALGO had a blanket no-cover policy for any unfilled post but how do you determine what that means exactly for, say, a typist post that is, say, one of a typing pool of four typists in an office? Do you black every fourth piece of typing whether it is a court report or a routine letter offering a client a duty appointment? Do you allow management to decide the top priority tasks, meaning that only the lowest priority work is not done thus rendering the no-cover action useless and allowing the Council to pocket the saving of the wages of the unfilled posts into the bargain? These were the kinds of issues which began to enter the discourse of local Government through the coming decade. Some workplaces ignored no-cover entirely, some blacked only lower priority work while some, like Craigmillar – and then later, more spectacularly, Pilton Area Office – refused to play the game and applied no-cover to all work including the higher priority stuff.

It took several months before a vacancy actually arose in Craigmillar Office, not for a typist but a social worker post. We could have done what many other workplaces across the Region were already doing – allowing management to re-prioritise work, keep calm and carry on. But not the bears in Craigmillar. ('The bears is no happy' is an expression I first heard a fat Glaswegian electrician shop steward say to a foreman on a building site I was working on in the late 1960s.) Much the same could have been said of the social workers in Craigmillar office in the early 1980s. There is a certain irony, too, in the fact that some other social work offices in Edinburgh with far more radical images than Craigmillar – like Leith, which had a Trotskyist Socialist Workers Party shop steward, Sylvia, who, for all her eloquent militancy, could not persuade her colleagues for love nor money to adopt a similarly unyielding no-cover stance as Craigmillar or Pilton. And this was so despite Jimmy and me constantly reminding the bears that we were the only workplace in Lothian then taking such unbending no-cover action.

There was, of course, another reality operating too. Our employer, a propped up Tory Council, was not going to sack anyone for carrying out official NALGO policy, thus risking even more industrial action and hence disruption to services. There were other disciplinary measures short of sacking which were, of course, still open to a determined senior management including the docking of pay, demotion and written and verbal warnings – which had time-limits but could impede your moving jobs in the short-term since it was put on your employment record for a period. There was also, of course, that other imponderable: one's own future promotion prospects. As the Left was only too aware, blacking posts was not the sole prerogative of the trade unions, for the blacking of worker-militants had been the modus operandi of the employing classes for centuries. With Mrs Thatcher now beating the same old drum, who knew what lay ahead for those prepared to stick their heads above the parapet in Edinburgh social work department.

Actually, what lay ahead, at least for the Director of Social Work for Lothian Region, Roger Kent, was a court appearance – having to explain to a Sheriff whilst standing in the dock himself why a Social Enquiry Report (SER) had not been prepared under statute by the social work department based at Craigmillar. Big Roger appeared in person because the Assistant Director of Fieldwork, Martin Manby, had 'forgotten' that the said SER had been blacked as part of our no-cover policy for unfilled posts imposed by NALGO. Unfortunately, Martin was so busy, he forgot to get someone else to do it, like Gus Campbell, who I think did it anyway after Big Roger's acquittal. The details of the no-cover action are still burned on Danny's soul. He recalls that NALGO (me and Jimmy) calculated six hours of work per court report so six reports equalled a week's work blacked to compensate for the unfilled social worker post, which was actually for a fostering resource worker. The court report that put Big Roger in the dock was therefore only the first of six SERs, mixed in with other types of reports, that would not get written until the post was agreed to be filled. It was, of course, immediately advertised/filled.

Needless to say, the bears in the Craigmillar office were ecstatic, so much so that, for the next several weeks, Jimmy and me were shuttling between George IV Bridge and Shrubhill House to meet Big Roger and the real NALGO bears – folk like Bill Heeps, Regional Convener; Archie Fairley, Service Conditions Officer; and Adam Ingram, the full-time official. Adam was a very hard nut who would later serve as an MP for East Kilbride and become a Minister for Northern Ireland with responsibilities for Security, then Armed Forces Minister in the Defence Department in the Blair Government. I would in fact write a poem about this in *Dancing with Big Eunice* called

'Work-to-Rule!', of me and Jimmy caught in that particular moment when trade unionism encountered the 'statutory responsibilities' of basic-grade social workers – which revealed some inability in the statutory social system to function too long legally without us.

Jimmy need not really have feared, for the Council, the unions and Big Roger were all basically bending over backwards to avoid igniting further industrial unrest. Craigmillar was so far the only Area office in Lothian showing such militancy. The social work post would become filled sooner rather than later but not before another outbreak occurred at the Pilton Area office in September 1982. Pilton had much the same social profile as Craigmillar and Wester Hailes. The non-replacement of a Criminal Justice social worker post led to the suspension of a Senior social worker and two social workers by the Area Officer, Angus Skinner, later Chief Social Work Adviser and then Chief Inspector at the Scottish Office 1992–2005. Angus had instructed a Senior, John McBride, to allocate a blacked court report to a social worker and the refusals led to the suspension of three of them. Whether this was done in consultation with the Directorate I do not know but I suspect not. The result was a complete office walk-out for several weeks, the striking social workers sending out speakers to every social work workplace across the Region stating their case and drumming up support as though they were miners or steelworkers. Angus succeeded where Sylvia in Leith had failed, sending van-loads of steamed-up social work militants across the land condemning the iniquity of the Tory Government for imposing 'cuts' on Labour-voting Scotland. It is doubtful whether the speakers would have told their listeners, often folk earning far less than they were, that they were on full-salary strike-pay paid for by NALGO which was something that Archie Fairley, the Service Conditions officer, fumed over none too quietly behind the scenes.

There would be further occasions for Archie to fulminate when the residential social workers went on strike nationally in 1983–4 for pay-parity with fieldworkers, which turned particularly bitter when some of the children's units began to withdraw emergency cover arrangements. Some senior managers volunteered to help out, including the ubiquitous Gus Campbell. I did not endear myself either to the residential shop stewards for publicly criticising the withdrawal of emergency cover. I cited my experience of managing the Emergency Duty service in Nottingham without social workers and suggested that giving up Union control of the emergency cover might also serve to justify the Tory Council bringing in some outside cover for which they would probably gain (and the union lose) public support. That made me about as popular as Gus but the action would lead eventually to pay-parity between field and residential workers, certainly across Lothian.

By this time, however, I had become Branch Education officer, with duties confined to organising training for shop stewards and health and safety reps.

I might add that I was not the only Senior social worker in Edinburgh who became active in the unions at this time. John McBride and John Stevenson in Pilton as well as Ken Morrison at the Royal Edinburgh Infirmary and the Clapton brothers in Craigentinny – Gordon and Gary – were also involved. Bryan Chatham, too, was a Senior in the Leith office, a terror on the five-a-side court being a rugby lout and finance secretary for the local Labour Party branch, all good preparation for his stint later as Director of Social Work for Edinburgh City. There were also Assistant Principle Officers (APOs) in children's residential services who became active in the later disputes. My finest hour was during a threatened social work walk-out leading to a huge meeting that filled the Assembly Rooms. Les McEwan came along to remonstrate as an 'ordinary' NALGO member, despite being Divisional Director for West Lothian. Les queued up to get to the microphone, so I just stood immediately behind him in the line. When he got the mic, Les gave it laldy about how he had been in touch with official NALGO HQ in Glasgow that very morning and how he had been assured that the action being proposed was entirely unsupported by NALGO official protocols and so on. Les endured the barrage of boos and jeers despite being perfectly correct in every word he said. I did not deny this when I got to the mic after him but merely said, 'I ask you, would you buy a used car from that man?' Never got a bigger laugh or cheer in my NALGO life.

Danny had to undergo much the same kind of treatment at union meetings in Craigmillar, which he attended faithfully to hear the feedback from the latest boxing match between Big Roger and Adam Ingram. At one meeting, Danny demanded a full debate on the next planned 'action'. I tried a few times to explain that this was out of order but Danny was not called 'Bovver Boots Deans' by Big Tam for nothing. So I said, 'OK, do you have a seconder for the motion, Danny?' Danny said, 'No.' I said, 'Does anyone second Danny's motion? – No? Sorry, Daniel, next business.' This would be when Big Charlie christened Danny 'Two-Hats Deans' in honour of an old tramp who used to walk around Edinburgh wearing two hats and so got called 'Johnny Two-Hats'. I cannot reveal what Danny called Big Charlie. The most militant Lothian NALGO meeting I ever attended, sitting on the platform, was in the Usher Hall, 2,000 members demanding action over planned 'cuts' – no, not to jobs but car loans, paid telephone bills, mileage rates, 'out-of-pocket expenses'. Aye, Lothian NALGO.

I will mention some of the vibe at the time around David Thorpe's study of juvenile crime cultures based on labelling theory, *Out of Control* (1980). Thorpe argued that social workers should be allowed to divert youngsters away from the English juvenile justice system in order to prevent them from starting on a criminal career, prison merely serving to provide a crash-course in more effective skulduggery. Sometimes miscalled 'radical non-intervention', Thorpe showed that the resort to penal disposals for working-class youngsters should be replaced by a kind of 'continuum of care', designed to keep them out of the custodial penal system by well-resourced diversion schemes. Of course, this was unlikely to appeal to the Thatcher government, whose larger political purposes were to be served by increasing tensions within working-class communities rather than tackling the poverty – occupational, educational, financial – on which youth criminality thrives. Indeed, shortly before I arrived in Craigmillar, Martin Manby had invited David Thorpe to Edinburgh to discuss his work and theories at a large conference.

Danny recalls that I began an initiative with our area Reporter, Alison Cunningham, based on diversionary principles already inherent in her role. We thus met regularly to help 'screen out' the referrals she received from police and other agencies before she considered requesting an Initial Inquiry Report from social work. Primitive, no doubt, but it helped reduce the volume of non-essential reports to ourselves while minimising contact between ordinary children and families and social work.

An extreme – indeed, verging on the catastrophic – version of diverting children away from residential care was concocted by the Fife Director of Social Work, Alan Bowman, in the late 1980s, which involved banning his staff from placing children in residential care altogether. This caused both mayhem and fury not only between social work and the Reporter and Children's Panel but in the social work department itself – often between frontline managers implementing this blanket policy and social workers who felt that residential care was being denied to kids who were assessed as needing it. Whatever its purpose – to save children from care or to save money or a good deal of both – the professional role of social workers was drastically circumscribed by a Director who was backed to the hilt by Fife Regional Council. An Inquiry Report was prepared but became overshadowed by being published at the same time as the Orkney Inquiry in October 1992. Bowman survived but many Fife social workers fled to neighbouring authorities, including West Lothian, some of whom I worked with. Fife Council became the North Korea of Scottish social work almost overnight – like the old sexist-ageist-racist joke about sex and Australia: everybody knew where it was but nobody wanted to go there.

Bowman seemed to think he was pioneering community care by doing away with care homes, which also kept the rates down, of course – more Dickensian than Lord Wheatley, I would have thought.

I thought social work's job was to work in the society that Mrs Thatcher said no longer existed. I thought our job was to work to keep those families she said did not exist from falling even further apart under the weight of her own regressive social policies. Maybe I was merely imagining the following case therefore, one that was all too familiar in places like Craigmillar – and Fife – in that decade and increasingly since. It featured a pair of young drug addicts and their baby, allocated to a young Intake worker who was assiduous in supporting them, visiting daily to monitor the child. The baby was on the NAI Register and under the Panel but the health visitor and other agencies were highly concerned and urging removal into foster care.

These agencies tended to have a lower risk-tolerance than social workers, mainly because we are governed by statutes more legally restrictive than either health workers or teachers seemed able to comprehend – and this persists to this day. The social worker was totally committed to this family and I supported her at a meeting we had with Gus and Danny who stated their own concerns plainly enough. Despite their professional reservations, however, they allowed us to continue. Not long after this, the social worker visited and came upon the couple doped up and the child crawling about on a carpet scattered with broken glass, which resulted in immediate removal and transfer on to a long-term team. Despite their own reservations, Gus and Danny recognised the complexity that always attends such assessments but trusted us, the professionals directly involved, to make these judgements. Social work is rarely a risk-free matter and those who think it should or can be better start forking out a lot more money for a lot more prisons, care homes and foster and adoption places. There are no shortcuts or quick fixes to reach the Promised Land of total safety for all, not even in Fife, let alone places like Craigmillar.

Later research into child protection work coined the term 'the rule of optimism' to describe cases where professionals tend to look for positives and down-play some of the negatives in assessing risk situations. This is not a rule, however, because it does not possess the scientific certainty it wishes to confer upon itself. The correctness of any judgement-call can only be determined in retrospect, certainly in child protection work. In the situation described, the child was not actually harmed but he certainly could have been. On that basis, of course, a lot of children in Craigmillar and similar areas could have come to harm, even those who were not already on the NAI Register or supervised under the Children's Hearings. So who can be trusted with such judgement-calls and how far might this extend upwards – the Area Officer, the Divisional Manager, the Director? Such grades can never get close enough to the detail of every case in their area to even begin to second-guess the judgements made by those professionals directly involved and responsible. Passing such decisions up the food-chain is liable to lead only to a different kind of risk-taking – namely defensive practice – likely to result in removing a lot more children unnecessarily from their parents or alternatively losing cases at proof hearing stages through insufficient evidence being presented to courts.

Of such practice there was quite enough anyway, whipped up by the hyena press. At that time in Edinburgh, there were no such media-orchestrated witch-hunts. I can deduce this from *The Glasgow Herald*, which reported on 26 October 1981 that a baby called James A from Wester Hailes had died earlier that month in the Royal Hospital for Sick Children. There was a history of previous fractures and of being known to social work and several other agencies over the last year. The Assistant Director of Fieldwork, Martin Manby, is quoted saying that an internal inquiry and report to the social work committee was planned and that 'we will look carefully at our part in attempting to provide services and see if we can learn any lessons. I say that without coming to any conclusions.' Impossible to imagine that today, certainly when Ed Balls was on the go (I will get to him later). Ed might very well have sacked Martin before the end of that press-conference.

But who knew anything about such a future, or Ed Balls, as Craigmillar Area Team revolved like a whirligig in a gale? Jimmy, the shop steward, suddenly became renamed 'Monsoor Jeemee' by Big Charlie for foolishly inviting the Intake Team along to witness him in an amateur dramatic production of a play by Chekov at Morningside Theatre. Halfway through the first act, Jimmy suddenly made his entrance via the French windows, dressed as a young Officer in Napoleon's *Grande Armée* – 20 years too old for the part. Nevertheless, Jimmy launched resoundingly into some lingua franca, his 1982 NHS black plastic specs glaring in the footlights, which rather undid his 1812 French Cavalryman's uniform and character, but we cheered him to the rafters anyway.

Jimmy took most things in good part for he got plenty of ribbing about his new specialist post – resource worker for the mentally handicapped. He was obliged to patrol its boundaries with all the fortitude of a nightclub bouncer. An infamous couple, George and Jessie, tested these boundaries to breaking point. A pair of alcoholics in their late 50s, they used to haunt the Intake duty-system on any pretext, often to indulge Jessie's fascination with the phone. Sitting in a crowded reception and with the ever-vigilant Donna momentarily distracted and the duty and stand-by workers up to their eyes in emergencies, Jessie would sometimes sneak into an empty interview room and phone people, any people, including a bewildered person in South Africa in the middle of the night, to talk mince, until she was detected and put out the door. Jessie had had all her children removed and a psychoanalytically-inclined caseworker once suggested that perhaps she was trying to contact them through this behaviour but, no, she did not have any room for Jessie on her own caseload. Neither did anybody else.

The Craigmillar Young Turks delighted in plaguing Monsoor Jeemee with the proposal-cum-accusation that he should be allocated George and Jessie which, of course, Jim stoutly refuted because he had far younger and more vulnerable cases to deal with. George and Jessie were housed and fed by the Salvation Army and the Cyrenians and, whenever they had drunk all their benefits, they were hardy enough to sleep under a hedge, in a doorway or on a park bench during the summer. So Jimmy went apoplectic the day Danny was enrolled by the Young Turks into pretending he was allocating George and Jessie to him. They had filled out the allocation papers in detail and Danny met an enraged Jimmy waving them at him after he found them in his pigeon-hole at reception. Danny tried to keep up the pretence but soon called it off because he thought Jimmy would either hit him or have a heart attack. In truth, we did not have the resources to deal with these cases, many having been released to the community from institutional care without proper backup support. Today such people still churn through the duty-systems, especially in the cities, but can be referred to private care agencies and supported-housing schemes paid for by the Council. Back then it was just the hostels and the charities – or Raymond, if he was on duty down in the Leith office.

We were in the Intake room at lunchtime one day when Donna phoned through to say Jessie had been put out and was lying outside the front door. We gathered round Sheila's desk, the lookout spot, where she and Jan were piloting what Big Charlie said was a new Intake initiative that he was thinking of writing a paper about and sending to *Social Work Today* – window-watching duty. Sure enough, there was Jessie lying on her back outside the front door. Suddenly, who walks up the path but Danny, briefcase in hand, just back from another big meeting at Shrubhill. We all chuckled – 'What's he going to do now?' What Danny did was look down and address a few words to Jessie's inert corpse. He then looked up at the sky, put his hand out as if testing for rain, addressed another few words to her before stepping over her body and in through the office door with nary a backward glance. We all looked at Jessie – 'What's she going to do now?' Jessie lay there for another 40 seconds, got up, straightened her clothes and walked out into the afternoon, also with nary a backward glance. We went back to eating our sandwiches, for later some of us would be off to Hearings, some to Court, some to prison or children's centres or List D schools or foster homes or high flats or hospital – all in a day's work. Danny has insisted on adding a codicil which he thinks will make him look better in this tale. After he had stepped over Jessie, he said to Donna at reception that Jessie was lying outside on the pavement and to give it a few minutes and, if she hadn't moved, 'tell the Intake Team they will have to keep an eye on the situation'.

And so we got on with whatever came our way. On Friday nights, workers and Seniors across the whole Team would gather at The Southsider pub for a pint and a blether for which the Childcare Senior, Ron McKenzie, was usually well to the fore. Ron was well-versed in his job but also had an unfortunate penchant for Cockney rhyming-slang so Big Charlie dubbed him 'Don McFrenzie' and he became 'Don' ever after. Going to NALGO meetings at the Assembly Rooms was also part of the social life, which would continue after in such watering-holes as the Café Royale and Mathers. Wee Jan, who was a potent mix of Mother Teresa and Rosa Luxemburg, and Big Charlie were both ex-Regent Roaders and their party-pieces included brilliant impersonations of Dougie Carnegie, now a legend amongst wave upon wave of social work and community work students passing through Moray House gates. It was difficult to beat the real thing, though.

Life continued in this kind of professional, politically charged and buzzing manner until the day arrived in March 1982 when Danny left Craigmillar to become the Area Officer at Bathgate. Naturally, the Craigmillar Team gave him a resounding send-off in the usual social work fashion. I read out a mock SER on his background, purporting to explain the growth of his two heads; Diane and Mary dressed up in pin-stripe suits with false moustaches and violin cases under their arms to represent The Falkirk Mafia, about to be reduced to a mere two, myself and Big Craig; Jeanna, the Admin junior, announced Danny had won the best Senior bum competition, myself coming a poor joint-third despite Jeanna's charming depiction of it as 'quite sporty'.

Until Danny was replaced, Penny was drafted in as acting Area Officer from her post as Principal social worker at Rillbank, Department of Child and Family Psychiatry, part of the Sick Kids Hospital. Penny was middle-aged, single and a tweedier version of Muriel Spark's Miss Jean Brodie, though more Liberal Democrat than Fascist. I enjoyed Penny's fluency and the occasional awkward streak she revealed. She was, after all, prepared to come from the relative shelter of a hospital clinic to embrace a brawling inner-city bourach, complicated further by the fact that cases were unallocated because of union action over an unfilled vacancy. I would sometimes meet her wearing different hats, rather like Danny, as Intake Senior and then office shop steward. When I went to see her about progress on the vacant post, Penny said she had written a memo about it which was in for typing. I said did she mention this and did she mention that, to which she kept nodding her head and saying, 'It's in the memo, yes, in the memo, in the memo', until she suddenly burst out, 'You know, you are a complete and utter bastard!' – to which I said, 'Eh, I suppose that'll be in the memo as well, Penny?'

I suspect Penny was more likely to have been in BASW, the professional organisation, rather than NALGO, although some social workers were in both. The history of this professional association is possibly a lot more interesting than the kind of people I thought tended to join it, often stuffy liberals and hand-wringers. BASW was formed from 18 former specialist professional associations in 1970. Almost 50 per cent of UK social workers were members in 1971 (8,539 in a 17,500 workforce). In 1974, there were also some 3,000 members in a sister body, the Residential Care Association. By 1975, the workforce was 24,000 and, by 1983, BASW's membership was 8,238, roughly 10 per cent of the 100,000 non-manual social services employees that worked in England and Wales (see *Striking Out: Trade Unionism in Social Work* by Paul Joyce et al, 1988: 115).

The online history of BASW from 1970 to 1990 by Andrew Sackville states that Dennis Gower was constantly complaining that the Scottish branch was starved of resources. Sackville supplies a useful breakdown of BASW's average annual expenditure over the period: 40 per cent for the journal *Social Work Today*; 34 per cent for Admin and Finance; 8 per cent for Tax; 3 per cent for Conferences; 9 per cent for Members Services. This last statistic shows why social workers preferred to join the trade union movement, which is not to disdain BASW's contribution to social work training and practice. Indeed, even now, Big Tam, a NALGO and Labour Party man through and through, can still come out with what would then have seemed an outlandish statement to us both, 'Al, we should have done more with the Professional Association' and, just as absurdly, I find myself agreeing. Still, the phrase 'herding cats' sprung very readily to mind when I read that it took a BASW Working Party the best part of three years (1974–7) to reconcile its diverse range of perspectives into a rather woolly definition of 'the social work task'. Likewise, the question of BASW including unqualified workers and which qualifications were valid involved similarly extensive disputes on the distinction between 'social work' and 'social services work'.

A major breech with NALGO was opened in 1979 when BASW set up a separate social work trade union, the British Union of Social Workers (BUSW), which crash-landed some six years later after which BASW reconciled with NALGO in April 1985. But the failure was predictable given the fact that between August 1978 and May 1979, some 2,600 social workers from a total of 100,000 went on strike in 15 different (mainly English) local authorities over pay and re-grading disputes. This represented 2.6 per cent of BASW's membership but only 0.5 per cent of NALGO's 1978 membership of 729,405. Bear in mind, too, that in 1984, BASW had about 9,000 members which represented a third of the profession while, in 1985, NALGO had a

UK membership of 20,000 field social workers and 25,000 residential workers. The NALGO strikers were maintained at or near full pay during these actions which at one point was costing the Union £500,000 per month and amounted to £1.6 million overall, an average of £700 for every social worker on strike (Paul Joyce et al: 129,130,134). Finances apart, white-collar trade union militancy was in its infancy, even within NALGO, never mind BASW spending three years over the definition of the social work task. And yet, could more not have been done?

Reading BASW's professional history more carefully than I ever did at the time shows that its Professional Development and Practice Committee established in 1979 acted as a watch-dog of standards in different settings and upheld core social work values and principles regarding good practice. A formal Code of Ethics drawn up in October 1975 was later amended to include matters of sexual orientation, racism and the exclusion of sexist language. It still survives, as do papers on confidentiality and one entitled 'The Management of Child Abuse' (1985), which many local authorities used to review their own procedures and practices. Such documents embodied professional practice values that employers and politicians could ignore but at their own peril. Professional social workers operating within the corporate structures of local and central Government and external regulatory inspectorates today may have more need of such codes than our generation because our role as professionals under the law was never challenged or undermined by the micro-management and regulatory controls now routinely applied to local authority social workers as though they are bin-collectors. No harm to them, of course – but they don't have to persuade their charges to jump onto the lorries themselves, do they?

I endorse Andrew Sackville's broad conclusion about BASW, therefore, that 'the grandiose claims for its powerful influence are dubious, but so are the views of the sceptics who dismiss it as an irrelevancy'. Of course, I never gave a second thought to joining it at the time and neither did most social workers of my immediate acquaintance. For me, the only game in town was statutory local authority social work and that meant joining the public sector unions. I had no illusions that NALGO was anything other than a collective defensive organisation for its members and for the public services as a whole. My work identity in the 1980s was not simply that of being a professional social worker but of something wider, a welfare professional or welfare worker employed in and by the welfare state – meaning health and local Government services such as education but linked with the police, fire-service, public transport and housing through an ethic of public service and localised democratic control. The national conferences I attended in the mid-'80s and also the monthly Saturday Scottish District Meetings in the Mitchell Library in Glasgow were therefore on behalf of NALGO rather than BASW. I think now, however, that the new generation should think more seriously about bringing both these organisations much closer together. No other collective is protecting their interests as a group or as individual workers, including the regulatory body, the Scottish Social Services Council (SSSC), which seems as protective towards professional social workers as Robert Maxwell was of his employees' pension fund. I note, too, that since 2012, BASW has had on its board Maggie Mellon, a feminist and social work activist of redoubtable repute with Children First and an old Regent Roader as well, if I recall right.

Back in Craigmillar, Old Peggy retired about the same time as Danny left. He would be replaced by David Cumming, a dapper, boyish-looking young man from Motherwell who, coming from Strathclyde, appreciated the kind of work we were faced with in the area. David was unfussy and suitably under-reactive (meaning not over-reactive) in the way that Danny had been, which enabled the Seniors and workers to get on with the job, prioritising who needed our scarce services the most. I could sense him looking at me and perhaps wondering why I had not gone for the Area Officer's job myself. I was not opposed to becoming a frontline manager but I knew I was primarily interested in children and families work and I still enjoyed the buzz of the Intake Team.

I liked David's affability though, leavened with management phrases like 'rainbow-to-rainbow', meaning people at the same level should communicate with each other directly rather than pushing things up to the next management level, a principle I still endorse. The only problem I had with David's management style, certainly compared to Danny's, was that his door, like his phone, seemed permanently open, so that discussions you were having were constantly interrupted by other matters. David seemed quite oblivious to this and, while Danny saw Craigmillar as a merry-go-round that revolved with him on board, I used to think that it must have resembled more of a kaleidoscope to David, the workplace unfolding frame by frame with no settled image ever fully forming before being dissolved into the next one. But I found David a supportive manager nonetheless, sympathetic to the difficulties of the work and he would later team up with Alistair Gaw and Angus Skinner in the new Care Inspectorate established in the early 2000s. He wrote me a cracking reference for the next job I applied for in March 1984, as NAI Coordinator at Shrubhill.

After four demanding and rumbustious years in Craigmillar, I was now looking forward to a new professional challenge that did not involve either going up into management or out into training. David's reference was comprehensive and informative – unlike most modern ones – and most of it was true, another novel feature of those now distant days. It ranged across my sound grasp of procedural links with a number of agencies which facilitated inter-agency working and threw in at the end that I had managed to combine two onerous tasks, shop stewards convener and Intake Senior, efficiently with no detriment to the service delivered or the support given to my staff before ending that 'it illustrates Alistair's ability to separate potentially competing interests while still maintaining as a priority direct services to members of the public'. He also added:

> In the course of this work Alistair first became aware of certain deficiencies in the present system of registration, and in conjunction with the previous Area Officer, an approach was made to the Area Review Committee by Mr Martin Manby (Assistant Director): it was possible to undertake a review of previous children living in the Craigmillar area. You will be aware that subsequently a wider culling was performed, resulting in a more accurate and up to date Register...particularly in the area of child abuse, [he] recognises that many of the difficulties in this acknowledgeably complicated area, stem from a lack of understanding of inter-agency practice. In terms of his ability to act effectively as a consultant to practitioners, one of his main assets is that in an area which inevitably generates much anxiety, he is able to respond calmly and thoughtfully which thus enables fieldwork colleagues both in residential and day care social work, Education, Health, etc to work jointly to an agreed plan.

I had forgotten I had done so much of that preparatory work with Martin Manby as regards the need to cull and computerise the At Risk Register, which would become my main focus for the first year or so in the Regional Coordinator's post. The Card-Index Register comprised a small box of hand-written cards kept on Martin's secretary's desk at Shrubhill. She answered phone queries during office hours from social workers and other designated agencies as to whether specific children were known to the Register. This task fell to the Emergency Duty Team outwith office hours which enlarged the chances of even more admin cock-ups. There was no proper registration form or review mechanism in place compared to the system in operation in Central Region even in 1975. I thus found that children's names had been placed on the Register simply from phone enquiries being made by GPs and beat police as to whether a child was on or not which were not followed up and so removed afterwards. This survey of the Register therefore led to the creation of the post I was now offered, jointly funded by social work and health. I was interviewed for the post by Les McEwan, recently made Big

Roger's Deputy, and the very positive Dr Helen Zealley, Director of Public Health for NHS Lothian. No one mentioned anything about 'used cars' and I got the job, for about three years – or so I was thinking in my own head. It would, in fact, turn into seven.

I no doubt received the same kind of treatment I had happily handed out to Danny when he departed from Craigmillar but fortunately I have no papers to consult. I do however have the mock SER I wrote for Big Charlie when he left the team around the same time, snippets from which may convey something of their spoof mickey-taking nature. The general rule of thumb in these things, however, was that the more popular the person departing, the more insulting their 'report' should be (at least that's what I told Big Charlie). Snippets from it include:

Birth: On the day he was born, Charles had a normal delivery – eight pints of milk, a carton of yogurt, two half-loafs and a six-pack of Les McEwans Lager. He was immediately placed in an incubator to prevent him from drinking all the other bairns' milk...

Attitude to Offence: Charles is somewhat aggrieved at the attitude of the Court but is confident it will not be repeated since he is leaving Craigmillar and will no longer be under the peer-group pressure of another well-known delinquent, Jimmy Johnstone.

Significant Others: Charles trained at Moray House and came under the spiritual guidance of one Dougie Carnegie who told him on their first meeting – 'you'll never meet a harder bastard than me!' – at which Charles burst into tears. He then developed an interest in Mental Health, mainly his own...

Things he says he learned from his Colleagues: Donna – patience; Mary – 7-card brag; Margaret – to keep his hands to himself; John H – thrift; Betty – a trouble shared is a trouble multiplied; Ian S – more thrift; Irene – more trouble; Bert B – 'Take No Prisoners!'; David – how to play the daft laddie; Mary O – how not to play the daft laddie; Danny D – obedience; Don MacFrenzie – everything; Mike M – nothing; Jimmy J – 'dignity, always dignity'; Home Care –'Take No Prisoners!'; Alistair – democratic management in theory; Big Evelyn – how to swear without really trying; Bebe – Dialectical Materialism; Penny– 'It's in the memo!'

And so, in a similar cloud of good humour and communal derision, I too left Craigmillar for Shrubhill, Social Work HQ, the bosses hang-out, situated halfway down Leith Walk and a new challenge. It was a new post, one involving no increase in salary but offering a great opportunity to develop the Child Protection Register system as a practice tool fit to meet the basic demands of frontline work. I also thought this should be done by someone with as much current fieldwork experience of child protection as I had accrued in Craigmillar – the kind of place where child protection was needed most and where it needed to function well, day in and day out and, above all, on an inter-agency basis.

10

Shrubhill: Hanging with the Bosses

I don't think wearing a kilt protects a baby much, do you?
Roger Kent, Lothian Social Work Director, 1988

The author discovers that social work bosses are human, mostly, and professionally committed. He offers some observations on the Directors, Roger Kent, John Chant and Les McEwan while computerising the Child Protection Register, writing practice guidelines and booklets on sexual and emotional abuse and organising inter-agency training in the wake of the Cleveland Inquiry (1987). He comments on the Orkney Inquiry (1991) and plays a lot of five-a-side football in Leith to compensate for the Communist Party disbanding itself and merging with Hibernian FC Supporters' Club in 1990.

I WAS GIVEN a long thin room at one end of the fourth floor of Shrubhill on which all the bosses and their Admin were located and which overlooked Leith Walk. There was a large garage in the forecourt below us with several petrol pumps which, had there ever been a mishap, would have incinerated well over 100 social work staff. No one gave it the least thought. At the other end of the corridor was a large square room where Roger Kent, the Director, held court. We sometimes passed each other in the corridor and nodded warily. During the Cleveland events of 1988, he paused one day and asked if I thought it could happen in Lothian. I said the chances were very much reduced because of the higher level of inter-agency working that we were developing and the role of the Reporter-Hearing system in Scotland, to which he listened closely like the old Children's Officer he was, before opining, 'Yes, but I don't think wearing a kilt protects a baby much, do you?' and continued on his singular way. A former naval officer, he was a commanding figure whose presence seemed to loom over meetings even when sitting down, never mind striding along the top corridor of Shrubhill. We certainly never discussed his court appearance or that blacked Craigmillar Social Enquiry Report or, indeed, the current state of adoption in Doncaster.

My direct line-manager was the Assistant Director Fieldwork, Audrey Lowe, who had been in charge of residential care prior to Martin Manby leaving. She was supportive without having much direct experience of child protection work in the community and so, for the first year or so, I reported to Les McEwan, Chair of the Area Review Committee. Iain Paterson would take over from Audrey and also become Chair of the Review Committee in due course. My initial task was to computerise the At-Risk Register. I met with a very young-looking, blond, curly-haired IT programmer – Richard? We stared at each other over what seemed to me a small TV screen, a monitor which sat on top of a rectangular box. He said, 'What do you want it to do?' and I said, 'What can it do?' and he said, 'Anything you tell it to do,' and I said, 'What can it do?' and he said, 'What do you want it to do?'

I think it was called an Amstrad and Richard said it did not like coffee or tea to be drunk or spilled in its vicinity. He handed me a wafer-thin 5x4 inch black floppy-disc, which looked like a square envelope for a birthday card. It was like Cortez showing the King of the Incas a cuckoo-clock. He told me that the Register information is stored in the rectangular box and can be transferred in a highly compressed form onto the floppy-disc every evening 'just in case'.

'Just in case what?'

'All the information gets lost or scrambled,' he said, 'so then you have the floppy disc to restore the information.'

He also tried to explain how to manipulate the statistical info using programming language. He said to forget all the science-fiction stuff about computers out-thinking human beings because the IT programmer's motto is 'spam in, spam out'. The personal computer or PC is not 'smart' just 'very thick'. It just does what you tell it to do, nothing more, nothing less, including incorporating any errors you may have told it to make by mistake. In other words, it was an annoying wee bastard and I was the only person in Lothian Social Work Department who had so far been given one to play with.

By this means, we began to obtain an accurate idea of how many New Enquiries were being made annually, by which agencies and how many proceeded to case-conference and with what result – cancellation of the Enquiry or Registration. We gathered data on Registered cases as to the primary type of abuse (because the same child can experience several forms of abuse) – physical injury, physical neglect, sexual abuse and so on. We also knew which agencies were attending, or not attending, different case conferences. I recollect that GPs, for example, would attend New Case Conferences when concern was at its highest but very rarely Deregistration Conferences, perhaps sending a letter or a report. Indeed, social workers often had difficulty getting even one or two other agencies to meet in order to deregister a case, as the procedures now formally required of them.

What did surprise me, and still amuses me in a way, is that in the seven years or so I spent coordinating the Register, there was not one single enquiry made to it about a child who happened to be on the Register. The original purpose of Registers following the Maria Colwell Inquiry was touted as being one where a lone professional might come across a concerning situation and so check to see if that child was on the Register. Of course, in practice, children already on the Register were likely to be known to all the local agencies anyway and these may have been noted on internal agency files, including police files. During investigations, of course, it was as important to know that children were not on the Register as to know that they were. In that sense, checking the Register was simply the first step in the process of investigation, for the whole point of the Register system was to ensure that key local agencies collaborated professionally with each other about a particular child in order to agree a plan that might reduce the need for registration.

My recollection is that we transferred about 150 cases from the old hand-written At-Risk Index Cards system to the new computerised Register, which increased over the next couple of years to about 250–400 cases for Lothian as a whole. The bulk of these cases were for physical injury and neglect, with only a handful of sexual abuse cases and no emotional abuse cases because emotional abuse was not seen as a separate category at that stage. The design of the At-Risk Registers until 1985 related to a single circular issued in 1975 by the Scottish Office (SWSG) – SW1/75. It did not specify the 'content' or 'form' that registration should take, other than that a child should be placed on the Register, reviewed and deregistered via an inter-agency meeting of local practitioners and reviewed at least annually. This reflected the state of knowledge at the time about abuse that focused primarily on the risk of physical harm and neglect to very young children, which relied on the capacity of medics to diagnose it as parental over-chastisement. In 1987, Cleveland would confirm just how limited that idea of abuse was and its reliance on medical evidence alone, since the discovery of child sexual abuse added a further layer of complexity to what was already a demanding area of professional intervention. Ironically, child sexual abuse and the moral panic that ensued propelled agencies like the police and education to become with social workers and health workers more 'equal partners' in the inter-agency identification and management of child abuse. This was what SWSG circulars had been stressing with little effect since the Maria Colwell Inquiry in 1975.

I produced a summary of the impact which the Cleveland (1988) and Orkney (1991) Inquiry Reports had had on the general field of child protection in an essay I wrote in March 1993 for a Child Protection course run by the University of Dundee and which was undertaken by all of West Lothian's children and family social workers and their frontline managers during the course of the 1990s. Nothing has changed that much:

Child protection seems to me a subject which has been pulled from the surgery where it was 'diagnosed' over 20 years ago and set within a multidisciplinary framework, then placed on the front pages of the tabloids for the alleged moral and political edification of politicians, pundits and punters alike. This has resulted in the front page becoming rather like the back page of these same newspapers, where they discuss the football results, and where everyone feels well qualified to express deeply held, although usually deeply partisan views, about children or football, until the former become virtually indistinguishable from the latter. At this point, social workers are often seen 'holding the ring', when not thrown bodily into it, between a confused and morally outraged public opinion and the individual children and parents involved – who are frequently pathetic and engulfed in human stress, pain and misery. The very neutrality of the profession may then be construed as condoning, perhaps even creating or not preventing, some specific child abuse event. One of the hard lessons of the Orkney Inquiry is how, when the subject itself has become so political, senior managers require to operate both professionally *and politically*. Orkney and Cleveland, in my view, were partly the result of a confluence of naïve social work managers and professionals who did not perceive the limits of their own power and knowledge bases or the hostility of the political environment within which child protection has to operate, certainly in respect of child sexual abuse. It is interesting how, when a member of the medical profession commits an error leading to a tragedy, it is dealt with as an individual failure but a similar incident somehow becomes the litmus for the failure of the whole of the social work profession. This should alert us to the real exercise of professional authority and power in society – who has it, who does not, and why?

In April 1987, in the midst of the events at Cleveland and four years before the Orkney Inquiry, I produced a 43-page Practice Paper on Child Sexual Abuse for Lothian Region, coloured yellow. It drew on talks given by around ten specialists in the social work, psychiatric, psychological, legal and academic fields dealing with children and abusers. I quoted some statistics with regard to Lothian showing that there had been a doubling of cases of child sexual abuse placed on the Register over a nine-month period, 35 cases in May 1986 rising to 70 cases in January 1987. By September 1989, this had risen to 86 cases of sexual abuse out of a total of 400 cases on the Register – of which 37 per cent (145) were for Physical Injury, 21 per cent (86) for Sexual Abuse and same for Emotional Abuse, 18 per cent (72) for Physical Neglect, and 3 per cent (11) Other. For the Register as a whole, only 30 per cent of cases could be classified as 'certain', meaning based on an admission or a court finding, which means 70 per cent were not. This snapshot underlines the general complexity of investigating, establishing, managing and even classifying child abuse, particularly child sexual abuse. This was and remains the great unspoken reality of child protection and assessment work and it is high time that whoever claims to be in charge of social work these days should make far more effort to explain that to politicians, press, public, parents and poetasters – as well as to professionals themselves. Professional complexity and legal uncertainty characterise all child protection work which staff are expected to undertake day in, day out, all the while hallooed by a hyena press-pack. The Inquiry Reports rarely help, mostly used as press fodder to second-guess already known outcomes in that familiar, retrospectively 20:20 vision way.

Being located in Shrubhill amongst senior managers enabled me to observe some of them at close quarters, sometimes beyond the scope of my own remit. My boss, Iain Paterson, was a tall, slim, rather taciturn man with a background in mental health. Iain tended to say little and think a lot. It is a wonder to me that he had time to say anything at all. He had a long table in his large office on which were laid columns of papers each a foot to 18 inches high, numbering 20–30 piles. These were his correspondence and reports concerning the main fieldwork matters of the day. In conversation, Iain rarely shared his own mind except through questioning and listening intently to what was said. The draft reports and circulars I prepared for the Committee or to go out in his name were subtly corrected for spelling or grammatical errors in a manner worthy of the old Latinist I suspected Iain was, all without comment on both sides. I occasionally ended sentences with a preposition, as one does in conversation, to reduce the formality of some of these texts but Iain was invariably formally correct.

Neither was he an alarmist or scaredy-cat. I was attending a field management meeting on one occasion, waiting my slot on the agenda with most of the Area Officers present, when the door bursts open and in storms Les McEwan, the Deputy Director, without knocking. He shouted across at Iain that he had just been phoned by a unit and the heating was not working and he needed to get it sorted straight away, then turned on his heel and burst back out again. In the stunned silence that followed, Iain was heard to remark, as if to himself, 'What does he expect me to do, go out and fix it myself?' but I also noted he remained seated throughout the rest of the lengthy meeting. As this incident may show, Iain rarely reacted to stuff or made long-winded statements of principle, though I do remember him remarking (possibly about some current bolshie residential social workers), 'If they are so dissatisfied with the Authority then why don't they just put up a nameplate outside their own doors?' It was probably the longest sentence I ever heard him say.

My Regional remit brought me into contact with Area Officers and Divisional managers across the board and I began to gain impressions of the various regimes they had each installed in their own domains. Edinburgh City had three divisions run by Anne Black, Gus and Malcolm McCallum, all of which were urban, busy, laid-back and collaborative. West Lothian had a rural mix of old industrial villages, small towns and Livingston New Town that was temperately managed by Mike Cairns and then Danny. East and Mid Lothian had similar demographics to West Lothian but seemed to me to be run more top-down and fussily by their veteran manager. I deduced this when he phoned me blazing-mad after I had met some Seniors in the Musselburgh office without going through him first. The meeting had been at their request and to get sex abuse training set up more quickly in their locality. Shades of Central Region and Little Sport and the Etiquette Syndrome floated back as I listened to him but I was sweetness itself. Nobody knew exactly what my job was but I reported directly to this Divisional Director's boss, Iain Paterson, so I was an irritant that could not be ignored entirely. I told him I was tasked to roll out Region-wide programmes and inter-agency training workshops on sex abuse with specialist speakers organised centrally through myself and Training and which had to be delivered to local workers in local settings in conjunction with local Teams. I could almost hear the death-rattle at the other end of the phone, the unthinkable, an initiative that crossed not only inter-professional boundaries but managerial ones. The Horror! And in Musselburgh!

I was sometimes requested by Area Officers for Register stats for their own and other areas. This would have been both time-consuming and statistically questionable given the small number of cases held at area and divisional levels. These figures would also no doubt have been cited in some cases to argue for more staffing, which would have altered their primary purpose, possibly creating a league table mentality which might then have led to lower-risk cases being placed on the Register. Why risk turning the Register from its primary task of managing the riskiest child protection cases on an inter-agency basis at local level? I thought it important to have the basic information Registers can provide, like the numbers, ages and gender of children placed on them, the categories of abuse and the relationship of abusers to the abused. I have already mentioned that the 'level of certainty' criteria – and the category of 'professional opinion' (the collective view of the inter-agency case conference) – would become even more prominent after the Cleveland and Orkney Inquiries for all cases and not just child sexual abuse.

Indeed, professional judgement had always been stressed in Lothian's guidelines as a cornerstone of investigation and intervention but Registration itself gave agencies no legal powers to intervene in family situations over and above what agencies like social work, health, police and education already possessed under their own legal powers. This was a common misunderstanding in case conference situations with agencies other than social work, who thought the conference could act on the basis of shared concerns when there were insufficient legal grounds to do so. This likewise bedevils sensational media reporting of major child death tragedies which rotate round an often astonished and plaintive public outcry that 'somebody should have done something'. To this, one can only reply, 'On what legal grounds?' Register statistics can tell you nothing of this.

The Director Roger Kent retired in 1989 but continued his work for AIDS victims begun by the Waverley Trust during his time as Lothian Region's Director. I attended his retiral in the conference room of Shrubhill where he was seen off by Senior councillors and figures like Alan Finlayson, the Regional Reporter, who caught Roger perfectly when he said that, when they first met a decade or so earlier, he had a terrible time explaining to Roger that he was not a member of his staff and that he had had the same difficulty ever since. Roger's obituary was written by Nicola Barry in *The Herald* which reported his death in Borders General Hospital on 22 March 2013. It details why he was held in such high esteem by most of the people he met and worked with before and after his time with Lothian Region:

Thousands of people can be grateful that a 12-hour drinking binge with Errol Flynn changed Roger Kent's life – and theirs – for the better. Kent, who died on March 22, aged 81, was one of Scotland's most vociferous advocates of social work. In his 20s, as a gunnery expert in the Royal Navy, he was, memorably, posted missing from his duties at the Royal Tournament in London's Earl's Court, after going on a gigantic bender with the Hollywood hell-raiser. Roger had just completed a year-long gunnery course and, being the era of Burgess and MacLean, hackles understandably rose. Charged with 'improperly absent', the tabloids went on to have a field day in the wake of the ensuing court martial, with his gunnery connection reflected in lurid headlines such as: 'Navy missile man vanishes', while others made do with, 'Champagne sailor sentenced'. The poor soul was bitterly ashamed of this unfortunate blemish on his CV and saw his later move to social work as a form of rehabilitation. He used to say he spent his years trying to make amends. Truth to tell, nothing gave him greater pleasure than the respect of his naval colleagues for whom he organised reunions and even continued to distribute a newsletter.

An extraordinary former Director of Social Work for Lothian, Roger Kent was born in 1931, into the Navy tradition. His father, Teddy, joined the Navy as a boy seaman, becoming Captain of the Victory in Portsmouth Dockyard. He died at sea while in command of a new minesweeper. His mother, Lucy, the daughter of a police inspector, died soon after her husband and seven-year-old Roger was an orphan. He never forgot the day he was handed over to his adoptive parents at London's Paddington Station. At his first meeting, his new mother asked him to call her 'mother' rather than 'mummy', he repaid her by calling her 'Mrs Kent'; yet, he always insisted they made wonderful parents, if strict. Many would say being adopted gave him the insight he put to such good use in social work. At 13, Roger joined the Royal Navy, starting at the Royal Naval College in Dartmouth. He then served as a midshipman in the West Indies, in the frigate Carisbrooke Castle as a Sub Lieutenant then as a Lieutenant in the destroyer Duchess, the frigate *Whitby* and in motor torpedo boats. Just 25 when the furore erupted over his Errol Flynn champagne antics, Roger always acknowledged that the Navy was extremely forgiving, allowing him to train young officers and seamen before going back to sea for two years in HMS *Whitby*. Highly regarded wherever he went, Roger's request to resign from the Navy in 1969 was not initially accepted. He took voluntary retirement at 30, studied at Durham University and earned a postgraduate diploma without a basic degree.

Then he fell into the arms of social work. Roger's rise through the ranks was meteoric. Rapidly promoted to Director of Social Services in the newly created Metropolitan Borough of Doncaster in 1975, he accepted the same post in Edinburgh five years later, where he proved an extremely popular and able leader of 8,000 staff. Roger felt his main achievement was managing to work with two separate budgets throughout the 1980s following mid-term rate-capping and keeping up morale during a time of serious financial restrictions. Roger could be scornful of certain schools of social work philosophy; reluctant at times to accept advanced thinking. He firmly believed that social work was on the periphery of everything but at the centre of nothing. He was wryly funny and loathed political correctness – once saying the PC Lobby had become so extreme that we would soon be referring to the dead as 'people with breathing difficulties'. Known for his rapid-fire delivery and obsession with statistics, journalists rarely interviewed him without a tape recorder in order to catch his mutterings about whole-time-equivalent home-helps.

Roger was also a cricket nut. As social work director, he was known for occasionally cutting short meetings in order to catch the latest Test score. In the final analysis, Roger was sometimes thought to be rather reserved. In spite of the respect he inspired in adults – whether at work or in his home life – he claimed he felt more comfortable with children and adolescents, never afraid to engage with them at their own level. In fact, Scotland's legendary social work director could be downright anti-social at times. Even with Parkinson's Disease, cancer, only one leg and a pacemaker, he was known to whizz through supermarkets in his wheelchair, in a somewhat ungainly manner. Roger was fond of saying he didn't grow up until he was 30. There are those of us who say he never quite managed it.

I don't know about you, but that image of Big Roger speeding through a supermarket in his wheelchair (skateboard?), a danger to himself and others, says something also about the helter-skelter turbulence that marked the 1980s decade and the social work generation of which I felt most part. The personalities of senior managers in social work matter at least as much as they do in frontline practice, perhaps even more so, certainly as regards the survival of social work as a meaningful profession working primarily with the poorest and most vulnerable groups in society.

This was very evident in Strathclyde and Lothian during the 1980s when the state, local and national, massively collided. Social policy is perceived by cultural historians as a contested space and the 1984–5 miners' strike was a particularly vivid example of this played out nightly on television screens across the country but which also impacted off-camera in places like Craigmillar.

I recall, for example, that Child Protection investigations were left in abeyance for months on end while police-leave in Lothian and the Borders was cancelled and CID officers put on uniforms to face picket-lines gathered round pits and power-stations all across central Scotland. Roger Kent in Lothian and Fred Edwards in Strathclyde would throughout that decade show their mettle at the height of Thatcher's attack on the welfare state, facing down the Government and Scottish Office in their duty to uphold basic social services. Fred Edwards famously told the Scottish Secretary, as he also enacted through Strathclyde Regional Council, that his staff were authorised to pay out Section 12 grants to the families of striking miners under statute. So, too, did Lothian and most other Scottish Regions affected by the strike, including Fife and Central. Social work, because of its statutory powers and responsibilities under the law, entered a political battle simply by being there and interpreting statute. I have no doubt it was this realisation amongst Tory and New Labour Governments that led to the diminution of the Director of Social Work role to that of Chief Social Work Officer in the move to District Councils in 1997 so making them accountable to corporate management bean-counters – about which I shall no doubt wax lyrical in due course.

In 1989, Lothian Region was fortunate to appoint another Director of similar stamp to Roger Kent in the shape of John Chant. He, too, was English and had also lost his parents at a young age. Big Roger was adopted and John would enter local authority care aged ten in his native Somerset. He was first apprenticed to a Wiltshire farmer then entered psychiatric nursing at Tone Vale Hospital, Taunton. He studied at Bristol Polytechnic and The University of Edinburgh, becoming a mental health officer for Bridgewater and then a social worker for Taunton. One of his strengths was cited as a capacity to view situations from the bottom up as well as the top down. He was appointed Director of Social Services in Taunton in 1974 and became a member of the Darryn Clarke Inquiry in Liverpool in 1979. As Secretary of the Association of Directors of Social Services in 1981 he came into contact with Senior officials in the DHSS, the English equivalent of the SWSG in the Scottish Office. In 1989, after 15 years as Director of Somerset, he came to Lothian fresh from Lord Butler-Sloss' Cleveland Inquiry into child sexual abuse. The Report contained many of his contributions both in its drafting and conclusions, which stressed that social work assessment is as vital as medical examination in these cases. Knowing Edinburgh since his student days, he would serve on National Task Forces examining some of the contemporary problems besetting it, such as HIV/AIDS in 1991 and drug abuse in 1994.

I had little immediate contact with John Chant in his first year at Shrubhill. As his early history might have predicted, he looked like a large congenial Somerset farmer, bluff and shrewd. I heard about him mostly from an impressed Danny, particularly after he became West Lothian's Divisional Director in 1990. Danny found him open and fair, always available for comment and advice but with a sting in the tail. He remembered being late for a lunchtime meeting at Shrubhill, called at short-notice, along with another outlying Divisional Director. Chant took them both aside at the tea break and said he wanted their advice: he had these two neighbours, one on either side whom he'd invited for dinner but neither had appeared. What should he do, cut them off? Danny immediately said, 'No, talk to them John', and Chant said, 'That's what I'm doing. Where the fuck were you?' There were no recriminations, support and good humour being more in John Chant's style, combined with an alert mind and reflective disposition.

As Child Protection Coordinator, I would have several conversations with him over the events in Orkney which began in November 1990 based on allegations of sexual abuse made by a child in the W family, whose seven younger siblings were removed to the mainland under Place of Safety Orders. They were interviewed by staff employed by RSSPCC and the Northern Constabulary in early February 1991, one of them a former experienced mental health professional in Lothian, a specialist who contributed to the sex abuse workshops I had organised a few years earlier. Three of the W family children made allegations that were interpreted as organised sexual abuse involving the parents and children of other families on Orkney, including the local minister. This was headlined in the media as 'Ritual Abuse' and led to the removal of another nine children from other incomer families. Such numbers for a small Island authority required police and social workers to be drafted in from Strathclyde and Central Regions, following a request faxed to them on 14 February 1991.

On 27 February, the children were removed from their homes on the island of South Ronaldsay by social workers and police in what was dubbed a commando-like 'dawn raid', legal authority for which was given by Scotland's most senior Sheriff. Following a local community meeting, some parents organised a support group Parents Against Injustice (PAIN) which invited further intense media comment. These children all denied any abuse had occurred and medical examinations revealed no evidence of abuse either. In most other local authorities in Scotland at the time, this is probably where the matter would have ended, the children returned home and schools, nurseries and the social work department left with low-key watching briefs in case any of the children later disclosed information on which to act. But this did not happen in Orkney.

In April 1991, after a single day, the presiding Sheriff, David Kelbie, dismissed the case and the children were allowed to return home. He criticised proceedings as 'so fatally flawed as to be incompetent', the repeated interviewing of children making their evidence unreliable and amounting to 'repeated coaching'. The Reporter appealed against the dismissal of the case to the Court of Session in June 1991, which upheld the appeal and criticised Sheriff Kelbie's handling of the case. The Reporter then abandoned the case given that the surrounding publicity had severely compromised any further proceedings. As a coda, it was later reported that objects seized from homes during the raid and later returned included: a videotape of the TV show *Blackadder*; a detective novel by Ngaio Marsh; a model aeroplane made by one of the children from two pieces of wood, which was identified by social workers as a 'wooden cross'. The minister was asked to sign for the return of 'three masks, two hoods, one black cloak', but refused to sign until the inventory was altered to read 'three nativity masks, two academic hoods, one priest's robe'.

An official Inquiry was established under Lord Clyde in August 1991 and the Report was published in October 1992, the social work assessor being Anne Black, a Divisional Director seconded by Lothian Region. With 194 Recommendations, the Report criticised everybody – social workers, police, the Orkney Island Council and the appeal against Sheriff Kelbie. Social workers' training, the methods they adopted and the judgements applied were particularly condemned as was the concept of ritual abuse, not only as unwarrantable but because it affected the objectivity of practitioners and parents. The interviewing team was slated for cross-examining children and being 'fixated on finding satanic abuse' and for using the interviewing techniques condemned by Sheriff Kelbie.

As for myself, I was horrified as the story unfolded in the newspapers, a car crash in slow-motion. I had spent the last five years of my professional life getting to grips with the complexities of investigating child sexual abuse exposed publicly by Cleveland and had blithely assumed that other authorities were doing much the same, trying to alert and prepare their frontline staff. Now the smallest authority in Britain along with the largest in Europe combined to over-react in the same ill-informed and imperious manner that had led to Cleveland. I was appalled if not entirely surprised both by the naivity and inexperience displayed by Orkney social work department and the gung-ho involvement of Strathclyde staff and local police who seemed to treat this isolated island community – which was, in fact, a complex mix of natives and incomers – rather like a drinking-den in Sauchiehall Street, breaking down doors in search of illicit booze. This was bad enough, only to have been followed by the ineptitude of the RSSPCC interviewing team, so-called experts, overly reliant on American literature then circulating allegations of ritual and satanic abuse fanned by evangelical groups in the USA – which were supported in the UK by the Evangelical Alliance and the NSPCC (Waterhouse et al., *The Independent on Sunday*, 19 March, 1990). Indeed, I later learned from contacts within the counselling community in Edinburgh that there were cases coming to light around this time of some women who claimed to have been subjected to abuse by white witches and covens. Of course, they were adults and, in a therapeutic environment, such matters cannot be dismissed out of hand but rather explored carefully through private counseling.

In Orkney, the children explicitly denied what another child had alleged under heavy questioning but had then immediately retracted, calling it a lie. Aggressive and untried repeated interviewing techniques were applied to children recently admitted to care and separated unwillingly from their families, which alone made them 'vulnerable witnesses'. RSSPCC interviewers seemed bent on a simple-minded quest to unearth 'the truth' behind 'the denial', whatever the emotional cost to the children themselves. In 2006, the Lothian-based specialist repeated her claim in a BBC2 documentary, *Accused*, that a child's denial should not be taken as proof that abuse did not take place:

> As long as it's a secret, denial will come. And the denials come for the same reason that the secrecy is there. They're keeping something safe.

It does not appear to have occurred to her or her colleagues that the something these children were perhaps trying to keep safe was themselves, their own emotional safety, which is their human right, and that this ought to be understood and respected by professionals. Indeed, she made much the same assertion at the Lothian workshops I ran a few years earlier. In the introduction to the Sex Abuse Practice Paper I edited, I quoted a similar remark she made that children who are disbelieved within an abusing family should be considered 'emotionally orphaned'. It is difficult not to conclude that this is exactly how these children felt when being on the receiving end of non-child-centred questioning. What should have happened?

In the same Practice Paper, Dr Vivek Kusumakar, an accomplished child psychiatrist, stressed that what most abused children want is for the abuse to stop, for themselves not to be taken away, the abuser imprisoned or the family broken up. This may not always be possible but investigations must still be handled sensitively, with the child's feelings and interests kept very firmly in the centre, a space being created around the child by all the professionals involved that allows whatever work is possible with that child to occur in a safe and supportive manner. He also stressed, vitally, that the secrecy inherent in child sexual abuse also

> means in practice the workers dealing with their own rescue fantasies, anger, despair and uncertainty. There is no standard model for helping such children and families but a team approach appears to be essential.

The events in Orkney contradicted all of that clinical expertise four years later and it staggered and angered me at the time. In reminding myself of the details surrounding Orkney, I came upon an article published by *The Therapeutic Care Journal* dated 1 August 2011, which seems to me to sum up many of the key themes of child protection intervention which still apply today – just as they should have back then. It mentions an evening prior to removing the children from their homes, during which a pair of mainland social workers raised doubts about discrepancies in the information given to them and were unhappy about the methodology and grounds for the operation, especially regarding the police role. After confronting Paul Lee, the Orkney Senior Susan Miller and staff from RSSPCC, these social workers only agreed to participate after a phone call with a senior member of their own department on the grounds that it would be less damaging for the children for them to participate than to pull out at that stage. This is what I would call the proper exercise of professional judgement and, without it, social work would be as well packing up and vacating the welfare field to the more rule-bound remits of the police, prison governors and social security officials.

For professional discretion is what all laws pertaining to children and vulnerable people presume and without which social work intervention risks descending into reactive responses rather than professionally informed case management with all that that implies. Social work is a professional space, located within public policy, precisely because more authoritarian approaches have been repeatedly shown not to work even as regards those people that the police and penal agencies spend most of their time and resources trying to detain and prosecute. Social workers occupy that space in which the law and social reality places them because nothing else has worked better or, indeed, at all. Such a complex and strenuous role requires professional social workers and frontline managers able and empowered by senior management to confront the complexities of such work, not shrink from it harried by a bunch of right-wing commentators and populist politicians.

My conversations with John Chant at the height of the media frenzy focused initially on the total silence emanating from the recently appointed Director of Social Work for Orkney, Paul Lee, whom John had been phoning to offer advice and support not only from himself but on behalf of the Association of Directors of Social Work. Instead Lee remained close-lipped to all suggestions that other Directors could come forward in the media to address the general complexity and delicacy of such investigations. This was especially needed given the full glare of public scrutiny and the one-sided narrative being broadcast daily by PAIN that was also roundly criticised in the Inquiry Report. I think Paul Lee was English-trained though he later became a district manager for Grampian Region for several years. I remember thinking at the time that he was supervising fewer social workers in Orkney than I had in Craigmillar but that Orkney had needed someone absolutely steeped in frontline management because there were no intervening management layers as was the case in all other Scottish authorities, except Shetland. BASW would fund Mr Lee's case to the tune of £1,000,000.

My main criticism of the whole sorry saga is the lack of humility shown by all of the parties to the affair – not only the professionals caught up in it but also the Parents Support Group, the media and the public – as to their own ignorance of child sexual abuse: its existence, its ubiquity, its difficulty to detect or prove in court. I particularly remember a Tom Morton, who may have been the radio disc jockey, loudly castigating the Hearing system by continuously demanding that criminal levels of proof, which are applied in adult courts ('beyond reasonable doubt') should be applied to children rather than the civil level of proof ('the balance of probabilities') which applies to the Reporter and Hearing system. This failure to even contemplate that the authorities had a clear duty to investigate such allegations was in itself a kind of denial, a level of disbelief surrounding child sexual abuse that was common amongst the public and other professionals like teachers during the period. It would take the historical unearthing of Jimmy Savile to blow apart that kind of innocence, that kind of naivety and that kind of unexamined level of public trust.

* * *

The structure of child protection work in Lothian encouraged a broader, more inclusive inter-disciplinary approach to child protection than Strathclyde. Throughout the 1980s there were distinct differences between the devolved multi-agency approach to child protection in Lothian compared to the top-down structure operating there. Social work in Strathclyde controlled not only the machinery of the case-conference and Register system but who actually got placed on the Register. In Strathclyde, case-conferences were chaired by Divisional managers at least two grades above the Senior social workers who chaired the case conferences in Lothian. These managers were able to Register or not Register children against the wishes of the other agencies present at the case conferences. The rational for this was that as the de facto lead agency in most child protection investigations, the social work department should have the lead say-so. Lothian saw this responsibility as shared between different agencies, even though social work undoubtedly had the lion's share of investigative and supervisory responsibilities in cases on and those not yet on, the Register. However, other agencies were constantly encouraged to honour their own responsibilities for monitoring and engaging with vulnerable children and their families as part of joint case-plans. If this sharing was often a kind of fiction at one level, it was a useful one through which a clearer understanding of each agency's remits and responsibilities in specific cases was created. Joint say-so may well have increased friction between social work and other agencies, but it also increased clarity, especially when child sexual abuse arrived on the scene. But a more inclusive approach widened inter-professional ownership of child protection matters far beyond the single-agency powers of social work acting or operating alone across what is a huge range of cases and diverse risk-situations.

My opposite number in Strathclyde, Phil Green, was amongst those dispatched to assist with the removal of the children from Orkney. I had come across Phil a couple of years earlier at a large conference in Edinburgh, organised I think by swsg, which included a distinguished cast of speakers, including Alan Finlayson, a Senior Sheriff and a speaker from one of the Scandinavian countries who mentioned that his country had a 'mandatory reporting system'. This meant that health professionals and teachers and the like were legally obliged to report any concerns they had about child abuse to social work and the police, basically overriding the claims that an older generation of doctors clung to in the uk about not compromising their doctor-patient confidentiality. I had often heard Alan Finlayson field this mantra with trainee gps during training sessions by pointing out that the child was their patient too, to whom they also owed a primary duty of care. So, in the middle of the Scandinavian speaker's mentioning mandatory reporting, the mischievous Phil interrupted him from the audience to say that 'Strathclyde already has a mandatory reporting policy – it's called a p45.'

Huge laugh, of course, but the remark perhaps also conveys a perspective not yet attuned to the subtleties and new realities that sexual abuse posed for all agencies, especially social work, police and health. I laughed as loudly as anyone at this gallusness which also reflected Strathclyde's traditional no-nonsense, knock-on-the-door, check-the-cupboards rspcc style approach to child protection, which some might also call 'the hairy-arsed approach'. But what might have worked when abuse meant something pretty obvious – physical injury or neglect – struggled with forms of abuse that were often far less evident, like sexual and emotional abuse, simply because there was literally nothing to be seen – no bruising, no empty cupboards, no lice. Indeed, another Practice Paper on Emotional Abuse (1992) would become my final contribution to Lothian's child protection system.

It followed on logically from the issues and implications arising for health and care professionals attempting to understand and case-manage the emotional and psychological problems arising for sexually abused children. Sexual abuse had served to raise in an acute way the emotional impact of abuse, highlighting it in its own right and not just as a component of physical abuse and neglect cases. Emotional Abuse, though legally difficult to establish in court, still needed to be understood and recognised by professionals as the consequence of inconsistent and unreliable parenting and it still does. By 1990, there was a growing concern that generic fieldworkers, especially in short-term Intake posts, needed to re-engage with childcare casework principles and theory if they wanted to maintain a role in direct work with children in long-term residential and foster care who had been emotionally damaged by abusive or neglectful or unreliable parenting. I closed my Paper by commenting:

> It is a further irony, worth noting here, that practitioners will often have the most professional concern regarding children about whom they may have the least legal or medical grounds on which to intervene.

That should be being shouted from the roof tops today.

In describing these matters, I have suddenly become aware of the extent to which I have been writing almost exclusively with a focus on community-based field social workers. I cannot remember being asked, never mind becoming involved in, organising training workshops specifically for child residential social workers or preparing procedures for them on sex abuse topics during this period. Individual senior residential social workers may have attended inter-agency workshops but I do not recall that and I cannot think of any specific training material being produced which focused on residential care scenarios. The priority at the time was to gear up the community inter-agency investigative apparatus and to roll out preventative programmes – 'Feeling Yes, Feeling No' – to schools across the Region. Indeed, I seem to remember that abuse allegations concerning children in residential care were dealt with directly by residential senior management rather than office-based duty workers and Seniors.

I can, however, cite some of Big Tam's experience of the difficulties he encountered as Assistant Principal Officer for Strathclyde's children residential services in the late 1980s-early '90s when he was reporting directly to the children's service director, our old Falkirk amigo, Ian Gilmour. It indicates the kind of holes in the old system that enabled unscrupulous and determined paedophiles to find employment in a sector notoriously under-qualified and over-burdened with work and stress. I will not name the units but the case concerned a male worker from London who got a job in a Catholic-run voluntary home which recruited its own staff outwith the local authority system. He then moved on to a residential school also in the central belt but outwith Strathclyde which had a few Strathclyde children placed in it as had the previous unit, and they were planning to place a few more. Big Tam was phoned by a detached youth worker from a city centre project in Glasgow offering outreach support to young, particularly male drug addicts and street-sleepers prostituting themselves, ensuring their health and welfare. Tam Baillie it was, who later became Scotland's Commissioner for Children and Young People in 2009. Some of the lads had recognised the predator from being in these units and he was now seen kerb-crawling the city centre area where they were living.

Big Tam consulted Gilmour, the immediate concern being the safety of the Strathclyde children currently in these homes. The formal investigative routes would take time with no certainty of disclosure by the children or other legal evidence, the bar for which was, as it remains, high. Investigations were still being dealt with by the CID along with other general work with no specially trained police family protection teams tasked and geared to deal with historic abuse allegations which has since become usual. Ian said that when the children went home from the units for weekend leave, they should be placed in other care units or foster placement or remain with their families pending further assessment. When the unit managers concerned phoned Big Tam, he had to parrot a pre-prepared sentence: 'Strathclyde will place children where their care needs are best met'. The unit heads then had stormy meetings with Ian Gilmour who basically repeated the same mantra, while Big Tam and the Human Resources managers were furiously tracking the employment history of this rogue character and how he had slipped through the net.

It was discovered that the paedophile had used a contact in London to supply him with an official reference form which he had filled in himself and the accomplice signed off with a covering letter to the Catholic-run voluntary sector care unit. It was discovered that there were ten-week gaps in his employment history he could not account for and so he was sacked for submitting false information to his employers. One is strongly reminded of Al Capone being jailed in the 1930s, not for murder and the rackets, but false tax returns. This was only the beginning of the realisation by the authorities of how insidious and easy it was for such people to infiltrate the children's residential care system aided, of course, by the level of unqualified staff both in the state and voluntary sectors, which is still uncomfortably high today.

* * *

Working and residing in the vicinity of Shrubhill, halfway down Leith Walk, would bring me into contact again with my old colleague, Raymond, now in the social work office at its foot. Raymond had a new Senior about whom he was very enthusiastic, Big John. I had encountered Big John when I was still in Craigmillar, for he had dropped into the office one day and asked to see the Intake Senior – me. He was very pleasant and chatted about nothing and then started telling me about a case until I stopped him and asked why he was telling me all this and was he considering a transfer, and he said 'Yes', and I said 'When?' and he said, 'Today.' Now, a transfer of a case typically took a minimum of three months into an area like Craigmillar, an exchange of background reports, a look at the casefile, a meeting with the client and a projected handover date, like the next Children's Hearing review. Big John soon departed rather disappointed from my poky wee office which was cluttered from floor to ceiling with cases for allocation and transfer-in requests.

Whenever I met Raymond thereafter I would make some disparaging opening remark about Big John and the 'Leith transfer system', which invariably amounted to 'the purchase of a bus-ticket up to Craigmillar'. This never dented Raymond's adulation for Big John. 'No, you've got him wrong there, Alistair, he'd no a guiser at all, just a very caring guy.' To which I would reply, 'Oh aye, I care about my old granny but I'd never drop her off at your door just because I was passing and expect you to take her in?'

Raymond now ran the five-a-side indoor football game every Wednesday evening at Leith community centre comprising social workers and Seniors and residential workers and senior managers from Shrubhill – no quarter asked or given. Raymond played in goals limited by arthritic hips but, as with social work, Raymond was totally committed. It came as something of a surprise when, after three weeks, Raymond announced his retirement from the game and nominated myself as his successor, and solemnly handed me an old pudding of a ball that looked like it had just survived the Battle of Waterloo. I accepted.

The first thing I did was purchase a proper ball, a light metro, and the second thing was impose a 'below head-height rule' which meant that if the ball went above head-height a foul was awarded the other team. In effect this stopped the game and took the 'heat' out of overly competitive matches. This was a form of professional football training which built up both ball skill and discipline. This was a drastic change from Raymond's regime – 'blootering the ball aboot the park' – which unskilled players major in. I explained that this new rule was basically designed to protect them from me. I was in my mid-30s and still pretty fit and robust and if I went for any ball in a confined space at any height somebody was going to get hurt and it was not going to be me. This soon became clear.

The 'below head-height rule' helped prevent many a potential blood-bath down at Leith community centre every Wednesday night between 6 and 7.00pm while slowly leading to an increase in all-round skill levels. Afterwards we gathered at the Windsor Buffet at the top of Leith Walk to chortle or grumble at awkward bounces, fluke goals and diabolical bad luck – Stan Godek, Kenny Dickson, Malcolm McCallum (a Divisional Director at Shrubhill and capped for Scotland at basketball), Bryan Chatham (a ruffian rugby player and a Senior at Leith, later capped Director of Edinburgh City), Bill Whyte (a Senior at Musselburgh, later Professor of Criminology at the University of Edinburgh) and countless others from a well-named out-fit called 'Unreal Portobello', notably Bill Guthrie, Jim Pattison and Brian 'Snake Eyes' Jennings. We even attracted some good players too. For some reason Gus Campbell (another Divisional Director at Shrubhill who was also capped for Scotland at basketball) and had been a regular during Raymond's time, never appeared and so he lived on in legend alone.

I had given up being Branch Education Officer for NALGO in 1986 and continued to study fitfully via the Open University. My political interests continued to be channelled through the Communist Party in Edinburgh, which I had joined in 1982 in response to Mrs Thatcher's Falklands War. It was now hurtling in free fall, a shell of its former self, which I would write about in Andy Croft's *After the Party* (2012). I was now 42 years old and had seen all I needed to from the fourth floor of Shrubhill. It was still interesting, of course, but I was beginning to feel professionally stale, like I had when I returned from England to Craigmillar. Iain Morrison used to say that you gain most in your first year in a job, in the second year you give most and in the third year you start repeating yourself. By now, after seven years, I was beginning to meet myself halfway along the corridor of Shrubhill.

So all of the cherries came up at the same time for me when a Senior post fell vacant in Broxburn Office in West Lothian in early 1991, Big Peter Harris being the Area Officer and Danny the Divisional Director. By then it had become apparent that a major re-structuring of the service was planned over the next two years, which would create separate children and families, criminal justice and adult care specialisms within the same unified Regional Departments. It seemed almost planned for me. I had already started playing five-a-sides through in Bathgate with my young brother and his pals on a Friday evening, some of whom were ex-Seniors and Juniors, so the standard was pretty good. I would also continue to play five-a-sides on a Wednesday evening down at Leith as well for the six months or so it would take to sell the Edinburgh house and move to Bathgate. The five-a-side ball was thus passed officially to Kenny Dickson, who accepted it, and no doubt replaced it with another big pudding.

And so I left Shrubhill without fanfare, no rude SER stuff, just Les McEwan, Deputy to John Chant, wishing me well and saying that he was always pleased when West Lothian recruited 'good staff'. I believe he had not been drinking. What I always admired about Les was his thorough sense of commitment to practice. When he managed the Emergency Duty Team headed by James Pinkerton, he often sat in on evening and weekend shifts, interested in what was actually happening on the ground, talking to workers direct.

I commuted to Broxburn for several months taking the back roads from Leith to Barnton and so on through Kirkliston. It was also agreed that I spend a day a week in Shrubhill finishing off the Emotional Abuse Practice Paper which was eventually published in January 1992. During this period, I had an extraordinary epiphany as I sat in Shrubhill one day, hunched over the keyboard of my PC typing up that Practice Paper. Suddenly a picture of the newsroom in my father's old office in the *West Lothian Courier* in Bathgate popped into my head. My hands were poised above the PC keyboard and, for a moment, it was as though I was looking down on the typewriter keys in the characteristic pose I had seen my father adopt all through my childhood. It was like one of those moments when middle-aged men catch sight of their face in the mirror and see their old man staring back. I suddenly had this shocked insight that writing had always been shadowing me in some form or other, composing essays and assignments for school, university, professional Practice Papers. Was my subconscious now speculating that I was going back to West Lothian of all places to write like my father or about my father, as I in fact would? Or had I simply been reading too many books by Melanie Klein?

I had another kind of epiphany or, at least, an out of body experience in January 1991 when I was still contemplating returning to West Lothian. My partner Sheila and I attended a Burns Supper at Linlithgow Burgh Halls at Danny and Jeanette's invitation, where she met Big Tam and Anne for the first time. The room was packed and the seating such that once you were sat down you could hardly get out. I noticed Sheila and Big Tam deep in conversation throughout the evening but was too far away to hear what was being said. Sheila later confided that she had been telling him all about her counselling training and the therapeutic work she was doing and so on, to which he listened attentively. The APO for Children's Residential Homes, Strathclyde Regional Council, then said, 'Yes, we have a word for that in the profession: keech!' Sheila was very much amused by this and so I did not bother telling her that he had not been joking. Well, not much.

11

Don't Panic

When you paint anything... you are painting yourself
as well as the object you are trying to record.
Francis Bacon, 1960s

*The author returns to his ancestral home in the parish of West Lothian, Sleepy
Hollow, for 18 months of sunbeds and hokey cokey while he tells workers
and Seniors that a Social Work (Scotland) Act came in in 1968. Specialisation
in Broxburn in October 1992 is unnecessary so the author is parachuted into
Livingston office as a Childcare Practice Team Manager (South Korea) in
order to be twinned with another Childcare PTM (North Korea), known only
by the codename 'Wee Jim'. New specialist teams are patched together which
leads to some unrest which wears off after ten years. The author describes
getting on famously with a medical adviser over the Adoption and Fostering
Panel but gives the new corporate management structure a right good
kicking. Admin is praised to the heavens because it still runs the place before
computers and robots take over (called corporate managers). Happily, all
survive to fight another day, and another day, except for Danny, the first Chief
Social Work Officer, who fights instead for a huge lump sum and pension.
A performance artist called Mr Gaddafi enters, stage right.*

GOING TO BROXBURN social work office in April 1991 was like returning
to 1971, 'Sleepy Hollow', as one of my new Senior colleagues there
dubbed it, Big Ronnie Barnes. The office comprised a tangle of Lego-like
Portakabins stuck behind the swimming pool on the main street, alongside
a set of lock-up garages and a tiny precinct of shops selling greetings cards,
flowers, ladies' haircuts and other things I never quite needed myself. Big
Peter was its genial, air-raid-shelter proportioned Area Officer, a working-
class Londoner who did his National Service in the 1950s in the company
of another cockney called Michael Caine. Peter started out with the NSPCC
and then trained as a Children's Officer. I had encountered him briefly as a
Senior social worker in Stirling at Regionalisation in 1975, from whence he
departed to become the Broxburn Area Officer for Lothian Region. Peter had
a fund of quite unbelievable stories from his London past which he would
relate in a Michael Caine fashion or perhaps Michael related his stories in
a Peter Harris fashion? One tale that still sticks concerned a teenage boy

who ran away from a residential home in London, eventually being tracked down – or is it up? – in Thurso on the northern tip of Scotland. According to Peter, with many diverting details thrown in, the boy travelled all the way at four miles an hour on a purloined petrol-driven lawnmower which also managed to survive the several weeks' journey unscathed.

In the weeks leading up to my first Christmas in the Broxburn Office in December 1991, the Admin staff, most of whom had been there even longer than Peter and the Portakabins (another good name for a punk-rock band), festooned its dim-lit corridors with festive bunting and an antiquated intercom through which traditional carols were transmitted all day long on a 'tinny' frequency in a hauntingly M*A*S*H-like manner. A Second World War Blitz atmosphere thus prevailed, prompting me to christen Big Peter 'Bomber Harris', though a less aggressive or violent personality one could hardly imagine. Peter was old-fashioned, old-school and upbeat no matter how dire things might appear. Much of the staff he had gathered over the years came out of much the same pod, along with a light sprinkling of bright young talented female social workers – well, three at least! I had one in my team which covered the Linlithgow to Winchburgh patch, Sue Power had two in hers which covered Broxburn and Big Ronnie had none at all in his which covered Blackburn and Stoneyburn.

Sue was a highly committed and experienced professional, a person of the utmost integrity, humility and openness in her dealings with both workers and clients. On the other hand, some people might have formed the impression that Big Ronnie, a future Chair of BASW, was a rather indolent character, possibly by the way he sat in his office all day at the intersecting point of three corridors, his sizeable feet planted firmly on the desk, hailing passers-by and chortling and blethering away while eating cake, while his veteran social workers recounted casework tales of misery and doom, all of which they had, through their own experience and fortitude, managed to patch up for at least another week. Big Ronnie was unstinting in his chortling praise and support for their selfless efforts on behalf of 'the parish', as he liked to call Blackburn, Stoneyburn and Seafield. But for me, Big Ronnie was not indolent, just Highland, having been born and raised in Inverness where they speak the most perfect English in the UK and 'relaxed' is a euphemism for 'passed on'. Big Ronnie had qualities that should never be discounted in frontline social work managers, namely, he chortled rather than panicked. If ever there was a Senior social worker who had the words 'DON'T PANIC' emblazoned across his whole demeanour, it was indeed he. Big Ronnie was decidedly not a Vogon. (See *The Hitchhiker's Guide to the Galaxy*, 1979: I fondly remember Wee Jan Aitcheson roaming about Craigmillar Intake room shouting oaths at the Vogons – 'the most officious and obnoxious creatures in the universe', apparently, and who, for good measure, 'you should never allow to read poetry at you'.) I never did.

I tried to convey some of this laid-backness in a poem called 'Emergencies' in *Dancing with Big Eunice*, which is based on an actual incident in the infamous Blackburn flats, long since demolished. What the poem does not say is that the parent was well known to Ronnie's team and had a 'history' of similar presentations. There was an element of 'calculated professional risk-taking' behind this unrhymed sonnet – written as a kind of 'found poem'. The poem shows something of the absurdity that sometimes confronts duty social workers and Seniors in the course of a normal working day and which, Sod's Law, usually comes in the middle of a very busy shift. On this occasion, Big Ronnie rose once more to the professional task:

> Big Ronnie was on the phone, and the client
> was crying and asking him what he was
> going to do because she was holding
> her child outside the window of her flat,
> three-stories up, so Ronnie asked her
> if she thought she would be strong enough
> to hold on until the fire-brigade arrived,
> but she thought not, so Big Ronnie
> agreed this was tricky and he'd really
> prefer more time to think about it, so
> she agreed to bring the child back inside
> and he'd phone her back in five minutes,
> which he did, only to find that the child
> had gone to play at a neighbour's instead.

Before coming to Broxburn, Ronnie had worked in the Falkirk office in the 1980s a few years after I left. He took over from my successor, in fact, and knew various other people I had worked with in the 1970s. Ronnie now supervised Miriam in Broxburn, who I am pleased to report was still the same thoroughly dedicated worker as in Falkirk. Miriam, of course, thought nothing of Big Ronnie's thoroughly relaxed management style and thought nothing of telling him so either. But in evaluating Big Ronnie as a Senior, or myself for that matter, one ought to be mindful of the composition of his team who were all thoroughly capable and experienced females – formidable, authoritative, honest and nurturing. Indeed, professionally, Ronnie did not need to do that much except chew his way through the cakes they routinely made and brought in for him and their colleagues to share. And while he listened and chortled, they told him about their latest catastrophes for which he became responsible, managerially and professionally, regarding the case issues arising through their interventions because of his supervisory function. For the critical factor of ownership of frontline social work decision-making was now moving inexorably towards Seniors being consulted by social workers ever more frequently and ever more thoroughly – but now before rather than immediately after the fact.

The kind of Senior or frontline manager one is depends, in my experience, not only on your own background and outlook but on the workers you are given to manage and the managers who manage you. The hand I was dealt in Broxburn regarding workers was quite similar to Big Ronnie's except that the complexity of workloads arising in relatively affluent Linlithgow and backwater Winchburgh did not really compare with that of his Blackburn team or Sue's Broxburn team. Of course, together, the combined caseloads of all three teams did not compare to the workload demands we had faced routinely in Craigmillar. However, since I was feeling my own way back into frontline social work after a seven-year sabbatical in Shrubhill, Sleepy Hollow suited me just fine and I suited it. I had gleaned from Big Peter that my predecessor had been a rather bright young woman full of new ideas and energy but this had not gone down too well with some of the old stagers, who were now my responsibility. I was thus faced with the same dilemma Tommy Docherty had in 1968 when he became manager of Queens Park Rangers and found that the older pros were effectively playing for themselves in a small on-field cartel that did not allow the young talented players to come through. Being 'the Doc', Tommy tackled this head-on by putting the guilty senior players into the reserves and the youngsters into the first team, with disastrous results. Losing games, the board did not back Tommy so he left after 29 days, moving to pastures new, which included managing a small outfit called Manchester United, but that's another story.

I did not need to go that far and for two reasons. Firstly, most of my team were pretty competent and experienced in their own specialist areas, though a couple were not fully competent or confident in the childcare-protection field. Secondly, they were nearing the end of their professional careers and, since Restructuring would soon return them to their former specialisms, well, it seemed a short-term problem with an obvious short-term solution. I therefore took the complex childcare and child protection cases off them and redistributed them around the other workers while giving them cases more suited to their actual experience. In a way, Restructuring came to these practitioners 18 months earlier than it did for their teammates or, indeed, for me. Context is all, in football or out, and if I had needed to take more stringent or immediate action, I would not have hesitated.

For example, I did encounter one social worker in one of the other teams who I would have sacked on the spot. This creature was a middle-class snob who saw themselves as above the common herd of both clients and other social workers. Exuding an air of ennui and superiority bordering on contempt, X read *The Scotsman* sat at a desk every morning, all morning, and then snuck off from work early by going on late visits, for which they could claim overtime. They routinely took extended lunch breaks and opted out of difficult visits by visiting people not needing them but which still let them claim mileage, overtime and so on. In short, X was a supercilious knob-head who coolly took every advantage of the openly trusting professional environment of the times, to everyone's detriment, not least the people they were meant to be helping. I heard all of this second-hand after I had begun to suspect it for myself. I now watched them like a hawk when I was on duty but, of course, never a word or foot was ever put out of place. A decade or so later, they got themselves stretchered out, medical retirement, enhanced pension, full lump sum, the lot.

In 1991, Broxburn was culturally and professionally much the same kind of place it had been a couple of decades earlier. The old family and cultural support networks had survived until the 1990s even if the full employment of its traditional industries of mining, steel-works, railways, brick-works, crisp and chicken factories, manufacturing and tractor-making of the 1970s had not. This enabled social workers to find a family member or reliable neighbour to care for a child for short periods if their parents were incapacitated through drink, drugs or mental breakdown. Criminal drug networks had not yet taken root as began to happen in cities and sea-ports and drinking culture still ran along gender lines, men drinking pay or benefits in the pub and women at home surviving on child benefits and mutuality loans supplemented further by borrowing from friends and family members. These have since been replaced by pay-day loans that ripple through the underclass world that social work still plies its trade amongst. Much of the drink and drug-taking is now done inside the home. Young children and teenagers are thus far more likely to witness or participate in this kind of sub-culture which is consequently far less visible and accessible to outside intervention than it had been before. But things had not deteriorated to that extent by the time I arrived in Broxburn in spring 1991.

Going to the Broxburn office also returned me to the area of my family and cultural roots. I was born only three miles away in the shale mining village of Winchburgh. When I qualified in 1973, I had never given a moment's thought to doing social work in West Lothian. My father was editor of the local newspaper and a public figure almost as well known as the local MP, Tam Dalyell. I had four brothers, three of whom had families locally. Starting out in social work there would not have given me the kind of anonymity I sought at that time. Apart from that, the county had no reputation whatsoever for progressive social work practice. Its Director was a nice man but had the kind of local welfare background John Murphy considered a by-word for inadequate professional leadership, vision and funding. It was not until the 1980s that the influence of Lothian Region directors of the calibre of Les McEwan, Mike Cairns and Danny Deans raised West Lothian's managerial profile above the mediocre and they improved the level of care provision accordingly.

My local family connections surfaced as soon as I arrived in the Broxburn office, where I was immediately pigeon-holed not as the 'Man from Shrubhill' but 'Jimmy the Van's Wee Brother'. Jimmy had become a local legend amongst Admin, OTs and Home-Help Organisers. He had worked for the department for a year or so delivering OT aids and chairs to old miners and ex-steelworkers across the county, amongst whom Jimmy's banter was often more prized than some of the items he delivered them. When Jimmy left, he had told me himself, 'Ali, it's the best worst-paid job I've ever had.'

He went to see the Divisional Director, Mike Cairns, to give him the bad news and Mike said to him, 'So you've finally finished your extension, Jimmy?' This was a reference to the numerous complaints Mike had received anonymously (Jimmy presumed from a local Bathgate councillor who lived across the road) that Jimmy was using the office van in the evenings and weekends to shuttle bricks, cement, timber, plaster-board, windows, doors, paint, tiles and other Findlay brothers, no doubt including myself, to erect an extension. Luckily, it was only a District councillor, who was responsible for housing, not a Regional one responsible for social work. Anyway, Jimmy had moved on to a much more boring but altogether better paid job, leaving me to chart my own course as best I could.

In summer 1992, West Lothian Division began reorganising staff along specialist lines – Criminal Justice, Children and Families (C&F), Community Care. This resulted in my being offered a post in the new structure as one of two Practice Team Managers (PTMs) for Children and Families based in the Livingston office alongside 'Wee Jim'.

'Who he?' I asked Big Ronnie and Big Peter, who smirked at each other and said, 'You'll see'.

Oh great, I thought, raking about in my old kitbag for the heavy-duty shin-pads I had not had on since Falkirk and the dog-days of Central Region. Big Ronnie would now become PTM for the district-wide Criminal Justice Team, also based in Livingston next door to my new office, with Big Peter becoming a sub-manager for elderly residential services. Danny had had a more senior role in mind for him when he phoned me earlier that summer to run a few names past for a list he was making for Les McEwan and Julia Ross, the Shrubhill Directorate in charge of appointing senior staff to the new structures encompassing Edinburgh city, Mid/East Lothian and West Lothian. Danny had known some names but not all on the draft list, especially the Shrubhill-Edinburgh mob, and so we spent some time with me saying 'yes' or 'no' or 'dunno'. Danny's preferred list for West Lothian came back completely altered, sometimes the same names but not for the positions he had proposed. There were some mutterings about Julia Ross, who would move on soon to become Director of a London Borough, for punting the promotion of young women irrespective of experience. This affected Danny's list too, for Les was left to cherry-pick the HQ and frontline managers for his own future patch, Edinburgh City. But who could blame him? They all would have done the same, especially Danny!

Broxburn office not only lost its veteran Area Officer but all of its Seniors and over half of its social workers. It went overnight from being the most stable workplace in the District to the least. If I have drawn Broxburn office as some kind of ruritarian back-water given Big Ronnie's affectionate irony, it might be as well to note that it also supplied one of its most experienced social workers in response to a plea from Orkney Council to send staff to work there in the aftermath of the crisis. Joyce Gunn spent four months dealing with the backlash of hostility that the social work department received from the local community, aghast at the scandalous attention it had received from the national press. Never mind, it did not stop us having a 'closing-down party' in the Broxburn office at the end of the first week of October 1992.

Myself and Big Ronnie billed ourselves as 'The Broxburn Blues Brothers', singing some naff songs I penned to entertain the troops who were either departing to other teams, coming from other teams or retiring. We sang an unflattering, quite gratuitous ditty about John Chant in which 'We'll Doo You John John' was substituted for The Crystals' epic hit 'Da Doo Ron Ron Ron'. This was followed by 'Ye've a' got tae go tae Whitburn' sung to the tune of 'Everyone's Gone to the Moon', with no apologies to its composer, Jonathan King, later convicted of child sexual abuse in 2001, about which we and the world were still blithely unaware.

> Rooms full of people, breakin' doon,
> Case files and rotas, scattered roon,
> Watch oot cries someone, they're on their way roon,
> Location Managers – Vroom! (meaning 'scatter')
> Long time ago, life was still fun,
> Everyone sat on their bum,

Noo it's all 'haw sir, it's your bloomin' turn,
Ye'vea' got tae go tae Whitburn'.
Long time ago, one door was one,
Everyone knew where tae come,
Noo it's a' 'Misses, ye've taen the wrong turn,
Ye've a' got tae go tae Whitburn'.

None of these ditties had the same edge as their 1975 counterpart, 'Clowns', perhaps because the singers would soon be 'location managers' ourselves, a job that would have more of a fieldwork practice focus than the Area Officer posts they were replacing. Facts, of course, should not be allowed to get in the way of a good lyric, and nobody knew how the new Practice Team Manager posts would pan out anyway. We finished with 'The Bleeper Song' which had some current references to staff safety when visiting clients in their homes. The 'hammer and bunnet' incident at Tymmeryet flats (about which I wrote a poem in *Dancing with Big Eunice)* had not required an 'incident report form' for the simple reason that these had not been invented yet. That incident had been followed by another involving a home-help getting locked inside a client's house, later released unharmed – the home-help that is, not the client.

This would lead to some discussion about introducing a pager system, personal alarms and other stuff such as giving workers a payphone card and them having to notify the duty Senior if they were going out on iffy visits and the like. The duty Senior could then decide whether this should be an accompanied visit or the visit cancelled altogether and the client seen in the office. This was a relatively new development, certainly in West Lothian, and it was evidently still capable of being treated with a kind of levity probably unthinkable now. But the norms of the job was still very much that social workers and Seniors themselves expected to visit all kinds of hostile or disgruntled persons in their own homes. 'The Bleeper Song', an obvious burlesque of Jim Reeves' 'He'll Have to Go', was pretty well-received, a good laugh, not to be taken too seriously and I am pleased to report that it wasn't:

Put your sweet lips a little closer to the phone,
Let's pretend we're no in Craigshill, all alone,
It's no gone three, it's no just me – and a psycho,
Before you hang up, you'll have to tell him, to let me go.
I can't hear the words you wanna say, my phone-card's in his hand,
And I've told him that he'll have to pay, but he doesnae understand.
I can't hear the words you wanna say, for your bleeper's out of range,

And you're somewhere in the Bathgate Hills, or passing Newtongrange.

And so I exited from Broxburn social work office in October 1992, singing, ready to become one of the two new Children and Families Practice Team Managers (C&F PTMs) based at Cheviot House, Livingston – since demolished – covering Livingston South. I met my new partner in crime, as it were, Wee Jim, C&F PTM for Livingston North. Jim had been Intake Senior for Livingston Area office for a few years and he had managed to retain most of his old Intake crew plus a couple of new young recruits. More importantly, he had also acquired in the restructuring process a highly experienced Intake Senior from the Bathgate office, John Howe. He thus had two Seniors, one a female recently promoted from within his group, most of whom already knew the area and the clients. I inherited a completely mixed bag of experienced and inexperienced workers, including a recent recruit to the Bathgate office who had been sent to Broxburn but had suddenly felt claustrophobic on entering the Portakabins – and who could blame her?

In the car crash that was Specialisation, therefore, Wee Jim was left sitting in the same neck of the woods he had been sat in for years, with a hand-knitted crew who knew the area and the cases. Myself, on the other hand, had suddenly become Para Handy, skipper of the vintage puffer, the *Vital Spark*, an old steamboat that had plied up and down the Clyde in the 1950s and '60s. I thereby acquired a rather motley crew of long-term Livingston caseworkers and an awkward Intake worker, two former Broxburn patch workers, a transfer from the Resources Team and an unknown phobic newly qualified female social worker recently appointed to another office and transferred to me – whom I could have refused as Jim would have, as he told me. And there you have it in a nutshell, what Big Tam would refer to as 'the psychological differential', a phrase that he picked up from Moray House days and had vested with shamanic qualities whenever he ran up against any strange or unexpected conundrum: 'Al, that is the psychological differential', he'd say, then take another long swig of his pint before lapsing into a momentous silence.

But how unusual, in fact, were Wee Jim and me in the Livingston office across Lothian Region as a whole both before and after Specialisation I rather doubt. In West Lothian, Seniors were allocated to the PTMs by Danny and the new client services manager. I thus inherited a recently promoted young female long-term Senior from within the Livingston office, probably because she was not wanted by Jim and vice-versa. I found her rather too keen to rush out to visit clients with her workers instead of learning how to supervise them from the personally less 'engaged' perspectives Seniors have to acquire regarding frontline work and angst. All new Seniors face this kind of transition – from making one's own assessment of clients to relying on those made by your social workers. For me she operated more like a skilled Senior practitioner than the Senior I had wanted. We were an unlikely pairing, neither of us being the other's particular cup of tea, but I doubted she would have fared any better with Jim. We rubbed along nonetheless and she would prove herself a supportive and competent Senior well able to stand up for herself and her staff, the base-line of any good Senior and frontline manager, even those you don't particularly get on with. I would much prefer if she had booted a couple of her new workers' arses, professionally speaking, a lot more often than she did but this simply underlines all that I have been saying about the reality of workers and Seniors bringing their own professional selves to the feast – for these are, and should be, in the plural.

Jim and myself were also plural PTMs in that location. He also had the management of a Senior social worker and a couple of workers based at St John's Hospital and so he had three full-time Seniors which helped him swan about a bit in the safe and sure knowledge that John was minding the store and Jim's back, back in the old Intake room from which John rarely moved. Meanwhile, I am doing a day's duty every week, supervising four social workers and a rather prickly new Senior while assuming control of the District Adoption and Fostering Panel after an absence of some 15 years. Sharing was not big on Jim's agenda for all his welcoming demeanour, which was a pity because, as PTMs, we shared a location, a duty system and a Senior practitioner, Anne Lind, an excellent social worker, probably the most accomplished I ever worked with. Anne was an ex-Bowman-Fife refugee and she had been acting-up in the Senior role in the period running up to Specialisation but decided it was not for her, unfortunately, though no doubt good for her own future sanity.

I began to get a fuller picture after a few days, for Jim was never out of my office, being helpful to the new guy, telling me this and that, until I realised that he had cautioned me to watch out for everybody in the building, including his own Intake team, especially some of his most devoted followers. On the credit side, Jim was an efficient frontline manager, albeit one intent on climbing the greasy-pole of middle and senior management. It also appeared that he had been passed over for promotion in the last few years, pipped several times to an Area Officer post, not by outsiders but by his fellow Seniors in the Livingston office. He had also worked hard to develop inter-agency child protection links with the police, education and health agencies in Livingston so Jim was no mug by any means, though I would find his evident desperation to shine, well, evident. But he was certainly respected by his own team, which always counts on the frontline. Unfortunately, his team continued to occupy the same rooms, desks and tribal attitudes they had occupied before as the old Livingston Intake Team.

I had learned a lot about tribal attitudes between Intake and Long-term teams in Craigmillar, of course, but that had been constrained by several factors, none of which applied to the Livingston situation: no overall boss onsite; two-thirds of the Senior group already having a history of pulling together; staff unity that came from the trade union response to defending the workplace from Tory-imposed council cuts to social services and jobs. That last facet had escaped Livingston, unlike the Broxburn office, which had formed picket-lines enhanced by cakes and scones made by Big Ronnie's 'Golden Girls'. John Stevenson is bitterly remembered by the Broxburn shop steward of the time, Emma Boothroyd, for having reported in the NALGO newsletter that the Broxburn office had formed 'picnic-lines' instead of picket-lines.

What unfolded was not all down to Wee Jim, therefore, who was no vicar but then I was no choir boy. But had I been Dame Eileen Younghusband herself all would not have been what you might call plain sailing between the two practice teams. I began to notice that Jim, if not exactly bolstering internal competition between the two teams, seemed unwilling or unable to reign it in. Reports kept coming to me from my lot that he was puffing up the North as the best at this or that, which they dutifully reported to me as though I should sort it all out. To this, I would either feign that they were indeed better than us or slyly ask, 'Does anybody really want to share a room with Eva Braun?' – the NALGO shop steward, a particularly demonic figure in Jim's group. The shared duty-system soon became a site of tension as some of Jim's old Intake hands began to patrol its operations like North Korean border guards. Any perceived differences in decisions made by duty-Seniors in my team, presumably including me, became wonderfully amplified if deviating one iota from the cherished practices of former days. This was the initial mindset and I studiously ignored it. I knew for a fact that most of these short-term Intake workers would have to get to grips soon enough with long-term casework skills that were second-nature to most of my team of former long-term and patch workers. Like Lenin and the old Bolsheviks, I trusted that history really was on our side and would only need a little time, and maybe a little push, to demonstrate that fact to the whole world.

The patch system we operated required both short- and long-term skill sets and since I already had the most experienced caseworkers as my core, I cared not a jot. If I had felt the need, I would have resorted to satire, dubbing them 'Jim and the Jim-Jams' and my lot 'Al and the Also-Rans'. I might have written a song and invited some of my old combos along to perform it – 'Raymond and the Brake-Blocks', 'Q and the Falkirk Seniors', and 'Peter and the Portakabins' – one huge resounding Battle of the Bands. Unfortunately, work got in the way. Things did settle down – work did get in the way – though tensions periodically surfaced.

Jim's other Senior, the bolshie one, Emm, came along to confront me one day in my room about some nonsense, probably some decision that me or 'my' duty-Senior had made or not made, that was not quite up to scratch, so I said, 'away you back out that door and take it up with Jim and he can take it up with me if he thinks it's worth the trouble'. Never heard a word back. She was one of those Jim had warned me about the most. On another occasion, my Senior got involved in a stand-up shouting match with her in the corridor halfway between the two Team rooms. By this time, Jim was acting-up and John was acting-up in his absence. The two of them were acting-up all on their ownsome. I came in at the tail-end of the harangue just in time to see John quietly closing his room door. Wise man, John, I thought, quietly closing mine.

So what do I think of all that now? Largely what I thought of it then: social work is not a church, candle-lit at Christmas, nor a stranger to wilful characters ballsy enough to bring order to social work's frequently febrile frontlines. Sometimes the subterranean emotional continent that runs through the social work task can spill over into florid confrontations with clients or colleagues and it is often the more dedicated ones who blow up because they are carrying the stress of the cases more or simply because they just care more. Social work is suffused with emotion, including one's own, and this kind of simmered away beneath the surface of the old workplaces, acknowledged in phrases like 'who cares for the carers?' that were once commonly banded about. But the days were long gone when I had heard Joe Gillen say in Hamilton Burgh in 1971 that if I felt I needed a break after dealing with some intense piece of work then I should just feel able to go for a walk or go home early. Yes, an early bath for the two of them but I wasn't going out to run it for them and neither was John, far less 'Wee Jim', no longer even there.

While Jim and I manoeuvred around each other and the new Livingston office, the person who actually ran it was the Admin assistant – or was it chief clerk? – Margaret Graham. Margaret was a Glaswegian and she had the approachable personality gifted to her kind. She was in the finest traditions of Rita and Jean and Wee Marion from Falkirk Burgh. She knew where all the bodies were buried in the Council; kept the Admin engine purring; smoothed out all of the glitches; organised the office Christmas party and any birthday celebrations; worked out TOIL (time off in lieu) and any kind of discrepancy that materialised regarding overtime, leave of absence or maternity allowance; sorted out the photocopier, the computer man, the fire drill, the sandwich man, the switchboard, lost files, reception, the waiting room, Hearing reports, forms, money, the phones, the toilets, the conference room, the stores, the karaoke machine; while keeping me up to date with the latest unofficial information flow plus any potential cunning ploys emanating from the vicinity of Jim, whom she constantly tried to convince me was a good human being after all, a father devoted to his children. Unfortunately, this happened to be true.

Margaret also had a brilliant singing voice and her only defect, apart from defending Jim, was an almost fanatical devotion to line-dancing, which she shared with the typing-pool. In pursuance of her duties, Margaret thus had to manoeuvre between four PTMs of equal standing but now from two different specialisms which required two separate duty systems for different patches serviced by the same receptionist. Margaret kept all of this in motion while telling the four PTMs where to get off in her own inimitable Glaswegian fashion. I think on occasion Margaret thought that some of the most difficult clients were a cake-walk compared to some of the Seniors and the social workers, though she would never say that, of course. Well, not to them. If there was any normality at all in the office, Margaret was largely responsible for creating and maintaining it through the 17 years that I found myself there. When John became group manager, he used to look at me incredulously: 'How the hell did you know that? I only got told this morning!' Margaret, of course, would have caught it in the wind weeks before.

Although a return to Specialism was widely welcomed in order to ring-fence resources for adult care and criminal justice to protect them from the predominance of childcare work, it was feared that the concentration of 'heavy-end' childcare and child protection cases amongst a smaller group of social workers might well prove overwhelming. In West Lothian, we gained an extra 14 children and family social worker posts to counter such concern. One may still ask where these posts came from if not Edinburgh City, which was already badly overstretched over childcare services. Perhaps half of these posts simply provided an expanded duty service across the District because, instead of three offices providing three generic duty Seniors, three duty workers and three back-up workers, they now had to provide, together with a separate duty system created for the Criminal Justice Team, seven specialist duty systems which meant seven duty Seniors and 14 duty-backup social workers – a leap from nine staff to 28 staff all told. West Lothian gained and Edinburgh, like Glasgow, did not, which is still the case today, both cities a quarter of a century later in a constant state of social care crisis.

On 2 October 1992, the gears started crashing in earnest between the offices and the new personalities parachuted in to manage and staff them. Just as there had been no chance to vet existing social workers or their Seniors by their assigned PTMs, the PTMs were themselves appointed to locations by Danny and the client services manager after the interview process, which

I cannot remember, and neither can Danny, though I got a great reference from Big Peter. The PTMs now had to interview for the 14 new social worker posts on an industrial scale. Posts had been frozen throughout the 1980s and vacancies had arisen only periodically since then. A bun-fight now loomed as we interviewed the candidates, mostly just off training courses, in panels comprising PTMs and Seniors. The lucky 14 were then allocated across the teams. Jim had only a couple of posts to fill and zeroed in immediately on a likely pair to slot perfectly into his lovingly honed New Livingston North Old Intake Schooner, recently re-painted. I had four or five vacancies and relied on my Senior's opinion since she would be supervising many of them. We hauled them aboard our leaky little craft, Big Vince's words echoing in my ears: 'Ye can only play wi' the players ye've got, Ali.' Aye, right enough, Vince. Shut it.

Two of our five recruits were duds, a couple were solid and one so-so. All were new to the game and the Senior worked hard, a helluva lot harder than the pair whose arses should have been kicked out the door every morning with a bucket-list and quizzed every evening as to whether they had done it yet. I called the brighter one into my room in the early days after reading through the duty-referrals, including those recommending 'no further action'. He had written a few details about a woman looking for money which he had then broken off mid-sentence by writing 'blah, blah, blah'. I tore into him for blatant disrespect for the people he was paid to help, his projected persona being Glaswegian-working-class-man-of-the-people. I said that if this woman ever got involved in a court case involving children the Sheriff might allow access to social work files which might threaten our case and invite a lawsuit against the council. The blood rushed from his face and I told him to rewrite it properly and submit all future write-ups to his Senior first. I still cannot fathom what he was about, for other workers in the team seemed to find him okay and there was no repeat of this, but I still found it disquieting. How could someone go through a full social work training course and yet still come out with guff like that?

I have since discovered that a major change in social work training occurred in 1989–90 when the Diploma in social work replaced the Certificates in social work/social services, a move criticised by professional academics and practitioners as shifting the balance more towards employers demands for 'practical job competences'. Lena Dominelli (*Sociology for Social Work*, 1989: 194) expressed this as 'a move away from training as an education process concerned with socialising professionals into the best traditions of the profession to the technical transmission of approved skills.' That chimes pretty much with some of the changes in practice and governance I will touch on in due course, which would see protective, investigative and assessment functions intensify while supportive casework roles became steadily hived off to third-sector agencies – resulting in what has since become a major de-skilling process in effect.

More gear-crashing. Big Moira, who had come with me to Livingston from Big Ronnie's team in Broxburn, refused to take on a complex child sexual abuse case left dangling by a former Livingston Senior and social worker, who recently moved to Broxburn office. The policy regarding the transfer of existing cases was that, on 2 October, all cases were to be written up and left for the incoming workers to pick up in whatever state they were left. Fair idea on paper. On reading the file, however, Big Moira discovered that a tricky home assessment had lain dormant for some time prior to the run up to the deadline. She was adamant it should not have been left for future workers to complete. Her Senior agreed and so did I, so I phoned the client services manager, the area officer at the time. She wrung her hands and said she would get back to me. I then got a phone call from the previous worker raging about the aspersions being made about her practice. I said I had nothing to say relevant to her. (I thought it was down to her Senior, of course.) While the field manager dithered, Moira's Senior offered to undertake the assessment herself, which is what happened, and I assigned another experienced male social worker in her team to it plus Anne, the Senior practitioner. They worked the case jointly over the next few months and a very fine job they made of it. One volunteer is worth ten conscripts in social work as in the military. It cost a bomb in overtime but so did Specialisation, and this was just another of the overheads. All Re-organisations have similar unplanned knock-on effects.

No matter, you could still laugh. Comic relief presented itself in the form of Wee Bill, the social work finance manager, who looked remarkably like son of Wee Bill from Falkirk days, with the same serene smile but no bottle-glasses. I liked Wee Bill, parachuted in from Shrubhill along with Big Grahame who had arrived from Shrubhill in October 1992 to work for Danny as residential children's manager, a long laconic character from Leith, on the ball, laid-back and capable. Wee Bill had a perma-tan because his wife liked holidays in the sun. I liked the way Bill grinned every time I took him my team's monthly budget print-outs, still with the same errors I had pointed out last month, assuring me there was nothing to worry about, Alistair, it would all come out right in the end, for he had the correct figures up here, in his head, they just weren't showing up properly in the print-outs. And I'd say, 'Why don't you get a new printer, Bill?' and Bill would smile that happy smile that I am told he is still smiling to this day in West Lothian's corporate financial emporium, the PLC, still in safe hands. What I liked most about Wee Bill as a finance manager is the same thing that I liked about Big

Ronnie as a frontline manager – they never worried about the incidentals. So long as the workers and the beds were there and no matter what it said on the print-outs, Wee Bill had the words 'DON'T PANIC' blazened across his whole demeanour

And I smile, too, as I think about Bob Stead, another DON'T PANIC t-shirt-wearer, a back-room techy who also got transferred from Shrubhill to West Lothian at Districtisation in 1995–6 to install a computer system called SID-SWIFT somewhere between Danny's and Big Grahame's reigns – for Big Grahame would take over from Danny in due course. Bob told me about 'Hughie's book', which was seemingly the only record that Lothian Region had of the number of children placed in and out of residential care – the so-called 'bed-book'. This legendary artifact had apparently provided the figures for Lothian Region's annual reports to the Scottish Office for statutory funding. The only thing folk ever thought about then was whether the beds were there when needed. Me too, I never bothered what it said or didn't say on the print-outs, so long as the beds and the staff were there and the cases getting worked on. For that's what Wee Bill represented to me, what 'value for money' actually means in professional social work – 'Hughie's book'.

So much for the comic relief. I suppose I need to mention something about the angst with a Medical Adviser over my appointment as Chair of the District Adoption and Fostering Panel. The Panel approved carers, matched children with families and provided professional advice to the District Director, Danny, regarding kids requiring adoption or long-term fostering. Such cases routinely involved convoluted case histories often stretching back several years of intense, tortuous work with parents and families and collaboration between health and voluntary agencies as well as all the legal apparatus surrounding Hearings, Reporters, Sheriffs and Courts. The Panel itself comprised experienced professionals drawn from social work, children's centres, resources (fostering team), a legal adviser and a group of medical advisers from the local paediatric unit at St John's. I did need to get back up to speed on these matters but, though the Permanency forms had changed over the years, the principles of working the cases certainly had not. There was likewise a standard agenda which the Chair could follow, setting out the topics to be covered and the sequence of issues requiring discussion. With this I had no problem, until herself decided to complain about my competence. She liked my predecessor better, it seemed, a highly skilled Senior no doubt but Danny had insisted on a PTM filling that role – me.

However, she started trying to get other Panel members to support her view and Danny said I should have a meeting with the Panel to discuss the issues, her included. I said, 'Discuss what issues – my incompetence?' and

Danny said 'Yes'. I said, 'Should the client services manager not discuss it with the Panel in private?' and Danny said 'No.' This was vintage Danny: face them up, see what they have to say, argue the case, see what turns up. I called a meeting and asked the Medical Adviser to make her points, then asked the other Panel members to make theirs, only to discover they did not share her concerns and, in some cases, quite the opposite, including other Medical Advisers. I reported back to Danny.

'Good,' he said.

I would have been quite happy to stand aside, for Chairing that Panel involved a tremendous lot of work every week, reading extensive reports in the evening. But Danny would have walked through fire before he let other agencies – police, health, housing, education, DSS – dictate to statutory social work how to carry out our duties, unless significant grounds were shown.

When Danny's successor as Chief Social Work Officer, Big Grahame took over in 1997, who had a residential care background rather than fieldwork, my reports to him from the Adoption Panel were basically waved through. Danny, a veteran of the generic care era, had scrutinised every line, just as he did every Guardianship Order. No shame on Big Grahame or his Masters in Business Administration but Danny was the last CSWO in West Lothian who could bring their own professional experience in such matters to bear meaningfully. I remember reporting back quite pessimistically to Grahame about a Freeing for Adoption appeal I had been interrogated over at length standing in the dock at Linlithgow Sheriff Court as an 'expert witness'. The defence lawyer asked me why the Panel recommended adoption rather than long-term fostering. I stood for ages in a mid-summer heat wave, all the doors of the court wide open, with an old electric fan roaring away above my head while a notoriously pedantic and deaf old Sheriff kept interrupting my testimony every few seconds to bellow 'speak-up... up... up!'

Big Grahame phoned me cock-a-hoop when he received the Sheriff's summation which stated he had been particularly convinced by my 'very compelling evidence'. This had involved a youngish defence lawyer asking me to name the actual research studies that informed professional decision-making over choosing between long-term fostering and adoption. I said that attachment theory informed the reviewing structure used by the local authority and that practice guidelines were issued periodically by Anne Black and Gerry O'Hara at Shrubhill, based on research by folk like Professor John Triseliotis and Dr Vera Fahlberg. The old Sheriff wrote it all down furiously as I bellowed it out at a fair rate of knots and decibels. Thus, I said, when a child comes into care there had to be an initial review within 72 hours to agree a care plan to return the child as soon as possible to the family with such supports as necessary. This is then reviewed in three weeks, then three months, then six-monthly thereafter. Parents are given practical assistance and encouraged to maintain visits and contact with the child as frequently as possible, and so on.

I cited national statistics showing that the earlier the child is returned home the better will be the prospect of full return but, if the child was still in care after six months, there was virtually no chance of that child being rehabilitated. I offered to supply the court with the relevant guidelines and the Sheriff nodded vigorously. I also explained the difference between adoption and long-term fostering, both of which could supply stability and security for a child and both of which could break down – or become 'disrupted' in the new lingo regarding adoption – but adoption was as close as it was possible to get to offering a child a 'normal' family experience, especially for younger children. If an adoption became disrupted, then Resources Teams and Adoption agencies could supply support to maintain the placement just as they would a foster-placement breakdown.

I did the job but there was no sense of elation or 'getting a result' – not in this case or, indeed, most. The mother of the child in question, a youngish overweight woman, had quietly sobbed all through my testimony sitting beside the young lawyer, though I could not hear her above the noise of the fan. These are knife-edged decisions and judgements to have to make in specific cases, specific lives, affecting the child certainly but also the birth parent and their family. This mother's mental and physical health will no doubt be greatly affected by such proceedings, which can never be shied away from, of course. But, in court, I saw the mother for the first time, not simply as a name on a pile of assessment reports written by others but a quivering mass, a human being not able to meet her own child's basic needs largely because of her own. It is this personal encounter that lies at the heart of social work assessments and is constantly under threat from being forgotten or not properly understood or no longer expected the further up the management food-chain such decisions have to go.

Such decisions had indeed increased from my early involvement with adoption practice in the mid-1970s. As the proportion of infants relinquished round birth by the parent reduced, so the number of older children 'freed for adoption' from the care system increased which likewise saw a rise in the number of 'contested adoptions' by birth parents. A Department of Health review noted this change in 1999 and a leading adoption agency, Scottish Adoption, spelled out the implications for practice:

This work is becoming increasingly complex as the population of birth parents/relatives requiring a service shifts from relinquishing birth parents to contested adoptions where parents/relatives may have complex needs

through drug/alcohol use, mental health issues and learning difficulties
(Clapton, 2012: 17)

All was not doom and gloom, of course. Another feature of social work office life that survived through to the late 1990s and was once quite central to staff relations and workplace harmony was the Christmas party, which both the Livingston children's teams attended *en masse*, plus community care and Admin teams. We had a karaoke machine, of course, blaring away in the huge conference room. I recall the first one when John, the North Senior, was quietly sitting at the door leading into the kitchen waiting on the show to begin, not intending to sing or dance himself, and he politely refused several offers from his team, I noticed, while I stood patiently waiting my turn to sing 'Danny Boy' with Pattiann and Joyce. A dramatic passodobla suddenly shot out from the karaoke machine and one of John's sonsy workers just as suddenly made an entrance and shimmied menacingly across the floor shaking her rigging to the pulsating beat of the music, homing in on an absent-minded John, who caught sight of her rather late and as he raised his palm to thank her for her kind offer but – she suddenly grabbed his outstretched wrist and yanked him out the chair and turned him into a veritable rag-doll for a wonderful next three minutes. John was held in a vice-like grip, trying to behave as though none of this was happening. But it was, oh yes, indeed it was. Highlight of my first year and possibly for the whole of the rest of my professional life in Livingston office.

Sexual relations amongst staff were not unknown in social work as in any workplace. Such relationships were studiously ignored unless they raised themselves awkwardly and, even then, they were downplayed as far as possible. For some reason, the relatively small size of West Lothian's social work network perhaps, a peppering of liaisons began to become public which for some reason seemed to result in one of the parties being dispatched off to another workplace, often Broxburn, which Big Ronnie soon took to referring to as the Betty Ford Clinic. Ronnie himself had relationship difficulties which he now blamed on having been 'released too early' from Broxburn and Big Peter's wise influence. These situations often involved married people and so this may have brought them to the attention of senior management with some need to step in.

I talked one worker, not in my team, out of announcing at a team meeting that they were having an affair with another worker, same sex, same team, but it was 'all over now'. I suggested their careers might be all over now as well as their marriages if the matter was raised in a public way because confession is the business of priests not Human Resources, whose business is sacking. Social workers are ordinary human beings, need I say, with an ordinary entitlement to live their private lives in private. I might add that the person in senior roles in respect of these liaisons were often females. Others may wish to consider whether this represents an advance in 'girl-power' in local Government along with the fact that when I retired in 2009 I was the only male Child and Families team manager out of four in the Livingston office. I likewise supervised the only two male social workers left in a staff group of about 25 to 30.

I eventually got an extra half-Senior's post for my team, for I was also supervising four social workers as well as chairing the Permanency Panel and countless children-in-care reviews for Broxburn and Bathgate cases for which there was no Admin support. Some of the older social workers retired and some new faces appeared. My Senior applied for a job in another part of the Region for which I supplied a reference and made the foolish mistake of imparting the truthful information that we had not chosen each other but still managed to form an effective working partnership because of her strengths and abilities. However, it transpired that the small jobby who chaired her interview expressed concern about some of my comments to our client services manager (who had of course installed her as a Senior in Livingston). The small jobby did not offer the post to my Senior, of course, for I knew him from when I was Intake Senior in Craigmillar and Convener of the Shop Stewards Committee. He had been an ineffectual Area Officer in Edinburgh, and his Senior group a renowned set of bolshies, very capable bolshies, who studiously ignored him. The idea he would have welcomed a bolshie social worker, never mind appointing one as a Senior, was therefore quite fanciful in the extreme.

The episode was a harbinger of what lay ahead as regards the content and structuring of references and job interviews. Human Resources (HR) now began to seriously hijack the format of job interviews and adverts: pre-interview visits by social workers to check out the workplace and possible future colleagues were banned as were informal discussions with team social workers; references were denuded of any revelatory professional-social comments; supplementary questions during interviews which varied from a pre-set agreed list were anathema; points were accorded by individual interview panellists for each 'correct answer' (which confined the questions to stuff like did they know what a client was); marks for each question were given then totalled and, while not binding, the panel had to explain why the post was not offered to the top-scoring candidate.

This pseudo-scientification never impressed me much. It is based on the kind of psychometric testing whose starting point is lie-detection – normative, behavioural, psychological. Its purpose is to factor out human difference. It is for folk who do not really get irony, who think Douglas

Adam's *Hitchhiker's Guide to the Galaxy* is just that, while the Secret of the Universe could well be 'the number 42'. As a profession, we perhaps needed to develop our interview style from that of the early 1980s, when Big Tam was asked by a candidate for a social work assistant post in Falkirk 'What about clothes?' – meaning 'Is there a dress code?' – to which he replied, 'Yes, we'd prefer you to wear some'. She got the job and proved very capable in the years to come – unlike, some might think, either of us. On the other hand, had Danny applied these new conventions with anything like zest, he might not have appointed one of his future successors as CSWO, Ian Quigley, who had a terrible interview, nervous and frozen in a way which belied his abilities. The same might be said of one of Big Ronnie's workers and later mine, Big Moira, whose non-PC straight-talking to struggling ex-kids in care drew them to her bosom like iron-filings to a magnet, cats to catnip.

* * *

In October 1995, I received a Certificate in Scottish Cultural Studies with distinction from the University of Edinburgh through its adult education classes run by Murdo MacDonald, later Professor of Art at the University of Dundee and the author of a great book on the history of Scottish Art. He arranged with Margaret McKay to have a copy of my Shale dissertation placed in the archives of the School of Scottish Studies, the University of Edinburgh. In July 1994, I also gained through in-service training a Certificate in Child Protection Studies from the University of Dundee, which all children and family social workers and frontline managers undertook through a programme rolled out over the next few years. One could say that, by this time, writing, reading, researching and studying had become integral to my life and temperament. I began writing *Shale Voices*, which would be published in December 1999. On Saturday afternoons for the next couple of decades, I could be found mooching around any number of second-hand bookshops in Edinburgh, Glasgow or Fife, browsing and ruminating on matters not defined or confined by social work mentalities at all. It was on one of these that I came across *Secrets of Strangers*, by Alice Thomas Ellis and Tom Pitt-Atkins, a remarkable book on personal and family identity, one of the most intriguing I have read.

If my writing life began to diverge markedly from my social work life, then that was once not so strange or uncommon in a profession which sought well-rounded people. For most of my career, the standard questions asked at job interviews had been 'Do you have a sense of humour?' and 'How do you balance the demands of your work and life?' Such queries showed the extent to which the profession simply assumed that social work marched to the beat of a drum different from most other local Government jobs, so focused as it had to be on the needs of others that one could easily lose sight of one's own needs and identity as a person – not a dilemma often faced, say, by a binman or housing clerk. I studied and wrote Scots poetry and social-cultural history, played five-a-side football and had a drink and laugh afterwards with lawyers and van drivers, and blethered with my mother.

Life was not all about social work, therefore, and my interest in studying literature developed into writing poetry following my departure from Edinburgh in the early 1990s.

I wrote a letter round this time to the novelist William McIlvanney, also a very fine poet, about his recent novel which I had found fascinating and I also included the recently written 'Fitba' Cliché' which I thought he might like (and no doubt secretly hoped he might pass on to some publisher!) as well as 'Brithers'. William McIlvanney, imbued with that spirit often referred to as literary Scotland's 'republic of the mind', sent me a brief note in reply, handwritten, dated 6 October 1992. It addressed me as though I, a complete novice, was a peer, which is one of the great qualities I discovered about our writing fraternity, its principled lack of elitism and openness to anyone trying to write, well conveyed in his reply:

> Thanks for your letter, which was a bandage for a sair day. Your appreciation is all the more heartening for being informed with such understanding. I especially enjoyed your poetry. I found 'Brithers' very moving, particularly because it confirms me in something I've always believed – that the nearest thing we have to immortality is how we live on in those who have cared for us, whose lives we have illumined, whose living sustains a continuing echo of our own. I like the way 'Fitba' Cliché' marries serious thought and ordinary experience, exemplified for me in making the high art of TS Eliot don a football scarf – 'In the room the punters come and go/Talking of De Stephano' – Keep writing. Thanks again. All the best.

Now I come to the way-going of Danny and the arrival of 32 new District Councils in 1995–6. Unfortunately, this means returning the reader to a time when Jeremy Corbyn was still a Lenin-hat wearing Lefty MP for Islington North and not remotely dreaming of the fate that awaited him a mere two decades later. It also means recalling a local West Lothian District councillor, a convert to the cause of New Labour nicknamed 'Gaddafi', presumably by those who knew him best. On the dawn of Districtisation, Mr Gaddafi had walked into his local area social work office and announced to the bemused staff that 'you work for me now'. Mr Gaddafi seemed oblivious to the fact that many of those whom he addressed had sectioned folk under the Mental Health Act for less delusional behaviour. Danny had visited that same office with John Chant in the months running up to the replacement of the Regions and they were taken round other places by Gaddafi, who always introduced them as 'the people who currently run social work in West Lothian'. Danny and John thought this might not bode too well for the future. Unfortunately, they were right.

I had bumped into Gaddafi myself a decade and a half earlier when I took over as Convener of the Lothian Social Work Shop Stewards Committee in the early '80s. He had been invited along to one of our weekly meetings at Picardy Place to give some input on shop stewards training, he being a tutor at one of the Further Education Colleges that provided courses for shop stewards and health and safety reps for NALGO and other unions. Although only an item on the agenda, Gaddafi proceeded to prowl round the room like a pole-dancer at a hen night, pouncing on some tongue-tied unfortunate who saw their role as merely representing their colleagues in traditional trade union terms – wages and conditions of service. Gaddafi verily gave them shit for not taking on the official trade union hierarchy, typical Ultra-Left stuff, but proffered in a coquettishly strutting manner that would have made Mick McGahey boak. It certainly made me boak. From Ultra-Leftist to New Labour neophyte, a new Masters degree in Business Administration in his hip-pocket, Gaddafi would then transform himself, as many in the 1990s labour movement would, from socialism to entrepreneurial fundamentalism in an era-long skidmark that took about two decades to come to a halt, if it ever has.

The replacing of 12 Regional Councils by 32 new District Unitary authorities in 1996 allowed the Tories to install into local Government Chief Executive-led corporate management structures which budget-managed skilled services like education, social work and health previously run by vocationally or clinically trained professionals. The title of Director of Social Work was changed to Chief Social Work Officer, thus making Danny legally responsible for the statutory delivery of services in West Lothian, the budget for which was controlled by a Corporate Manager qualified in, yes, Housing. The professional direction of statutory social work had thus been taken over by budgetary management principles, from which position it has not wavered since. The Devolved Parliament in 2000 controlled by New Labour created another layer of accountability which ham-strung local Government spending in ways that the old Scottish Office under George Younger and Michael Forsyth could only dream of. And it was Scottish to boot! A report by Tom Gordon in *The Herald* on 27 January 2018 illustrates the path down which social work and all other local Government and health services were about to amble:

Scottish councils reckon 58 per cent of their budgets are effectively off limits to cuts because of SNP Government priorities such as education, childcare expansion, and integrated health and social care. So all cuts fall in the other 42 per cent.

Welfare was becoming an ever bigger political football.

As far as most frontline social workers and their managers in West Lothian were concerned, April 1996 probably felt like nothing much had changed as a result of the Districts taking over from the Regions – another small bump in the road. Danny was still the boss of social work, only responsible to a corporate manager who also managed Housing, David, more in need of social work input I thought at that time, being a Hearts fan forced to watch them at Tynecastle during the reign of Vladimir Romanov. I met David once in 13 years, one less time than I had John Murphy in two, all by accident. But once was enough, for David did not know one end of a client, or any section of any Social Work Act, from a Brillo Pad – and why should he? What could we have talked about – budgets, bringing back prefabs, Willie Bauld? I think not. Besides, Danny was paid to talk to him and Wee Eck, who was now the Chief Executive, an accountant who had grown up in the 1950s in Fallside in Bathgate where one needed to know how to get and keep hold of a penny. Eck had risen to become Chief Tight-Purse for the old West Lothian District Council, in with the bricks, and thence put in charge of the new West Lothian District Council's treasury. Danny got on well with Wee Eck, both no-nonsense characters focused on doing what they were good at – their own jobs.

If the move to Districts for frontline social workers and managers felt painless, for Danny it felt more like time to pull on his old 'bovver boots' and start 'clugging' – primarily his former Regional boss in Edinburgh, Les McEwan, who had taken over as Director from the ailing John Chant who sadly died of cancer in October 1995 aged 57. One of John's last pieces of advice to Danny regarding the new District authorities was to make sure he got a seat at the Corporate Managers Group, otherwise he was 'doomed' (though he used a word beginning with 'f'). A few such words passed between Danny and Les in the coming period, especially over children and families, the key clash being the cost of the foster-places West Lothian charged Edinburgh, and for 'extra' services such as specialist placements for children with disabilities, problematic behaviour and special needs. West Lothian had most of the foster families given its plethora of old mining working-class communities, while Edinburgh City had most of the kids requiring such families. On the other hand, Edinburgh had control of the main Assessment Centre with 'secure' beds and Wellington List D

School to which West Lothian needed access, so Danny had to battle with Les, a renowned clugger himself, in a struggle which puts some of the Brexit negotiations in the shade.

Such matters were kept well away from frontline workers and their managers, however, who to all intents and purposes were left pretty much alone to make the same kind of assessments for care as they always had. There was certainly no question of finance intruding into our professional calculations and opinions regarding meeting need. Childcare agencies and charities like Barnardo's also began recruiting foster parents in West Lothian and elsewhere, as did a local private residential children's home – which later employed (or stole) two of my experienced workers in order to recruit families from all over Scotland, Fife, Lanarkshire and the Borders. One of them would continue to recruit and manage foster-placements herself on a small-business basis but it would take until 2005 before anything like a private-market evolved in this sector, the main providers for children's services remaining the local authorities.

A parting of the ways eventually transpired between Danny and the Council or at least the small enclave who led it – the Council leader (a senior transport executive whom Danny could never get hold of, him being away 'doing an MBA'), Gaddafi, David the Hearts fan and Wee Eck. It all came to a head around August 1997 over budgetary control and a change to the internal social work structure about which Danny had not been consulted and disagreed with when he was. Danny refused to give an oath of loyalty to remain within the budget and not go to the Committee if it happened to run out. He said that need determines the social work budget and he would not leave children or old people in situations of risk as defined by statute – because it is the Chief Social Work Officer, not an unqualified Corporate Housing Manager, who is responsible for the professional delivery of social work services in law. The other feature of the dispute was the proposal that Domicillary Care – home-helps etc – would now be line-managed by Gus Campbell despite his post being in policy planning and not operations. With Gus reporting directly to David and not Danny, this would take service delivery outwith the orbit of operational management as it applied to all other services including the rest of community care, criminal justice and C&F.

Danny had already been excluded from the appointment panel for a Domicillary Care Manager post as well as from attending the Association of Directors of Social Work (ADSW), the most powerful professional social work body in local Government, which David the Hearts fan had decided to go to – with what knowledge, professional authority or grasp someone like me finds it impossible to even contemplate. On reflection, maybe the ADSW were all housing managers by then, apart from Les McEwan.

Anyway, the Council Quartet then brought forth a package, a very golden package, that Danny took all of ten seconds to consider. Goodbye, West Lothian Council. Danny got a call from a senior 'Old Labour' councillor who said that the Labour Group in West Lothian knew nothing about this and he could get it reversed immediately. Danny asked if he could get him a seat at the Corporate Managers Group as well but he said he could not. So Danny phoned Securicor to send their biggest van along to collect his early-retirement package.

Danny was given a great send-off, the back hall of the West Port in Linlithgow packed out. I did the speech which incorporated a slideshow with old and spoof pictures purporting to illustrate the story of Danny's life. I had photos on acetate sheets and a projector throwing them onto a huge screen behind me. It opened with a photo of the aftermath of Hiroshima (yes) which I had placed on the projector and covered up with a blank sheet of paper. I then opened by saying that Danny was born and brought up in the mining village of Bonnybridge and here was a picture of it – Bonnybridge before the war (I uncovered then recovered the devastated scene) – Bonnybridge during the war (ditto, same scene) – and Bonnybridge rebuilt (ditto, same scene). 'Eva Braun' also appeared as a 1930s blonde screen-goddess on her way to a NALGO crisis meeting with Danny – and so on and so forth. Big Tam, Wee Marion, Raymond and the rest of the Falkirk crew and some faces from Craigmillar and Edinburgh also turned out. It was like a valedictory address, a symbolic gathering of the old generically trained, one-door school of social workers, managers and directors bidding farewell to one of their own. Danny would in fact have a great time thereafter – back to writing court reports as a freelance social worker for Clackmannan, then chairing its adoption and fostering Panel until a couple of years ago. He likewise chaired a foster panel for Foster Care Associates, a private care organisation in Glasgow and now drives patients for hospital appointments and the like as part of a local charity volunteer scheme in the Falkirk area. Big Tam says he ended up doing more social work after he retired than he ever did before.

Which brings me to Shakespeare or, more specifically, *A Midsummer Night's Dream,* which is famous for its 'play within a play' plot, the outer play comprising a set of fairies who impishly bewitch the humans – the skilled artisans – who are rehearsing their own play, the main character of which, Bottom the Weaver, is fooled into believing he is an ass (or donkey), the outer play thereby invading the inner one to much glee, confusion and mischief. Eventually they all wake up. Commentators have seen the play's underlying theme as 'not playing to the rules' with Bottom also a key figure in that respect. In the charmed world of West Lothian District social work in 1996–7, however, no one was in the least duped into believing that they were either an ass or that local Government could be run as though it were a private company by the ideological fairy-dust sprinkled first by the Tories and then New Labour. Folk like Danny and his tall successor, Big Grahame, refused the role of Bottom the Weaver – one of the 'rude mechanicals' – as comic fall-guy for the fairies. In their own ways, neither Danny nor Big Grahame stuck to the official script that the local politicos and their nose-wipes had in mind for them. Nor would Gus Campbell, or me at a much humbler level, just by doing our jobs.

Social workers did not see themselves as working for Gaddafi or Wee Eck, far less the Hearts fan David, only a handful of whom would have recognised them in any case. Social workers never saw themselves working for politicians, national or local, but for their immediate Seniors, courts, hearings and tribunals – the 'inner play'. Most social work is expressed in statute as 'duties' or 'powers', the latter giving local councils discretion to provide additional services, such as meals-on-wheels, if they can find the money. The new District Councils did what the central state funded them to do, mostly mediated through quangos. 'Quango' would become a term of political abuse from both Left and Right over the years but history shows that in perilous times it is often wisest to view one's enemies' enemy at least temporarily as your friend. The respected journalist-writer Andrew Marr noted in the mid-1990s that the Thatcher and Major Governments had created a 'quango-state' while telling lies about creating a democratic one:

> It has been estimated that there were in 1994 up to 63,120 non-elected new magistrates as against just over 25,000 elected councillors. The reorganisation of local Government into single tiers would strip away the ranks of the latter still further ... But the ministeriate didn't have the courage to hand down the political power as well. They tried to devolve the work, while keeping the control. They recognised that unelected quangos couldn't be given utter freedom, so they piled on the national controls, still exercised privately through Whitehall. They managed to combine a lack of democracy with bureaucratic inertia, the worst of both worlds. So the effect has been most odd. (*Ruling Britannia*, 1995: 96-8)

That effect included quangos protecting the public interest by acting as custodians for individual human and civic rights. Quangos can protect minority rights against majorities, including the elective majorities that periodically produce Gaddafi and his ilk or boot them out. But professionals – 'the rude mechanicals' – persist as public officials charged with upholding these rights, whoever is in or out of power. Gaddafi should have read more Shakespeare, methinks, and set far less store in Total Quality Management

(TQM). Which reminds me, the European Centre for TQM closed a few months after I retired in August 2009, a casualty of the Great Recession – TQM, that is, not me. But the point persists that quangos function as 'semi-public administrative bodies outside the civil service but receiving financial support from the Government which makes senior appointments to them'. The Hearing system is thus a quango, as are Mental Health Tribunals and the Care Inspectorate. These public institutions possess statutory powers whose inner workings politicians have no right to interfere with except through funding levels or changing statutory powers through parliamentary legislation. That is what determines professional social workers' duties within local authorities, not the preferments of their employers or council chiefs. Social workers assay their remits directly through Courts, Hearings, Mental Health Tribunals and, somewhat more obliquely through the Council, Care Inspectorate, Triple SSSC and Social Work Scotland (the old Association of Directors of Social Work, the ADSW). Somewhere, relegated to the bench, now sit BASW, UNISON and the other white-collar unions: is it not time they were brought back into the game?

Regional social work departments once operated like quangos located inside local Government run by powerful and respected Directors. Regional councillors, including those on the social work committee, were not allowed within a mile of frontline social work staff, nor statutory decisions regarding individual cases. The extreme scenario of Fred Edwards paying out Section 12 money to single striking miners in 1984–5 (£191,000 loans were paid to unmarried miners later judged illegal) revealed the extent to which politicians could not ignore, far less try to command, how professional duties should be exercised. The Scottish Office backed off from personally surcharging Big Fred for fear of sparking further public protest. Fred Edward's professional statutory authority posed a real dilemma for the Scottish Tories because it was certainly more in tune with public opinion than they ever were. The same applies to the health service where the expertise of medics remains a key part of the narrative, the 'play within a play'. Gaddafi, his head up his ass, would finally wake up to find that it was the politicos in Westminster and Holyrood who still controlled, ring-fenced and targeted local Government funding – not him, dreaming his dream of ruling the roost in West Lothian Council PLC.

12

The Golden Thread

The [New Labour] Government had more targets – over 6,000 on one count – than Stalin. By March 1999, Blair dedicated himself to a twenty-year plan to abolish child poverty. At a less sublime level, councils were instructed on the annual gross weight of dog turds they were expected to scoop. 'It's just not technically feasible, never mind desireable, to have so much centralisation,' noted Tony Wright, the impeccably New Labourite chairman of the Public Administration Committee: 'If everything is a target, nothing is a target.'

Andrew Rawnsley, *Servants of the People*, 2000

2018 is the ideal time to hold tight to the golden thread from the 1968 commitment to the value base of social justice, prevention and the power of the community and ensure that that thread can be woven into the integrated contemporary landscape.

Interviewee 50th Anniversary Report Social Work (Scotland) Act 1968
Brigid Daniels, Jane Scott, 2018

Big Grahame takes over from Danny and plays a blinder. A new punk rock band is introduced, 'The Purchaser Provider Split', lead singer, Sid Swift. New Labour politicos are given another monstering by the author who also traces back the introduction of new technology and the complaints system. The first Care Inspection and the infant Triple SSSC are discussed but resemble Picasso's Blue Period – namely, monochromatic shades of blue only occasionally warmed by other colours. Punitive-populist legislation is critiqued by the author who sounds almost clinically depressed. He cites a load of academic and professional authors aghast at the impact of neo-liberal social and economic policies and even says a few things about social work. He even starts quoting Big Tam and Big Ronnie.

MRS THATCHER'S HOSTILITY to public services was blatant in the way she spoke of 'cuts' so John Major, Tony Blair and Gordon Brown hymned 'targets', a new rhetoric for new times, 'cuts' through the back door. New Labour's new business techno-lingo confused even its own true believers. In reality, Blair-Brown finessed the Thatcher-Major 'purchaser-provider split' – softening their moral authoritarianism while deploying the more resonant language of social inclusion, social justice, diversity and choice. This concealed rather than reconciled the contradictions within the discourses of welfare by conflating what John Clarke called an 'apparently cuddly notion of partnership with its attachment to the harder-edged entrepreneurial techniques of cost-cutting, target setting, performance monitoring and competition' (John Clarke et al., *New Managerialism New Welfare*, 2000: 17,19).

Thatcher's list of 'achievements' would ultimately prove 'ambiguous and contradictory' and thus never fully 'trusted' by the public (Clarke, 2000: 5). The same could be said of Blair and Brown and their embrace of 'spin' – a new word to add to the synonyms for 'lying'. Between John Major's launch of the fraudulent Citizen's Charter in 1991 and the birth of its step-child, Tony Blair's Best Value in 2001 – 'fair competition, regulation, joined up working' – it became clearer that their idea of citizenship meant turning people into consumers of private services. In the social work world, that meant treating clients like 'customers'. The trouble with that is that urging people on the verge of suicide to 'have a nice day' neither works nor costs any less, never mind making a profit. Social work's mission is in fact to do itself out of business, not create more of it – fewer not more junkies, fewer not more criminals, fewer not more kids in care. Thus, the drive towards privatising social care mostly created the dog's dinner of half-truths, unrealistic public expectations, underfunded services, bed-blocking and the food banks on view everywhere today. As John Clarke, one of the radical welfare academics linked to Stuart Hall's Birmingham Centre for Contemporary Culture, noted of the 'New Welfare' model emergent by 2000 (5):

> [Thatcherism] had limited impact on controlling overall public spending; it shifted, rather than reduced, the tax burden, away from income and corporate taxation; it did not 'roll back the state' in any simple sense – though it certainly changed the capacities of the state and some of its relationships to the market and civil society; it 'set people free' in some limited ways but 'rolled the state forward' through the expansion of policing powers, criminalisation and the number of people in prison; it increased the scale and gradients of inequality in the UK while refusing to recognise the link between poverty and social problems; it attempted to change the meaning of welfare and the role of the state but had to go to considerable lengths to assure the public that cherished welfare provisions were 'safe in our hands'.

Oh dear, all that blood and snotters and it hadn't even worked. Well, maybe it had for the majority but certainly not for the underclass with whom social work is primarily engaged. In 2007, a UNICEF report confirmed that 22 per cent of children in the UK were poor compared to 13 per cent in 1977 (Iain Ferguson, Michael Lavalette, *Social Work After Baby P*, 2009:17). Gordon Brown would deregulate the banks while Blair regulated the professionals within the welfare state, sidelining the biggest critics of the retreat from 'universalism' – the main means by which the poor are effectively linked to social wealth increases through progressive taxation, fair wages and full employment. All of this was ditched when New Labour embraced the private market as a means of 'modernising' the welfare state. All of this is detailed in Andrew Rawnsley's archly funny but devastating critique of New Labour, *Servants of the People* (2000:292) and *The End of the Party* (2010). These confirm the arrogance and mind-boggling level of dysfunctionality at the heart of New Labour, bouncing unevenly between Blair's vanity – who thought he felt the 'hand of history' on his shoulder, which unfortunately belonged to George W Bush – and Brown's vaunting ambition and hubris. He claimed to have solved capitalism's boom-and-slump cycle just as the Great Recession hit, after which he had to try to solve it all over again.

It remains unfixed, aggravated further by Austerity. New Labour's failure to reduce the working-poor created by Thatcherism and strengthen those workers' rights removed by Thatcherism enabled the Tories-Lib Dems to impose another decade of cut-backs on essential public provision including health, transport, education, housing, social care and prisons as places for education and rehabilitation. Trends which were only spectral or vestigial in the closing decade of my professional life have since crystalised, some of which I wrote poems about for *Dancing with Big Eunice*. This included the introduction of new technology for the purposes of bean-counting and to 'target welfare spending more effectively' – which morphed instead into 'cutting more efficiently'. The main effect of new technology on frontline social work has been to speed up referral rates. Social workers and their frontline managers now have to keep abreast of vastly increased volumes of unfiltered daily referrals received from other agencies, particularly the police. This has turned duty-shifts into day-long hamster wheel marathons which require that workers read and sift referrals before doing nothing with most of them. Too much 'non-information' cascading and recycling, too much bumf, too much arse-covering, too much defensive practice, too much senior-middle managers thinking more stats justifies their existence. And, in this new world of spin/virtual reality/targets, they might just be right.

Nothing like that in my time. Big Grahame took over from Danny as CSWO in 1997 and was highly computer- and IT-literate. He asked me to become the children's link to a small working-group created to bring in a new computer system called SID, whose love-child would be called SWIFT. It dragged on unnervingly slowly, the IT stuff being done by the stats person, Bob Stead and Ralph Brown, a techy minded ex-community care Senior. Our task was to help install The Purchaser-Provider Split – another punk-rock band, lead singer Sid Swift? 'Tell Sid' had been a popular slogan for a TV advert the Thatcher Government deployed to sell off British Gas in 1986 and it seemed strangely apt to find it helping introduce IT into corporate local Government through the 1990s and 2000s. Devising and installing SID and the oxymoron SWIFT was the usual nightmare. They were basically glorified electronic card-indexes that entailed complete upheaval of the existing Admin paper-file system, which ran in tandem with the new computer system for some years thereafter. Folk printed out the referrals they had just put onto SID/SWIFT but kept a paper copy in the file because nobody trusted, or understood, how long SID might last. The thing about computers, of course, is that they add nothing at all to the professional task of meeting need and delivering effective social work support in any qualitative sense. They provide information for use or misuse by senior managers and politicians, described by Sapey in 1997 (cited by John Harris in his *The Social Work Business*, 2003:69–70), which I precis in the following passage:

The primary task of the organisation may also be changed... from one of welfare provision to the collection of data to regulate and determine eligibility for such provision... Social workers will find themselves... part of a machine that has achieved an objective reality. Such systems will inevitably result in greater control over the interpretation of data and consequently over the activities of practitioners. Some of the consequences of this for social work were also noted by Harris including adding 'a form of surrogate 'continuous' surveillance... previously possible only in the running of factories' (71); supervisors 'acting more like progress-chasers than the peer-consultants associated with the permissive supervisory relationships of the pre-business era' (73); the steady replacement of social worker 'discretion' by a battery of controls 'expressed in manuals, direction and guidelines... standardised and repetitive systems; tightly defined criteria for eligibility for services; standardised assessment tools; interventions which are often determined in advance from a limited list; minimisation of contact time; micro-case management and pressure for through-put. Key decisions about social work provision are made by managers, rather than by social workers. The fragmentation of social work tasks and their redivision between qualified and less-qualified staff mean both de-skilling and a loss of social worker control over the process, turning the social worker 'from semi-professional to state-technician' (75)

What price Lena Dominelli's opinion that social work training was becoming 'the technical transmission of approved skills'? A study by UNISON (*Still Slipping Through the Net?* www.unison.org.uk) in 2009, the year I retired, found frontline social workers in England particularly critical of a system called Integrated Children's System (ICS) supported further by independent academic study of children's social work by Sue White, which sounds frighteningly robotic:

> ICS's onerous workflows and forms compound difficulties in meeting Government-imposed timescales and targets. Social workers are acutely concerned with performance targets, such as moving the cases flashing in red on their screens into the next phase of the workflow within the timescale. Switching off the flashing red light bears no relationship to protecting a child. That is something of which social workers and managers are acutely aware, but slippages carry sanctions.
> (Iain Ferguson et al, *Social Work After Baby P*, 2009:26)

The UNISON study roundly condemned 'the cult of bureaucracy imposed by the managerial reforms of the past two decades. As one worker put it:

> The focus of social work has become entirely procedural and the meaning of the work has been lost. The needs of children have become secondary to the needs of agencies responsible for protecting them. The contents of assessments appear insignificant as agencies are far more concerned about whether they are completed on time. (Ferguson, 2009: 27)

That may be a tad strong for I can report that the state machine never managed to make a machine out of me or those who worked for me – though that was a decade or so ago. I knew about society being a machine back in 1970 but never expected to have it sitting on my desk instructing me what to do. Social work had proved an escape for many of us from the alienation of the production line with its progress-chasers, stereotyping and thirst for averages, the measurable over the ineffable, the sensed over the unquantifiable in social existence and individual lives. I would remain resolutely 'pre-business era' throughout my social work career. So, too, would Gus Campbell, who had been slotted in as head of policy planning in West Lothian through the disaggregation process from Shrubhill and he began to line-manage the domiciliary care service after Danny left. He received periodic memos from David the Hearts fan and Wee Eck requiring him to reduce the home-care budget. They failed to discern that Gus had been a Senior Regional social work manager – and a Morton fan – and was therefore disinclined to take lectures from referees and similar non-players.

Gus's lieutenant, the domiciliary care manager, kept bringing in the cheques, which Gus to her amazement just kept signing and, when she reminded him one day that the budget would never be reduced if he kept signing the cheques, Gus remembers telling her, 'Now you've got it, Marjorie, now you've got it'. Computers and budgets may have confined social workers' professional discretion to some degree but it still had to be lodged with somebody who had some sort of social work qualification and professional sensibility – social workers, frontline managers, middle managers, senior managers or Chief Social Work Officers. The play within a play still had people who were able and prepared to take the part of 'the rude mechanical' and, hopefully, some might even be doing so to this day. The Vogons were wrong about their assertion that 'resistance is useless' because resistance never goes away, it just varies its ways and shapes. I found that by doing my job, exercising the professional judgement and experience I had acquired as a frontline manager became a form of resistance itself, under statute, under the noses of the non-qualified and the over-superannuated. My highest authority remained the Chief Social Work Officer, not the Council, though he might now be surprised to hear that himself.

Big Grahame did his job, a kind of creative accountancy in the cause of maintaining service delivery, preserving his budgets for the next dozen years or more by producing more rabbits out of more hats than Paul Daniels. I should have nominated him for a Queen's Award for Ingenuity rather than sending him provocative emails describing his latest Draft Service Plan as 'less a plan, more a shopping list in search of a trolley'. He later told me he had checked with Human Resources about trying to discipline me but decided against it, though he was urged constantly to do so by an IT manager to whom I sent cheeky emails when the Council's computer system flagged up that I had been using the word 'sex' in emails. I merely pointed out that paedophiles avoided using words like 'sex' in emails for obvious reasons, whereas C&F social workers and managers used it because it was our business. I can track this to 2003, in fact – the year my first poetry collection was published, *Sex, Death and Football* – the cover of which the publisher had sent to my workplace for approval. I did not mention that mind you. Big Grahame procured a very good deal for social workers' pay in 2002 through the Single Status job and pay evaluation for Scottish local Government which lifted social workers to within a hair's breadth of the starting salary of team managers, so that, today, workers earn up to £36K, which is where team managers start on a scale going up to £42K tops, no paid overtime. This has created a workforce further down the line that is unwilling to apply for the TM roles because they can see the daily pressures on frontline managers dealing with complex frontline cases unsupported by middle and senior managers who have now managed to distance themselves from such quotidian griefs.

Another trend emerged, the raft of new legislation appearing through the 1990s and 2000s which slowly altered professional practice across the board giving it either a market or protectionist veneer. This included domiciliary care for the elderly, using the privatising principles set out in the 1990 NHS and Community Care Act, implemented in 1993; the 1995 Children's Act, which reviewed the Children's Hearing system for the first time since 1968 and it now acknowledged that 'public protection' could on occasion qualify the 'best interests of the child' (section 16.5), which had been the cornerstone of child-centred practice for 35 years; and the 1995 Criminal Procedure (Scotland) Act, the 1997 Sex Offenders Act and later the 2003 Criminal Justice Act all bringing in agendas focused on protecting the public. All of this legislation would be passed by Tory and New Labour Governments which cumulatively served to make the law, once seen as only marginally relevant to social work practice, central to its operation (Deborah Baillie et al, *Social Work and the Law in Scotland*, 2003). This latter point in my experience means influencing the preparedness of senior managers to take 'iffy' cases to court where the risk was deemed high, even if the legal grounds were judged by council lawyers to be low. Judges often disagreed with these legal predictions on the basis of compelling 'care' evidence from social workers or home-helps. Social workers once acted on the basis of what they thought the 'best interests' of those 'without capacity' to be, based on a 'professional judgement' of risk, not the precept of doing so only having the certainty of established legal proof.

The legal framework surrounding child protection had grown after Orkney in 1991 but further measures and stipulations mushroomed under New Labour – the 1998 Human Rights Act, the 2003 Protection of Children (Scotland) Act, the 2005 Protection of Children and Prevention of Sexual Offences (Scotland) Act – and continued after with the 2009 Sexual Offences (Scotland) Act and the 2011 Children's Hearings (Scotland) Act. For young people aged 12–16, there was the 2004 Antisocial Behaviour (Scotland) Act. In the year of my retirement, the sheer scale of all this legislative mania was noted by the children's charity Action for Children report in 2009 which criticised the Government for the massive rise in care policies over the previous two decades:

> there have been over 400 different initiatives, strategies, funding streams, legislative acts and structural changes to services affecting children and young people over the past 21 years. This is equivalent to over 20 different

changes faced by children's services for every year since 1987... Half of the developments identified began in the past six years. Three quarters have come in the past 10 years (*Adoption and Fostering in Scotland*, Gary Clapton and Pauline Hoggan, 2012:xii).

And this is just the legislation affecting children and young people.

No one could accuse the Scottish Parliament of not being against crime and punishment – never unpopular with the Scottish public – except that the Children's Commissioner warned that tagging children under 16 could be in breach of the UN Convention on the Rights of the Child. The same contradictory messaging was rolling out across the UK. In his book *Chavs: the Demonisation of the Working-class* (2011), Owen Jones shows the perils that attend when social policy is made on the political hoof primarily to appease popular opinion without consulting or ignoring those actually dealing with alienated youth cultures on the basis of well researched and largely welfare informed perspectives:

> Originally, New Labour promised that under-eighteens would only have ASBOS (Anti-Social Behaviour Orders) served under exceptional circumstances but, as it turned out, year on year, around half were imposed on the young. Overwhelmingly, those on the receiving end were both poor and working-class – and, according to a survey in 2005, nearly four out of every ten ASBOS went to young people with mental health problems such as Asperger's Syndrome. In one case, a child with Tourette's was given an ASBO for his compulsive swearing.

The law, which had once provided the background for our work, began to make social work its servant and keeper rather than its meet companion.

I say 'the law' but what this actually means is the people who make it and the pressures they are trying to appease, the politicians and the public. Welfare academics began to see in this legal re-framing a tilt towards 'popular-punitive' and 'penal-populist' measures, particularly after 2000 with the creation of the Holyrood Parliament. In an extensive analysis of 'Criminal Justice in a Devolved Scotland', Hazel Croall, Professor of Criminology at Glasgow Caledonian University, noted the tensions and shifts that became an evident feature of contemporary Scottish criminal justice policy emanating from the Scottish Parliament (Gerry Mooney and Gill Scott, *Exploring Social Policy in the 'New' Scotland*, 2005:193). Other essayists discuss children and adult care:

> Before devolution, there was a clearly distinct set of policies in Scotland,

with a criminal justice culture showing a greater commitment to welfare as opposed to punishment, to inclusionary rather than exclusionary penal strategies, and which had resisted some of the excesses brought about by popular punitivism. Since devolution, criminal justice policy has been politicised and there are clear signs of penal populism, seen most clearly in the Executive's seeming determination to forge ahead with unpopular proposals such as the single agency and antisocial behaviour legislation in the face of strongly voiced concerns from practitioners and other experts. Whereas until recently, informed commentators were optimistic that the welfare tradition would survive, some now fear that the effects of punitive policies may undermine key elements of the system. The Kilbrandon Philosophy of the Children's Hearings for example could be threatened by the more punitive policies and tone of electronic monitoring, ASBOS, fast-track hearings and youth courts and a correctionalist turn in relation to criminal justice social work could threaten holistic forms of social work intervention. (Based on McNeill and Batchelor, 2004)

In reality, this tilt towards public protection took another decade or so to impact seriously on frontline practice. The people who were really being targeted by New Labour and then the SNP and Lib Dems were the electorate, not the client groups identified by the old Social Work (Scotland) Act – 'the mad, the bad and the sad'. There was an increasing focus on the burgeoning care needs of an increasingly ageing population. Fine and necessary but was it not also a subtle shift back to meeting the care needs of the deserving poor while the 'undeserving' were offered 'control' and 'care-management' – workfare instead of welfare? The onset of Austerity would lead to lesser funding cuts for the elderly – certainly in maintaining pension levels and entitlements – than the traditional social work client-groups. Universal Credit (or Universal Discredit) has recently been admitted to be unworkable by a Brexit-distracted Tory Government. It didn't stop them trying though, did it?

In my final decade as a frontline manager, I would run the same kind of ship I had always run, occasionally poking fun at folk like the IT manager, which was nothing compared to Big Grahame sending up Wee Eck at meetings of 30 social work and housing frontline managers. Grahame would try to enliven some dreary management by feedback mimicking Wee Eck's famously local demotic speech, which must have got back to him in some fashion. Big Grahame seemed not to care, droning on about budgets with nobody saying much or asking questions. Whenever I turned up to these, I could see his face light up. I arrived late one time and he said, 'Oh, come in, Alistair, glad you could make it.'

I said, 'Oh, I can't stay long, got some work to do, know. I just wanted to check what we're calling ourselves these days?'

It was in fact Social Justice, after plain old Community Services, after which would come Health and Care Partnership – (HCP.PLC?). If asked, my preferred option would have been 'The Department of Doubt and Uncertainty'. No one did.

Politicians, local and national, now began to stumble across my path more frequently. My view was that they were members of the public. In other words, they could give you information about individuals but not receive anything confidential in return, unless you approached them as Justices of the Peace to swear out warrants. Otherwise, like lone golfers, they had 'no status on the course'. For the most part, they were well-intentioned civilians wandering about in a minefield. For the first quarter century of my career, I only remember one phone call from a local councillor, a Tory district councillor, when I was Intake Senior in Craigmillar. He had a newsagents shop and wanted to complain on behalf of one of his constituents about a social work client, and he wondered what I was going to do about it. I said if the person was known, I would pass the info to the social worker's Senior but if his informant wished to speak directly to a social worker, they should arrange an appointment with the duty social worker. He thought this not good enough and I said it was to do with confidentiality and lower staffing levels caused by council cuts as a result of Tory Government rate-capping, which did not please him much either. I need not have said the latter, of course, but it signifies the extent to which there was, and still officially remains, a fire-wall between politicians and state professionals like social workers, based on rights of confidentiality enjoyed by all citizens, even those being complained about by – well, who knows whom?

In April 1996 when folk like Gaddafi entered the scene – 'you work for me now' – the unions were alert to the issue and a protocol was agreed with councillors that they should not contact frontline workers or managers directly but should go through Danny, the Chief Social Work Officer. Thus, Danny would phone me if a councillor spoke to him about a case and I told Danny the detail and he told the councillor what he thought appropriate to tell them – because the rules of confidentiality applied as much to him as to fieldworkers. Any councillor phoning me direct was simply asked to go through Danny. The same protocol was maintained under Big Grahame for the next decade or so but may have begun to slip as regards community care frontline managers who began to give information direct to councillors and MSPs, who sometimes spoke directly to social workers. Some even tried their luck with C&F frontline managers. I wrote a poem about one such instance when a local councillor, who later became leader of the Council, contacted the duty Senior of C&F, who happened that day to be my colleague, Margaret Kalashnikov, asking her to send out a duty social worker to a family upset at finding some condoms in their back garden and she did send out a worker. I went mental when I heard, told her she should be charged along with the councillor for wasting frontline social work time (just as people can be charged with wasting police time). I may even have meant it. Yes, I did mean it and the poem, 'Monday Morning Duty', explains why:

> It's Monday morning, again,
> and, yes, I'm duty senior, so
> I've read all the Emergency Referrals
> – the Unrulies, the Self-Harms,
> the Runaways, the Admissions,
> the general round of Domestics and
> Violations of the Peace – whit, in this dump?
> Anyway, between the Forensic Medicals
> and Joint Interviews, the ordinary mayhem
> and clatters roond the heid, and the weans
> found drunk in charge of their parents,
> and the alcohol, crack and cocaine,
> my eyes came upon this, a message from
> a councillor, no, not a person offering therapy,
> but someone definitely in need of some, yes,
> a local *politicien*, worried, so he says,
> about his constituents, who have found
> some condoms in their back-garden – can we
> please go round there straight away? Why –
> to pick them up, make sure they're no his?
>
> But now for some tea, and a read at the papers,
> something to cheer me up, perhaps, the work
> of the Scottish Government, Afghanistan.

The role of politicians, local and national, is to make laws and fund them adequately, not second-guess those whose job it is to assess and deliver the statutory services without fear or favour. I never encountered a Holyrood MSP during my time but I received the odd letter from the MPs Tam Dalyell and Robin Cook during the 1990s and 2000s. As a frontline manager, I wrote the draft replies and passed them to Danny then Grahame to edit and send on as they thought fit. One case horrified Robin Cook, which shows he would never have made much headway as an ordinary frontline local authority C&F social work team manager. It was a particularly tragic case involving a young mother in her early 30s with two children at primary and a baby a few months old. The mother was all but paralysed from the neck down.

A well-heeled family: the father/husband left her and the children abruptly to return to the leafy English suburbs of his parents' home, offering to take the children to live with him so long as the mother agreed. She was receiving psychological and physical therapy from St John's Hospital, a psychologist's report supporting her capacity and desire to keep the children 'with support'. The mother was able to sit in a chair in the house with the baby placed on her knee by an au pair while she took the other children to nursery and day-school. The mother's relatives lived on the west coast and came across to help out at weekends, thus far. I visited with a social worker to see for myself. I phoned the father to clarify his position, which remained the same, and he insisted he would make no attempt to take the children away legally from their mother unless she agreed. I was now dealing with three sets of denial – the mother's, the father's, the psychologist's up at St John's – and perhaps now a fourth – Robin Cook's down at Westminster?

I spoke to and then wrote a detailed letter to the mother after I had held an inter-agency meeting with her, members of her family, the psychologist, school, nursery and au pair in which I sought to clarify who did what and when regarding the care of all the children and what more might be possible. The father would not attend. My letter effectively said that, by asking the local authority to intervene, we had a statutory obligation to assess the best interests of all the children and went on to itemise all the varied options of support to consider from home-helps to foster care to Children's Hearings if matters deteriorated.

A copy of the letter was sent to the father in England, for both parents remained in the frame. Big Grahame phoned. He had just received a shocked letter from Robin Cook regarding the 'blunt' tone of my letter to the family. Grahame wondered if this new thing that had just come along for Community Care cases – direct payments – enabling people to organise their own care might be worth considering. This is now termed self-directed support, which came into force around 1997 but was then entirely new. I said I could see how adults could organise for their own care needs but this concerned the needs of the children, including a baby, and the father seemed prepared to finance it so payment was not really the issue. The problem was the precarious and fragmented nature of the care network presently sustaining the care of young children and a baby given the incapacity of the mother, the geographic distance of both the father and the mother's relatives and the almost total reliance on a young au pair who was due to depart soon. My letter had indeed been blunt, if that is another term for truthfully honest and clear-eyed about the actual care needs of a baby and a couple of youngsters. I was paid to be blunt with parents or anyone else over the adequacy of care arrangements because the law bluntly required that children's needs came before theirs, irrespective of postcode. The bluntness may indeed have had an effect, as was intended. The mother moved with the children to be near her family and relatives on the west coast and I soldiered on, blunt as ever, in Livingston.

As the 1990s wore on, a year or so after Danny's departure, another round of internal management re-structuring abolished the role of PTM. I saw this as a window of opportunity to change my role to supervising a group of social workers while keeping my PTM grade and dropping my working week down to four days. For some inexplicable reason, Big Grahame talked me into applying for the new group manager post, saying my request to do it on a four-day basis was no barrier. I wrote an application which bristled with contempt for any middle-management approach that did not protect the professional discretion of frontline staff and their supervisors. So, it was a great relief when Big Grahame said I could indeed become the 11th man, a four-day week Senior in the Livingston office, formally relegated to the sub's-bench but still getting paid the same as the first-team – every old pro footballer's dream. Indeed, so regretful did Grahame appear at this halt to my career that he agreed I could take an MPhil in Modern Poetry at the University of Stirling attending two days a week from September 1998 to December 1999. For the rest of my career, I would work 32 hours per week, Monday to Thursday, 8.30am to 5.00pm with half an hour lunch break, until I departed on an 18-month sabbatical in August 2007, courtesy of a writer's bursary from the Scottish Arts Council to write *Dancing with Big Eunice*, published in 2010.

I was now a Senior, later team manager, for half a dozen social workers with access to a couple of assistant social workers. In football parlance, I had dropped back down the park, playing well within myself and defending the specific areas I still thought worth defending. I felt in many ways like a well-paid Senior in a large office collaborating with three other children TMs while the group manager did all the donkey work: budgets, meetings, the swamp called performance indicators and waffle called 'joined-up-working' that was invisible to the naked eye and mostly irrelevant except when agencies worked together in specific cases. My colleague Seniors/TMs were decidedly less experienced than myself and, from the late 1990s to early 2006, there was a constant churn amongst the other three Senior and TM posts who flitted through the workplace in which I remained a fixture. I was duty Senior every Monday (the busiest day for dealing with weekend SCET

Emergency Referrals) and I chaired child protection case conferences for any worker who asked me, most of whom did not hesitate, for I was an assured and assiduous chairperson.

The Seniors came and went – Big Emm, Norah, Jane, Gillian, Angus, Ian, Pauline, Sheila, Carol – until finally the fog cleared in the mid-2000s to reveal the batch who would see me off the premises, so to speak. All were well-grounded in the craft, meaning they took no shit from anyone, including and perhaps especially me, which also suited me just dandy. One could not defend independent professional judgement in general then complain when it got deployed by Margaret Kalashnikov, Sister Sarah and Phoebe from *Friends* – which I secretly thought defined Judith's qualities – seeming otherworldliness round a core of Geordie iron. It is customary to say that a person's bark is much worse than their bite – well, not in Margaret's case. As for Sarah, an earlier career in nursing, possibly in the Crimea, made her busy and effective despite being distantly related to the English Poet Laureate, Alfred Lord Tennyson, who famously wrote 'The Charge of the Light Brigade', which, quite frankly, I could have seen all three of them leading. Fine, for the oyster of social work needs some grit in it and I am pleased to say we all supplied our fair share, sometimes wholesale, always for free and most likely unasked for.

Protocols changed, sometimes even for the better, despite drawbacks like child-rescue. As child protection procedures began to become more formalised in the 2000s, Initial Referral Discussions (IRDs) became standardised, forms being completed by the duty Senior on child referrals received from a range of agencies such as schools or children's centres. We now had to have phone conversations with the police family unit and the local paediatric unit at St John's to agree whether a joint-interview by the police and social work was required or a single-agency follow-up by police, medics or ourselves, or left with the school or agency which referred the matter. If no action was agreed, we still filled out a form and logged details on the computer. It formalised what had now become common inter-agency practice when investigating CP referrals and I had no problems with it in principle. In terms of social work, I felt it tightened up the initial stage of investigation by allowing the key protection agencies to agree there was enough concern to proceed and state those features of the situation which worried us most and so gave the social worker and police officer assigned a clearer focus for a visit when required.

In practice, however, there were paediatricians who had far lower 'thresholds of concern' than I did and usually the police rep who was routinely involved in these discussions, Wee Neil. There was rarely a referral that did not seem to qualify in some estimates for a 'full joint-interview'. Since social work or the police were most often the first agency to receive such referrals, I made sure I phoned Wee Neil first and he me. We were, after all, the prime social investigative agencies based in the community outwith the confines of a hospital precinct. A child-rescue mentality – a knee-jerk impulse to remove or protect a child from an alleged but not fully assessed situation – can present problems for proper inter-agency collaboration, an over-reaction not proportional to the initial risk presented. A family or a person has a statutory 'right to privacy' which obliges social work and the police to always ask if they in fact have good reason to knock on that door. Sending a social worker out on a visit always seemed to me a significant step to take, not a blanket one. My awareness of the importance of balancing individual liberty against overweening state power no doubt influenced my views here, for we do not have *carte-blanche* to enter premises, remove children or get medical examinations without sufficient legal cause being shown. I was interested primarily in the medical opinions of hospital doctors, not half-baked views on families, social and cultural matters or myself. I decided the social work response and no one else, for who else knows better what our job is? Let them get on with their own business and leave me to get on with mine – the messy stuff, not very neat, the weighing of options, particulars, duties, resources, powers, anxieties, 'risks'.

Collaboration does not mean total professional agreement, a will o' the wisp, it means sharing information and opinions. Making a decision not to do anything is still a decision. Lothian Region's child protection guidelines were prefaced during the 1980s and '90s by two instructions to practitioners: first, before doing anything else, read the guidelines; second, if the guidelines are not followed in some respect then write the reasons in the case notes. Guidelines were intended to aid professional judgement, therefore, not replace or restrict it. In other words, the guidelines presumed the operation of professional judgement. The law presumes the same: the exercise of responsibility. As an example of the stuff needing weighed by care professionals, I cite a recent Supreme Court ruling on 1 March 2017 in the matter of a permanency order taken out on EV, a child, versus West Lothian Council, finding against the Council. The court discussed the 'threshold for intervention' and cited approvingly Lord Templeman's summary from an English case in 1988 (para 50):

> The best person to bring up a child is the natural parent. It matters not whether the parent is wise or foolish, rich or poor, educated or illiterate, provided the child's moral and physical health are not endangered. It follows inexorably from that, that society must be willing to tolerate very diverse standards of parenting, including the eccentric, the barely

adequate and the inconsistent. It follows too that children will inevitably have both very different experiences of parenting and very unequal consequences flowing from it. It means that some children will experience disadvantage and harm, while others flourish in atmospheres of loving security and emotional stability. These are not the provenance (province) of the state to spare children all the consequences of defective parenting.

I spent four decades differentiating the abusive from the eccentric, the barely adequate from the inconsistent – because somebody has to and it will not be hospital-bound paediatricians, who know nothing of subcultures, deprived communities or childcare law in process. I cited Dr Kusumakar some time back regarding the necessity, particularly in sexual abuse cases, for professionals to be able to deal with 'their own rescue fantasies, anger, despair and uncertainty. There is no standard model for helping such children and families'. This basically is what my practice experience showed and which I upheld against all-comers, snooty hospital consultants, a professor of social work quoting 'the law' at me, while I quoted the latest finding of a fat wee deaf Sheriff in Linlithgow, who makes the law in Scotland with every judgement he makes, case by case. Social work's job is to weigh risk, which is a relative concept, and 'judgement', a professional one, in collaboration with other professions, but who do not share our exact responsibilities. Indeed, many of them are sometimes quite grateful that they do not.

Thresholds of intervention, like risk assessment in child protection investigations, should be active rather than reactive, specific and particular, never general or routine or rule-driven. I lived with risk all my professional life and I evaluated it all my working life and in a way that never got either myself or the Council into the headlines. I recall one particular occasion in 2005 when I was duty manager, unusually for me on a Friday, my normal day off. I had asked a colleague to cover while I went to a meeting. Just before I left, a child protection call came in regarding a situation: the school had some concerns about a child, the mother of whom was not agreeing for him to be seen by a medic. I had to hand it to my colleague to pursue and when I returned, the situation was that I was to meet the duty Sheriff in Edinburgh who was holding on until I dashed through to get an Emergency Child Protection Order signed. Friday evening Edinburgh traffic meant I got there at about 5.00pm. The Sheriff was as iffy about the whole thing as I was but I told him all I could. He signed it and buggered off home to Barnton, myself going back to Livingston, one of the posher areas.

I had arranged to meet a social worker and CID officer, Phil, outside the house but, just as I turned the corner, my car shuddered to a halt! I had to push it the last 20 yards or so to the house. We were greeted at the door by a genial black man in a brilliant dark blue suit and invited into an immaculately furnished, large modern-built house. Several happy, equally well-dressed children lined the stairs smiling at us. He was graciousness itself, a high-ranking health manager. He said that his wife had not understood the earlier discussions which she thought had meant the child was being taken away – English not being her first language. We talked more. I clarified that he was saying there was no objection to them now taking the child for examination at the hospital, accompanied by the police and the social worker. I briefly conferred with my colleagues in private and we agreed this was the 'least damaging alternative' to the child in the circumstances. And that was that. I pushed my car to start it and was phoned later to say the medical was fine and the parents were happy to have a social worker follow the matter up on Monday.

My colleague who set up the Child Protection Order was most unhappy on the Monday that I had not 'complied' with the warrant but chose to 'abandon' it – as she thought 'illegally'. My view was that to have done otherwise would have abandoned the child to a weekend of needless separation from the mother and the rest of the family. There was a cultural question involved, too, of a parent perhaps quite literally not understanding the law or trusting the legal authorities in this country, the police in particular. Compliance for limited purposes, like a medical, rather than blanket removal, had perhaps not been inserted into Child Protection Orders by then as happened later but I took the view that the warrant had been most reluctantly issued by the Sheriff I spoke to and it had already achieved that purpose. Compliance in this case was a means, not an end, and certainly not one that involved placing unnecessary further stress on that child. If harm came to the child over the weekend, I would have to answer for it. And I am sure the old Sheriff in Barnton, whose brandy-chaser I had delayed for perhaps half an hour would have agreed with me. As it was, I was more relieved that my car had not stalled halfway up the Mound on Friday afternoon than I was about any further repercussions. It was followed up on the Monday, held open for a short time and then closed. As a codicil, a friend of a friend of mine, not a social worker, recently met someone who had worked with me in Craigmillar in the early 1980s. She said that I gained a reputation for 'cutting corners' – though 'in a good way', in order to support clients. I can live with that. I did live with that.

I met need by using my professional judgement, authority and experience in real time as I had been trained and required to do for decades. I responded proportionally to the risk identified and I avoided potentially greater risks accruing by not removing a child for three nights from a home which a police officer, a social worker and I had just visited – and my colleague had not and one can perhaps wonder why. 'Playing safe' is never a viable professional option. There is no such thing as a riskless option. Taking a child into care can often be judged a 'safer option' in the immediate term but it is never an entirely safe one if applying longer term perspectives. When I made that decision I had worked in long-term, intake, emergency, patch, generic and specialist environments, all of which brought different timescales and perspectives to removal decisions. Child protection requires openly weighing up doubt and uncertainty as regards all the options available, including most of all removal. But 'safe uncertainty' and 'authoritative doubt' are what the family therapist Barry Mason says practitioners should always keep centre-stage, along with the understanding that 'positions of safe uncertainty' are never 'a fixed place'. He also warns that the effort to avoid marginalising the client's discourse should not risk practitioners marginalising their own expertise, of vacating their own judgement. The moral panic that now routinely surrounds childcare 'failures' has made it more and more frightening for workers and their managers to maintain that 'fuller exploration of doubt and uncertainty' which all care assessments of risk involve. But trust and building on it, rather than a blanket mistrust, is the basis on which a broader modern child protection service must be created, sustained and justified.

* * *

Complaints. My introduction to the Council's first complaints procedure occurred in 1998, a 15-year-old girl who was suspected of having a sexual relationship with a 20-year-old man, who may once have been in care. The girl's mother objected and the girl, highly wilful, set up home with him, a particularly possessive and controlling figure. The Hearing put her on supervision and she was placed in care. There was some police intelligence that worried us about this guy and other young girls which could not be shared either with her or the Panel. The Senior and social worker found it difficult to speak to the girl alone without him present so when they both appeared at the office and demanded to be seen together, I was called in to persuade the girl to be seen alone.

I opened the door of the waiting room, which had a security lock, and called her in, letting her through but barring his way, saying that the workers wished to speak to her alone about her supervisory conditions. He should therefore sit quietly in the waiting room or I would call the bizzies to remove him. The waiting room was deserted. That was the end of the story until a complaint came in about myself 'abusing' said citizen. The case was to be chaired by Alan Finlayson, the former Regional Reporter. I was kind of looking forward to seeing how he handled it: impartial, no doubt, as I had seen him at Hearings and when co-training medical students, witty and not over-formal. It got called off when it emerged that two of our office Admin women, on hearing of the matter, had recalled the couple barging past them on their way out of the office on that particular day with him shouting, 'I'll fix that big b, Findlay'. The wee rat thus convicted himself out of his own sizeable mouth and without the need for a video-replay.

Some social workers are worth complaining about, as I have already detailed, but this reached new heights when events revealed that I had in effect appointed a rogue social worker. I had chosen him despite the wishes of both my female Seniors. He was a middle-aged man, who had worked for a few years with a voluntary agency but not in statutory social work. I thought he might add something to the range of workers we currently had. He certainly did that but at the bottom end of the spectrum. After about six months, alarm bells began to sound – three to be precise, all around the same time, which was approaching Christmas. He was managed by one of my Seniors and had somehow become involved in a minor way with a complex sexual abuse investigation she was managing, allocated to an experienced female social worker. During the early stages of trying to establish these concerns in court, the rogue social worker stated during cross-examination that he had heard the Senior say to the allocated worker before going into a meeting with the couple that the man 'made her feel sick' or words to that effect. It was thus every bit as damaging as the accusation made by Sir Geoffrey Howe during his resignation speech in Parliament that working for Mrs Thatcher had been 'rather like sending your opening batsmen to the crease only for them to find, the moment the first balls are bowled, that their bats have been broken before the game by the team captain'. This numpty, too, had potentially stumped his own side before it got out of the pavilion.

Just prior to this, I received a phone call from reception saying that a woman client had called in and wished to make a complaint about this social worker. I spoke to her, a middle-aged woman, who gave a compelling account of her own childhood sexual abuse, which she concluded by handing me an A4 sheet of fullscap on which she had written, in large primary-school handwriting, the kind of vivid 'conversations' she had had with her teddy-bear, Big Foot, the only 'witness' she had told her abuse to at the time. She then said how this worker had dismissed it, his disbelief now reflected in some kind of court report he had written. I assured her I would look into it straight away. I discovered the report – which may have been part of a custody hearing – had only recently been sent. I arranged for it to be recalled and/or supplemented by another report done by another worker at my request, Sheila Morris, a Senior in the Broxburn office who I had known as a long-term social worker from Craigmillar days. Sheila said later that the woman told her that the meeting with me was the first time she had ever truly felt 'listened to'.

Christmas suddenly seemed upon us and, when I returned to the office in the new year, I learned that a mother in a case that was either still open to, or only recently closed by, this worker had been murdered. The case seemed to have been a fairly minor supervision of a young boy, the youngest of several children. Emm, Jim's bolshie Senior, had been on Emergency duty over the period and had done a sterling job sorting out the several placements of these children with local relatives, many of whom had 'problems of their own'. She would remain involved for a further short period because of what happened next. I sought out the social worker and asked to speak to him as soon as he had caught up with the information flow himself. My office was directly across from the team room and I could see a lot of other workers coming up to his desk seeking info but him rather enjoying the attention rather than shooing them off. I went through and told him more directly that I needed to speak to him urgently about this stuff and asked him to come through in the next few minutes with the papers and reports. Unknown to myself, he then gathered up his coat and case and left the building.

He subsequently signed off sick with 'stress' for the next several months. Unsurprisingly, he would prove as difficult to dislodge from Council employment as a bogey on the end of a tadpole. Subsequent reflection on my part as to why he had got so under my radar was the realisation that, in my presence, he had been adopting an almost obsequious attitude (to authority), the reverse of which he tended to show towards women, including his Senior, colleagues or clients – as was now becoming clear in the case of the court report. I read it with mounting anger, it having no sense of impartiality, no sense of a neutral officer of the court reporting information he had gathered, more a refutation of her 'evidence', point by point, like a fiscal prosecuting someone in the public interest. The court ignored his report for the far more skilled assessment undertaken by Sheila. But now, of course, I had other more important matters to consider, like the fate of the several children he had effectively walked out on in the wake of their mother's violent death and their various complex needs. Work never stops and the case was transferred to me and one of my veteran workers, Liz, for the next ten years.

Complaints, complaints. I even caught my new group manager complaining about me, inadvertently, in an email after a meeting with me which she sent to me, its subject, by mistake instead of to her boss, Bill Atkinson, the children's services manager. She used a phrase which did not fit me at all I thought – 'drama queen' – which just confirmed how far off the beam she was about me. She clocked the error straight off, coming into my room immediately to apologise – for sending it, not writing it – just as I was reading the thing. I just shook my head. What else was being drip-fed back to the centre? I sent a few words of my own to Bill, mainly disappointment at the behind-the-back nature of the remarks, the lack of upfrontness which I always extended to anyone I worked with or for, ever hopeful it might be reciprocated in like manner. Bill phoned to say this was not typical of the feedback he had been getting and how problematic emailing had become in general with people using sloppy, personal, emotive language on subjects which require far more considered and formal responses. I said I was disappointed because I thought she was doing a decent job and had excellent qualities herself: practice-based, clear, though a bit humourless and contained herself, certainly around me. I knew Bill from ten years earlier when we met in 1990 while undertaking an exchange review between Lothian Region and Grampian of our respective child protection systems with Les McEwan and Iain Paterson. Bill impressed me and I told Danny so when he joined West Lothian in 1997 and he became a CSWO later for another authority. When I spoke to the group manager after the incident, I found myself saying I had no interest in doing her job or undermining her but my views were my views. It was never referred to again and we both just walked around it, another dressing-room dust up. The real game continued, of course, on the park.

We had entered an era where the numbers game was what the bosses were being judged on, not the quality of the professional work or maintaining the internal balance between present and new work. Waiting lists now threatened to become transformed from a sign of too much demand from over-cautious Reporters or new beat constables to being 'the fault' of frontline workers and Seniors. Waiting lists were something to be avoided rather than a sign of real demand and hence a need for more staffing and more resources. It just so happened that I maintained an allocation rate of about two to three weeks from referral to allocation for the whole of my 17 years in the Livingston office – a figure they never measured but a figure that ensured through-put, certainly, but also enabling workers to maintain that winsome thing – quality. I say winsome because, like a lot of social work practice in action, it is very difficult to measure vertically compared to being sensed by someone actually doing it or making sure it is done effectively. In social work, it is not just what you do that counts as a worker but what you are up against, what you face – the client culture and the management/ political culture, not just the professional culture.

Why does this matter? A particularly high-end child abuse case hit the headlines in 2007, the death of a 17-month-old London boy known as Baby P. Everyone will recall the hysteria. *The Sun* ran a petition calling for the sacking of the social workers, signed by over 850,000 people.

The Government set up a child protection review under Lord Laming. Ed Balls, the Children's Secretary, suspended and then sacked Haringey Council's Children's Director, a former Education Director, for daring to 'defend' frontline staff, some of whom were also sacked. A future Industrial Tribunal would find that she had been sacked improperly for which she was compensated but her career was over, while Ed's career was – well, we all know what happened to Ed's career. Of course, nobody was the least bit interested when Polly Toynbee pointed out in *The Guardian* on 18 November 2008 when the mother and boyfriend who had actually tortured and killed the child were convicted, that the number of children killed in England and Wales had been steadily falling – by 50 per cent – since the 1970s. At that point, Britain had been the fourth-worst nation for such deaths; now it was among the best. You'd never have guessed reading the press.

Lord Laming had also identified chronic issues of cash-cuts, unqualified staff, lack of supervision, high vacancies/turnover rates and dangerous case load levels in the Inquiry into Victoria Climbie's death in 2003, also in that Council's area. A poll of 751 health visitors in 2015 thought a similar death was either likely or very likely. Of course it is and for a hundred different reasons in an open society, even despite the best health and social care vigilance and support, for these are by and large criminal or disordered acts.

In 2007–9, I was writing the poems that would appear in *Dancing with Big Eunice*, including one on a Dundee child, Brandon Muir, who became known as Scotland's Baby P. Listening to the constant radio phone-ins made me realise the extent to which social workers, inside our own professional bubble, had become hated – and I mean truly *hated* – by the public at large. For this I think our press and politicians share the blame and the responsibility, as do the Councils, Social Work Scotland (the old ADSW), the Care Inspectorate and the SSSC – for not refuting the guff more openly because they are too busy defending themselves. It must be admitted, too, that in comparison to Ed Balls' 'improper' response to Baby P, the Scottish Government's handling of the Brandon Muir case was calm, measured and proportionate. Of course, the SNP minority administration was still being restrained by its Lib-Dem partnership and so could not grandstand in the depressingly familiar fashion that became a defining feature of New Labour's reign at Holyrood. Well, not yet. New Labour does deserve credit for introducing free personal care – though that was a maverick act totally against the grain of Blair/Brown's neo-liberal agenda and their devious mission to turn welfare into workfare. One week it was Surestart, next week smoking ban, the week after next ASBOs, then invading Iraq – a morass of hype and hyperactivity profoundly disorientating to live and work through.

As for Care Inspection and the SSSC, I had very little to do with either of them. Their joint function I see now was to fill the space vacated by Regional Directors of social work, whose professional authority and clout was axed and replaced by corporate management regimes installed by Westminster/ Holyrood in local District civic centres. The demoted Chief Social Work Officer post was left legally responsible for the effective delivery of social work services, while the Chief Executive and Corporate managers were responsible for the budget spend, 60 per cent of which is dictated by central Government today anyway. Meanwhile, frontline social work professionals were being instructed to always answer our phones with the same blurb, 'This is West Lothian Council. How can I help you?' Like Kunta Kinte in *Roots*, I kept saying, 'This is Alistair Findlay' to remind myself who I was.

Although I had nothing to do with Care Inspection or the sssc, I am now prepared to believe anything I am told by a reliable sort of person. Indeed, I penned the following terse note to myself in my work diary on 11 October 2006:

Off to Paisley for 10.00am review, a 14-year-old girl in Secure, then back to afternoon Duty. It's a disgrace the way they are taking resources from the frontline for this Inspection and pathetic everyone's going along with it. I've refused to touch it but the other TMs are volunteering to read and sort the files out so I end-up doing the extra duty cover – they've been away reading files for the last 3 days. All bollocks!

There is a further comment about the duty work I came back to later that afternoon:

Horrendous duty – major Child Protection stuff, plus 3 other CP referrals, one to progress today.

I had no qualms about Care Inspection, just with the way it was being measured and whether it would reflect anything other than the fact that the Council was throwing vast amounts of overtime payments at frontline managers and Admin to get the files up to date. The Data Protection Act had come in about a decade earlier and Children's files had not been altered to comply with that so it was now all hands to the pump to correct (or conceal from the Inspectors?). It certainly wasn't my idea of an Inspection – six months notice and a list of what they were going to look at, with unlimited overtime and an incinerator working full-time round the back. My admittedly primitive idea of an Inspection was for a wee guy or gal who knew the score dropping in unannounced one day and asking to see files A, B, C and D, speaking to the workers and the team manager and going out to speak to the clients and asking me what the problems were – in the team, with the staffing, with the Hearings, with the Reporter, with health and education and the bloody councillors, with the quality and availability of resources and with what I thought of ASBOs (even though they were operated by an ex-policeman and had nothing to do with social work).

Instead, what we got was Admin on constant weekend overtime for four to five months and then the Council only goes and wins the bloody Best Wee Bloody Council of the Year Award in 2006 and we had to read all about it in the Council's good news bulletin, 'Pravda'. And I thought I had left all that behind when the CPGB folded in 1991. I have been told that over 100 employees from across the Council were dedicated for months during that period, service development officers and others producing documents full-time to satisfy the requirements of Tony Blair's 'Charter Mark' to prove that Council workers were doing what the Council said they were doing (and they were, apparently). I am also reliably told that there are now a dozen members on the Management Board of the Care Inspectorate, only two of whom have any social work background. I leave the reader to ponder the full significance of that while I get on with wondering whether the profession has perhaps become, whatever the intentions, over-regulated and under-inspected by folk who actually know nothing truly worth measuring any longer about clients or current frontline practice – neither its joys nor its pitfalls.

Ho hum. It is time I signed off. I had forgotten I cared that much. I will comment on Social Work Scotland's 50th Anniversary Report of the Social Work (Scotland) Act, however, authored by the respected academics Brigid Daniel and Jane Scott, which cites some opinions about a golden thread traceable from the Social Work (Scotland) Act in 1968 to the present. I understand the hopefulness of their report based on a review of the literature and interviews of participants going back to the '60s. What the report says is commendable but what it largely leaves out is the key role of the public sector unions, BASW's bare knuckle fights against managerialism and the ditching of education-based social work training for employer-led demands for 'job training', which were in part intended to shelve the 1968 Act's 'duty to promote social welfare'. This dislocated the balance envisaged by the Act's architects to both 'care and control' the recipients of social care. Thatcherism thus promoted social work's control function while narrowing its care function, focusing purely on individuals rather than targeting communities and the wider social system. The writings of the Birmingham School (BCCC) helped show that the Right's purpose is to control welfare professionals even if they cannot control the underclass that their own neo-liberal social-economic policies are busily expanding.

Impartial and fair-minded academics poring over the small print of social policy papers coming from Holyrood have perhaps been less directly exposed to the 'jungle quality' of the corporate management systems installed over the last quarter of a century in Scottish local Government. Social work departments were the outcome of a centre-Left coalition – some might say an unholy alliance – of 1960s welfare academics, public intellectuals, progressive Scottish civil servants and senior Labour politicians like Judith Hart. That coalition proved broad enough to combine the interests of public sector unions, BASW, ADSW and CCETSW, sufficient to withstand Thatcherite attacks on Scottish local Government and the health service for half a century up to the millennium and after. This would give way to a centre-right coalition which now rules at Westminster and Holyrood via ring-fenced budgets and by controlling public sector professionals through shallow business-model regulation and inspection.

It has at any rate failed to win professional credibility on social work's frontline, whatever Holyrood might boast or imagine. A BASW-sponsored survey into the working conditions of 1,600 social workers in June 2018 found that 52 per cent of UK social workers intend to leave the profession over the next 15 months, 55 per cent in the case of children's workers. Such figures indicate professional despair of a density I never encountered at any time during my own four decades doing the job.

For those perhaps interested in a collection of views by academics and practitioners on the current landscape of professional social work in Scotland, I would recommend *Social Work in a Changing Scotland* (2018), edited by Viviene E Cree and Mark Smith. Another excellent thematic history of English social work from the 1970s to the present is Terry Bamford's *A Contemporary History of Social Work* (2015). A former chair of BASW and editor of its journal, a Director of Social Services in Northern Ireland and the London Borough of Kensington and Chelsea, a member of the General Care Council and a social work trainer, he provides an informed view of the most recent literature analysing contemporary social work and its pressing need for renewal (vi-vii):

> Undoubtedly the most influential works have been those taking a critical stance on the neoliberal trends in social work... Those who seek a smaller role for the state have a deep hostility towards the public sector. They are hostile to public expenditure on welfare provision, believing, as did the Victorians, that this fosters dependency and rewards idleness. Thirty-five years ago, a delegation from BASW, of which I was a member, met Margaret Thatcher, then leader of the Opposition. She opined that children's social work should be handed over to the NSPCC, the children's welfare charity (Mrs T did not

ask – she stated). The idea has not gone away... Radical social work has been a hugely beneficial influence on social work in general. Its critique has helped drive the recognition of the factors leading to social exclusion and the marginalisation of many of the people with whom social workers come into contact each day. It offers a potent challenge to the neoliberal trends of public policy and to the 'depersonalisation' of the social work role in an age of managerialism... This book suggests that [social work] can do both ['rediscover its humanity as well as its radicalism'] once it accepts that radicalism does not demand a particular world view, class analysis or the denial of the importance of personal relationships. Radicalism requires a challenge to the established order.

Big Ronnie has just whispered in my ear that I should advise the new generation to join BASW which has a braw new personal indemnity insurance scheme, while Big Tam has shouted in the other ear that they should also join the unions and it's still my round.

13

End of

None of us ever go to our graves remembering the great emails we sent.
Kevin McCloud, *Grand Designs*, 2018

The author is clearly trying to be hopeful for the future but fails pretty badly.

BY 2006–7 I had become decidedly wearied, even jaded, less by the pressure of work than a sense of the decentring of operational practice by consultants, service development pen-pushers, sub-contractors and proto-regulators who had not seen an angry client for years. I published a new collection of poetry, *The Love Songs of John Knox* (2006), which slagged the bum-clenching banalities of Donald Dewar and Jack 'the lad' McConnell's New Labour Devolved Parliament. Tony Blair's war in Iraq dispelled any notions that he represented anything beyond a neo-liberal private-market threat to the universalist welfare state. Far from providing an escape from the day-job, my writing became fascinated by the Janus-faced inauthentic nature of Scottish politicos, local and national – what the 1950s and '60s Existentialist writers like Camus and Sartre called 'bad faith'.

The occasional phone calls from Joyce Wood lifted the spirits. She was a Senior of Danny's in Bathgate in the 1980s, then PTM for Leith office in the 1990s when she was Raymond's boss. Her phone calls usually opened with her raging at some perfidity on my part over some disputed case-transfer. Joyce always had that vital biff so it was never advisable to argue with her at the outset but try to coax her onto more conducive territory like, 'You'll never guess what they bastards are up to now, Joyce'. And Joyce would pile in about the latest antics of Shrubhill, probably Bryan Chatham, the ex-rugby player, then boss of Edinburgh City and a former Senior in Leith. Joyce's phone calls at least confirmed that there were still recognisable life forms left on planet social work.

If Big Grahame ever regretted putting up with any of my stuff, he should have exchanged notes with Bryan about Joyce. Indeed, they could have swapped us every six months or so to give each other a break. Joyce and I, although very different personalities, shared a professional ethos with our generation, which included senior managers, despite an increasing casualty rate. Joyce and myself were what I would call 'trouble-managers' rather than trouble-makers, frontline decision-makers who made sure that our own agency used every office and orifice at its disposal to engage with the troubled people we were meant to deal with, while insisting that all other agencies deploy their resources towards the same end. It was our job to hold everyone to account, not just ourselves but our staff, managers, authorities, the clients and any other agency – the police, health, education. Corporatisation, such as it was, simply went on around us, us ignoring it and it ignoring us – or trying to. We were what the profession had made of us from the beginning.

Oh dear. I sense the shades of Morrison and Carnegie circling, the yin and yang of the Social Work (Scotland) Act. Dougie is smoking a fag and 'chuntering on' (another favoured expression) about how the new generation of social workers, the Millennials and Generation Z (the iGeneration, Post-Millennials, Homeland Generation and Plurals) have been far too bloody uncritically accepting of all that's come their way, good and bad, without questioning the half of it or probing, prodding and pummeling the other half to death with the blunt end of logic. Morrison is standing looking at me full in the face, an enigmatic smile playing round his lips, the one that says, 'Who am I to judge?', all the while screaming, 'Who the hell else is there?' I leave them mulling over the fact that, in 2003, entry to the profession got changed to a three-year social work degree course which does not require an interview to evaluate vocational suitability.

I do not wish to leave the reader here in the doldrums. The buoyancy of good practice continued between the cracks in the pavement long after I packed it in and no doubt still does to this day in pockets. There is the community care manager for adult mental health in West Lothian who, during the reigns of Big Grahame and Ian Quigley, pulled on her wellingtons to hike through woods somewhere in the Broxburn area to assess the living quarters of a single, elderly man, low paranoid, who feared living in houses because he believed the electricity wires were threatening him (not an uncommon fear for that kind of condition). After a time, he got to trust her enough to reveal his secret living quarters in the woods – his 'hide' – which she saw had been beautifully fashioned out of branches and ferns. She tracked down the President of the wonderfully titled Royal Scottish Agricultural Benevolent Institution, a farmer in Perthshire, and took him to the hide, him in kilt and green wellies. There he had a great chat with the man, who was an ex-woodsman, about all things open air and leafy. The President would channel the funds she could no longer get from the council or health board to purchase blankets, stoves and other basic equipment which sustained the man in his dwelling of choice for the next several years until he, 'the wood man', agreed to go into a local flat to be fed and offered companionship through a local community café run by volunteers.

Such work has not been offered by local Government social work for the last five years through pressure of work and sadly that is unlikely to change, even if it got past the regulators. That doubt is perhaps the most depressing feature of all. That and what I hear today of how they are putting mattresses down on the floors of the Royal Edinburgh Psychiatric Hospital. The frontline care manager who worked with the man in the woods has recently quit council social work altogether and been welcomed onto the board of a local mental health advocacy project for her knowledge and advice, a position she could not have taken when with the council because it would have been classified as a conflict of interest. Whose interest exactly – the clients? She had no role in awarding contracts and suchlike to third-sector operators. This provides a concrete example of how the focus of social work management changed to upholding principles that enabled traders equal access to the market over the primary welfare principle of ensuring client access to the best possible services. And the worrying question is, does anybody really understand the difference anymore, up there?

Sorry, I meant to end on a more uplifting note. I departed the social work coop myself in the summer of 2007 after it occurred to me that I might apply for a Scottish Arts Council Writer's Bursary to write a collection of poetry on Scottish social work while I was still up to my neck in it. Though technically I could have returned to my post at the end of the sabbatical, it was clear to me and my team that I would not. I had by then accrued a substantial body of published work and, lo and behold, I was awarded such a bursary. It may be a matter of opinion the extent to which I had outgrown social work or it had left me behind but an escape hatch suddenly opened before me into which I did not so much climb as hurl myself bodily through. I stood blinking in the sun.

I received the typical team send-off of the kind I had inflicted on Danny and many another of my departing colleagues over the years, a public humiliation punctuated by humour and innuendo. I had revelled on such occasions in hyberbole, exaggeration and downright lies. My farewell speeches had always been well-attended, including by Admin, drawn to hear some of the terrible things I was bound to say about people with such a po-face and degree of certainty that made them wonder themselves whether it was true or not. I said of Hughie, for example, that 'he sets himself very low standards which he consistently fails to meet'. And 'professionally, Hughie has a full six-pack but he lacks the wee plastic thing that holds it all together'.

I could hardly complain when I was given the same treatment. The standard Children's Hearing Social Background Report was duly read out. Under the heading 'Financial Situation', it listed:

Is he being paid to go? Did the Council have a whip-round? Did inter-agency colleagues contribute? Did Big Grahame re-mortgage his house?

There was also a 'Peer Evaluation' section, beginning with a table of 'Positives':

A Legend; Kindly; Helpful (good when cars don't start); Laidback; Unconscious; You can wait a long time but the occasional flash of insight is really worth it; Excellent at delegating and good at taking advantage; Poetry in motion; At least he's got a bit of personality; A voice like Sean Connery; Sean Connery in a cardigan and a bunnet; One colleague anxious not to be named did admit – 'Once when drunk I did think he looked sexy in that black shirt'.

Unfortunately, the 'Less Positives' read like they were all written by Wee Jim personally and who could blame him? These included:

A Dinosaur; Is he still in the Seventies?; Opinionated; Obnoxious; Confrontational; Aggressive; Gruff; Avoidment; Work-shy; Crabbit-faced; Slithers out of any work that comes his way; A man who does not need his ego boosted; A bit of a ladies' man, particularly if young, impressionable and not demanding; Reads reports in the toilet.

I have to say all true, except for the remark which may confuse my feminism with some kind of lechery. I grew up with feminism and sexual politics. I wanted social workers to talk and fight back, male or female, in a profession which was largely female and is now even more so. My mother was a red-haired Borderer with a whip-lash tongue, biting wit and complete disinterest in taking any prisoners, perhaps the template for the kind of women I was most comfortable with. I was never interested in doormats of whatever gender. Unless they were clients. Clients were the job. I related to most of my work colleagues in and through our work with the clients in all its glorious technicolour.

I liked the comments allegedly contributed by inter-agency colleagues: 'Is there anyone else I can talk to?' (police inspector); 'I owe a lot to him, he has been an inspiration to me and has, I think, made me look good' (hospital doctor); 'What's his home address?' (sandwich man). There was a fair amount of badinage during the course of it, comments from the floor. Joyce Ormiston, a fellow PTM for community care in the office and later a group manager, took me to task over a dispute she had had with me over desks in the early 1990s. I argued that my workers needed the desks unlike her OTs because they visited folk in their own homes and so the cupboard in the middle of the landing would be fine for them to keep their walking sticks and other aids in. I was joking, of course, but little did I suspect that desks would surface in a rather different context a decade after I retired when I visited Alistair Gaw, head of social work for Edinburgh City, to discuss some reminiscences for this book. He said he had booked us an interview room for an hour because he and the Chief Executive no longer had offices to call their own and he was not joking. I sat watching as a queue formed outside the door for the next scheduled meeting as our discussions came to a close. I then rushed home to re-read *The Hitchhiker's Guide to the Galaxy* to help figure out where the profession was heading next.

My departure was much as I expected except that it inspired a rather fine poem about me, unsigned, which a literary friend thought contained an ironic allusion to Hugh MacDiarmid's 'A Drunk Man Looks at the Thistle' with its reference to me as 'a defiant dandelion'. The office had three main public occasion rhymsters – myself, Sister Sarah and Christine Powell, from the typing pool, whose composition it was. The 'paper' referred to is, of course, the *Morning Star*, a beacon of truth and hope in a world of greed and spin, while 'organised chaos' is a nod towards the surface of my desk which I now see from an old photograph resembles my father's paper strewn newsdesk at the *West Lothian Courier*:

Ode Tae Alistair

How do I compare thee? Alistair Findlay.
A defiant dandelion pissed on by the odd rogue mongrel,
An Addiewell park bench. Sat on, shat upon yet constant and enduring.
A man whose facial hair was more alarming than inspiring,
A stained dirty tea mug that had seen better days, and that paper!
A dinosaur that had defied extinction.
Yet sharp, vibrant, bullish we have 'kent you'
A wise wizard, kindly uncle, your views would be heard!
A man who could be all things to all people, whether they wished it or not,
The acerbic wit, the e-mails, the dodgy music, the organised chaos
That is Alistair Findlay.
And now 'as the end is near' and you fuck off to the potting shed,
We will remember you... and oddly
We will miss you!

I could not have asked for better and no doubt deserved a lot worse. Reading Christine's poem now I think it captures that vitality and bullish disregard for the beige po-facedness I had always felt threatened our vulnerable little craft, from within and without, which I had not so much given up on as thought to myself – well, it's up to the next lot now. It always is. Me and my generation were history even as the ink was drying on the poems I wrote for *Dancing with Big Eunice*. That man with the alarming facial hair and stained tea mug could have been any one of us, including most of the women. I close, therefore, with an apology, not for the many colleagues I have left out of this memoir but to those I have found it necessary to include. Please forgive me.

14

The Bald Truth, Boldly

That might be a useful note to end on?
Iain Morrison, Moray House, September 1970

Dancing with Big Eunice was published in 2010 and its title poem was chosen for *The Forward Book of Poetry 2011* in the Highly Commended category. At the launch of the book in the Canons' Gait, the old Blue Blanket pub where generations of social work students and lecturers used to socialise just up from Moray House in the 1970s to 1990s, some of the stalwarts from Falkirk Burgh came along, including Wee Marion and Big Eunice. When I tried to explain to the assembled company that 'Big Eunice' was a metaphor for clients – well, all Hell broke loose.

Jen Hadfield was the youngest ever winner of the TS Eliot Prize for Poetry in 2008, whose youth and brilliance doubly pleased me when she found something sufficiently worthy in my own writing to select the poem 'Mrs McRobie' for the Scottish Poetry Library's *Best Scottish Poems 2010*. She also wrote a review of *Dancing with Big Eunice* in 2011, the full text of which can be found on the website of the online literary magazine, *The Recusant* (www.therecusant.org.uk/jen-hadfield-on-findlay/4566240212). I am pleased to say that 'Mrs McRobie' can now be found in a place neither of us ever expected to find ourselves when we first met in Falkirk in 1973 – the Scottish Poetry Library, Edinburgh – except perhaps hoovering the floor. Jen Hadfield also commented favourably on 'No Problemo':

> For me, child of the era of political correctness, Findlay's inability to be mealy-mouthed is both admirable and shocking. I find it hard to accept his likening of social work managers to 'Nazi war-criminals' ('The Senior Social Worker'); his outrage is most effective when his language is plainer and cooler and his tone more satirical. In 'No Problemo', Findlay gets the balance right, and the effect is heart-breaking... These are barely fictionalised, human encounters. As he put it himself in an email to me: 'direct, strong (often 'confrontational') language/emotions is the very stuff of social work practice [...] you would not earn the respect of the people we deal with unless you told the bald truth, boldly!'

Mrs McRobie

Caught sight of Davie McRobie bunking off school
  while sitting at the traffic-lights,
Graham's Road, saw his beatific face go from
  shock to delight when I,
his social worker, crunched into the tail-lights of a
  truck that had moved off
then stopped, saw the wee bastard tug his mate's
  coat, then run like fuck!
Mrs McRobie'd say: 'Whit kin ye dae, Mr Findlay?'
  Well, you might open the door
when I come up? – 'Aye, right enough.' She had five
  more, lived on fags and beer,
and wore a constant peeny, cleaned half the office
  blocks in Falkirk,
morning, noon and night – the Ice-Rink, Sheriff Court
  the Broo and Polis Stations,
locations not unfamiliar to her clan and brood although
  she never stole a thing in her life,
going from office space to office space like a coolie
  changing paddy-fields,
and giving her great lump of a man her pay packet,
  unopened: 'sair hodden doon'
her doctor might say, but as she told me herself, Tam,
  a liar and a thief,
was a bloody great lay! 'Whit kin ye dae, Mr Findlay?'
  'Aye, Mrs McRobie, right enough.'
So they took Davie away, and she gret every single day
  until they took him back.

No Problemo

Getting too old for this game,
holding onto an eight-year-old
spit-ball in the car-park
after a hearing that would not
send him home, so now he's
venting his wrath at the pavement
we are both now looking down on
my fourteen stone draped round
his shoulders while he questions
my parentage, my manhood
my professional credibility.
I feel his heart thumping against
my frame as we stand, or rather
crouch, in this foetal exchange
the world, and now me, weighed
round tiny Quasimodo-shoulders
until he breaks into a sob and rushes
forward to his carer demanding fish
for tea later. In the car not going home
he tells me that in three weeks time
the Panel will see it his way
and Celtic will win the League again
no problemo.

Timeline: Social Work

1968–9   Social Work (Scotland) Act replaced juvenile courts with Children's Hearings based on the care principle of 'a child's best interests' and civil law 'balance of probabilities' administered by the new post of Reporter, not requiring a law background. On 17 November 1969, the 52 new social work departments opened their doors in cities, counties and large burghs. Less than half of their directors had any social work qualification. Overnight, the Act turned 281 Probation, 97 Mental Health, 305 Children's and 276 Welfare Officers into 959 generic (one-door) social workers, only 300 of whom were qualified. By 1989, there would be 5,000 field social workers in Scotland, all of them qualified.

1970–5   CQSW Diploma/Certificate 3 and two-year non-graduate social work courses started at Moray House and a one-year graduate course at the University of Edinburgh and several other universities and colleges, including the University of Stirling, Robert Gordon's College, Aberdeen, and Jordanhill College, Glasgow, etc.

         British Association of Social Workers (BASW) formed, nearly half of the UK workforce being members and *British Journal of Social Work* launched in 1971. By the 1980s, 10 per cent of UK workforce joined compared to 75 per cent in the unions.

1973   *Children Who Wait: A Study of Children Needing Substitute Families* by Jane Rowe and Lydia Lambert (BAAF) coined the term 'drift' for around 6,000 children languishing in residential care homes.

1974   Maria Colwell (Brighton) Child Death Inquiry: all agencies criticised for 'unfocused' visiting.

1975   Richard Clarke (Perth) Child Death Inquiry: agencies criticised for assuming others were doing something about general concerns.

Community Care magazine launched, free, carried articles and job adverts.

Regionalisation: created 12 two-tier Regional/District unitary Authorities, districts retaining control of housing.

Non-Accidental Injury (NAI) Registers set up in the dozen new Regions.

Children's Act expanded powers to remove children and to modify parental rights to consent to adoption.

1976   IMF Loan required Labour Government to cut public spending by 4 per cent, restored two years later. Mrs Thatcher used this as a precedent/prelude to privatising all of the public sector. Kozo Yamamura's recent authoritative summation (*Too Much Stuff*, 2018: 137): 'By any objective standard it is indisputable that Thatcherism, based on supply-side economics, was a failure.'

1978–9   Community Service by Offenders (Scotland) Act: key pressure group role played by SACRO and its first development officer, Paul Morran.

Social work strikes over pay and re-grading in 15 English authorities. 2,600 out of 100,000 members on full strike pay cost NALGO £0.5 million every month between August 1978 and May 1979.

1980–3   Rate Capping: Regional Councils in Lothian, Stirling, Dundee had their Rate Support Grants cut by Scottish Secretary George Younger for not implementing spending cuts. NALGO members in Edinburgh social work offices applied no-cover policies for vacant posts in Craigmillar/Pilton, the latter striking for several weeks after some staff were suspended.

1984–5   Mental Health (Scotland) Act: new post-qualifying role for approved Mental Health Officers with new powers within generic social worker post.

Section 12 grants to Striking Miners: Directors like Strathclyde's

Fred Edwards, Roger Kent in Lothian, and Fife, Central, other Regions defied government by authorising payments to single miners (without children), later deemed illegal. Government backed off surcharging the Directors.

Jasmine Beckford (Brent) Child Death Inquiry: social workers criticised for focusing on the parents and not the child.

Tyra Henry (Lambeth) Child Death Inquiry: white social workers criticised for being too 'trusting' because the family was black.

1987–8 Cleveland Inquiry Report: over a few months, 121 children from 57 families diagnosed by two paediatricians of being sexually abused and placed in care; most were returned to their homes after the Inquiry. It showed limits of medical diagnosis in such cases and how it ought to be combined with social work assessments.

1988–90 CCETSW replaced certificates in social work and social services with a Diploma, criticised by academics as part of employer attempts to assert bureaucratic control over the broad professional support for social action.

Griffith Report argued that local authorities should be enablers of social care not providers; community care assessments for old/vulnerable aimed at keeping them in the community on basis of what is needed not on what is available; created the 'purchaser-provider' split.

1991 Orkney Sexual Abuse Inquiry: infamous cock-up by all agencies (reporters, sheriff, police) leading to new legal process for Emergency Place of Safety Orders being issued by Sheriffs rather than Justice of the Peace warrants.

National Objectives/Standards in Criminal Justice System funded by SWSG.

Citizen's Charter: John Major's scheme to make all services publish clear targets for service levels, NHS patients to have agreed time limits, 'Charter Marks' for public bodies – abandoned 2011. Criticised for applying business methods to the public sector while reducing the money needed to fund it.

1992   Skinner Report – *Another Kind of Home: A Review of Residential Child Care*: number of homes fell by 52 per cent between 1980 and 1990 from 294 to 154; 86 per cent of kids in residential care were over 12 in 1989 compared to 33 per cent being under five in 1977. Thus a massive increase in foster care took place.
Return to Specialisms in October '92 in Criminal Justice, Community Care and Children and Families teams; specialist in-service training for each group.

1995   CCETSW Assuring Quality in Diploma in Social Work, government-led review of social work education now to be based on 'practical, common sense, down to earth' practice – 'multi-culturalism' not 'anti-racism'; the dominant trend of social activism, of challenging oppression and racism was modified and itself ruled out by Tories and employer interests/demands.

Children's Act: reviewed Children's Hearings for first time since 1968 and said 'public protection' could sometimes qualify 'best interests of the child'.

Criminal Procedure Scotland Act, re: court orders in mental health cases.

Disability Discrimination Act 1995 and 2005 and Equality Act 2010 set out important rights protecting people with disabilities or health conditions.

1996   Districtisation: 32 new District Unitary Councils created by Tory Secretary Michael Forsyth to destroy Labour's electoral power base in Strathclyde. Introduced Chief Executive-led corporate management structures to limit local government spending through budgetary management controls, changed 'Director' to 'Chief Social Work Officer', no longer part of senior management council committees, made responsible to corporate managers for spending even though their background was in housing, education and administration.

1998   Blair Government agreed a Devolved Scottish Parliament with social work, health and housing devolved but social security reserved to Westminster.

Human Rights Act, mainly Article 5 'right to liberty and security of person' re: detention under mental health/reduced capacity; Article 8 'respect for private and family life, home and confidentiality', relevant to removal from home.

1999   Aiming for Excellence, Modernising Social Work Services in Scotland by creating new bodies – Scottish Social Services Council – register workforce, codes of standards, raise training and so raise professional standards; Care Commission, new independent regulator of care standards through inspection.

2008–9 Baby P (Haringey) Child Death: aftermath exposed expediency of Ed Balls for improperly sacking the Director (determined by an industrial tribunal).

Brandon Muir (Dundee) Child Death: aftermath found death could not have been predicted, social workers were more worried about other cases; despite public outcry, Scottish Government response calm, measured, proportional.

2000–18 Scottish Parliament became a paper-mill for new legislation and guidelines, described by academics as 'punitive-populist' and contrary to the 1968 Act's basic 'social welfare' principles. An Action for Children report in 2009 criticised the 400+ different initiatives, funding streams, legislative acts during the previous two decades, the bulk occurring in the last decade.

The Scottish Government established the Regulatory and Inspection bodies, the SSSC in 2001 and the Care Inspectorate in 2011.

Social Work Scotland's 50th Anniversary Report by Brigid Daniel and Jane Scott offered a wide overview of the literature and professional opinions stretching from 1968 to 2018.

Luath Press Limited

committed to publishing well written books worth reading

LUATH PRESS takes its name from Robert Burns, whose little collie Luath (*Gael.*, swift or nimble) tripped up Jean Armour at a wedding and gave him the chance to speak to the woman who was to be his wife and the abiding love of his life. Burns called one of the 'Twa Dogs' Luath after Cuchullin's hunting dog in Ossian's *Fingal*. Luath Press was established in 1981 in the heart of Burns country, and is now based a few steps up the road from Burns' first lodgings on Edinburgh's Royal Mile. Luath offers you distinctive writing with a hint of unexpected pleasures.

Most bookshops in the UK, the US, Canada, Australia, New Zealand and parts of Europe, either carry our books in stock or can order them for you. To order direct from us, please send a £sterling cheque, postal order, international money order or your credit card details (number, address of cardholder and expiry date) to us at the address below. Please add post and packing as follows: UK – £1.00 per delivery address; overseas surface mail – £2.50 per delivery address; overseas airmail – £3.50 for the first book to each delivery address, plus £1.00 for each additional book by airmail to the same address. If your order is a gift, we will happily enclose your card or message at no extra charge.

Luath Press Limited
543/2 Castlehill
The Royal Mile
Edinburgh EH1 2ND
Scotland
Telephone: +44 (0)131 225 4326 (24 hours)
email: sales@luath. co.uk
Website: www. luath.co.uk